Women/Cancer

CONFRONTING CANCER, CONSTRUCTING CHANGE

Women/Cancer/Fear/Power series

Midge Stocker, editor

Volume 1

Cancer As a Women's Issue: Scratching the Surface

Volume 2

Confronting Cancer, Constructing Change: New Perspectives on Women and Cancer

Women/Cancer/Fear/Power series, volume 2

CONFRONTING CANCER, CONSTRUCTING CHANGE

New Perspectives on Women and Cancer

Midge Stocker, editor

Third Side Press

Chicago

Printed on recycled, acid-free paper in the United States of America.

Cover art by E.G. Crichton. First published in *Out/Look Magazine*, spring 1988.
Cover design by Loraine Edwalds and Midge Stocker
Text design and production by Midge Stocker

We gratefully acknowledge the following for permission to reprint previously published work:

ANDRÉE O'CONNOR: "A Rose in Cancer's Thorn" appeared in abbreviated form as "One-Breasted Woman" in *Ms.*, vol 3, no 2, September/October 1992. Reprinted by permission of the author.

BETH KUPPER-HERR: "Living with Ovarian Cancer" appeared as a three-part series under the pseudonym Selena LeRoy in *Ovarian: Newsletter of Ovarian Cancer Prevention & Early Detection Foundation*; vol 2, no 7, November 1992; vol 2, no 8, December 1992; vol 3, no 1, January/February 1993. Reprinted by permission of the author.

ELLEN CROWLEY: "Grassroots Healing" appeared in *Woman of Power*, issue 22. Reprinted by permission of the author.

JEAN HARDISTY and ELLEN LEOPOLD: "Cancer and Poverty: Double Jeopardy for Women" is an updated version of an article of the same name that appeared in *Sojourner: The Women's Forum*, vol 18, no 4, December 1992. Reprinted by permission of the authors.

LOUISE LANDER: "Coming Out as a One-Breasted Woman" appeared in *Lesbian Contradiction*, no 30, Spring 1990. Reprinted by permission of the author.

PAMELA FERGUSON: "Drawing Circles: The Zen of a Mastectomy" is an updated version of an article of the same name that appeared in *Sojourner: The Women's Forum*, vol 16, no 7, March 1991. Reprinted by permission of the author.

RITA ARDITTI and TATIANA SCHREIBER: "Killing Us Quietly: Cancer, the Environment, and Women" appeared in a previous version as "Breast Cancer: The Environmental Connection" in *RESIST*, no 246, May/June 1992, and in *Sojourner: The Women's Forum*, vol 18, no 4, December 1992. Reprinted by permission of the authors.

Library of Congress Cataloging-in-Publication Data
Confronting cancer, constructing change : new perspectives on women
   and cancer / Midge Stocker, editor. — 1st ed.
     p. cm. — (Women/cancer/fear/power series : v. 2)
   Includes bibliographical references and index.
   ISBN 1-879427-17-6 — ISBN 1-879427-09-5 (pbk.)
   1. Cancer—Social aspects. 2. Women—Diseases. 3. Feminist
theory. 4. Feminist criticism. 5. Lesbian feminism. 6. Breast—
Cancer—Social aspects. 7. Mastectomy—Social aspects.
I. Stocker, Midge, 1960– . II. Series.
RC281.W65C65 1993
362.1'96994'0082—dc20   93-16998
                                                CIP

This book is available on tape to disabled women from the Womyn's Braille Press, P.O. Box 8475, Minneapolis, MN 55408.

                              Third Side Press
                              2250 W. Farragut
                              Chicago, IL 60625-1802

ISBN: 1-879427-01-X Women/Cancer/Fear/Power series
ISBN: 1-879427-02-8 volume 1 paper (*Cancer as a Women's Issue*) $10.95
ISBN: 1-879427-11-7 volume 2 paper (*Confronting Cancer, Constructing Change*) $11.95
ISBN: 1-879427-17-6 volume 2 cloth (*Confronting Cancer, Constructing Change*) $24.95

First edition, June 1993
10 9 8 7 6 5 4 3 2 1

To Audre Lorde,
1943–1992

Contents

Preface

Midge Stocker

This amazing collection of writing by women with cancer and cancer histories, the second volume in the Women/Cancer/Fear/Power series, reveals some of the growth of the feminist anti-cancer movement in the U.S. in the early 1990s. As an editor, I always worry about including references in any book that will date it, but the time-setting of this book is important.

When *Cancer as a Women's Issue: Scratching the Surface*, volume one of the Women/Cancer/Fear/Power series, was published in May 1991, members of the four founding organizations of the National Coalition of Feminist and Lesbian Cancer Projects had just met for the first time (see "The Politics of Cancer" for Jackie Winnow's words on that day). No one was ready, or had time, to write about how the organization of the groups was working, even though personal essays by founding members of several of the groups were included ("Lesbians Evolving Health Care" by Jackie Winnow, "No Big Deal" by Jane Murtaugh, "Fighting Spirit" by Nancy Lanoue, "CAUTION: IVF May Be Harmful to Your Health" and "One Day at a Time" by Rita Arditti, and "Lifestyles Don't Kill. Carcinogens in Air, Food, and Water Do" by Sandra Steingraber). But the groups were beginning to do life-changing work—from providing direct services and support groups to doing political direct action and setting up cancer information resource libraries.

The feminist periodicals, particularly *Sojourner*, that helped spur women to work in this movement, to challenge the medical/research/pharmaceutical establishment continued their excellent reporting, encouraging more women to speak up and join together. Other books on the subject were published, most notably *Cancer in Two Voices* by Barbara Rosenblum and Sandra Butler and *1 in 3: Women with Cancer Confront an Epidemic*, edited by Judith Brady. The beat goes on.

Now, Chicago's Lesbian Community Cancer Project, the youngest of those organizations, is two years old, has its own office/meeting space, has held two major fundraising events, the first netting more than $20,000 and the second netting nearly $30,000—vast amounts of money on a relative scale—operates several support groups, has a free gynecological health clinic one night a month and a free therapeutic massage clinic another night, provides direct services to women who call the hotline, and is working on setting up a whole foods cooperative. This volume includes essays about the reasons for and methods of development of those organizations ("The Politics of Cancer" by Jackie Winnow, "Grassroots Healing" by Ellen Crowley, and "Bringing It Home" by Lynn Kanter) as well as essays by members of the groups, writing about the work they are doing with the groups and/or the work they were doing that drew them to the groups ("'If I Live to Be 90 Still Wanting to Say Something'" by Sandra Steingraber, "Cancer and Poverty" by Jean Hardisty and Ellen Leopold, and "Killing Us Quietly" by Rita Arditti and Tatiana Schreiber), and a demand for action issued by the Boston group (the Women's Community Cancer Project's "A Women's Cancer Agenda").

Cancer as a Women's Issue: Scratching the Surface did its job: it scratched the surface. Its focus on moving personal narratives with a sprinkling of striking political analysis brought women out of silence and into the anti-cancer movement. *Confronting Cancer, Constructing Change* takes a more activist stance, including personal essays that have a decidedly targeted rage (in "Part One, Confronting Cancer") and political analyses borne of a widening awareness of women's underserved health care needs (in "Part Two, Constructing Change"). There will be at least one more volume in the Women/Cancer/Fear/Power series, a volume whose focus has not yet presented itself, that will develop as our need to speak to one another changes.

Working on this book, and on the series, has been emotionally overwhelming at some times and overwhelmingly gratifying at others. I thank all of the women whose articles are included in *Cancer as a Women's Issue* and in *Confronting Cancer, Constructing Change*—Ada Harrigan, Andrée O'Connor, Ann Mari Buitrago, Beth Kupper-Herr, Beverly Loder, Carol Gloor, Dian Marino, Ellen Crowley, Ellen Leopold, Elissa Raffa, Helen Ramirez Odell, Jackie Winnow, Jane Murtaugh, Jean Hardisty, Laura Post, Louise Lander, Lynn Kanter, Merida Wexler, Nancy Lanoue, Naomi Glauberman, Nicky Morris, Pamela Ferguson, Portia Cornell, Rita Arditti, Sandra Butler, Sandra Steingraber, Selma Miriam, Suzanne Joi, Tatiana Schreiber, Victoria Brownworth, Virginia Soffa, and Wendy Ann Ryden—for their courage, their openness, and their generosity. In particular, I thank Rita Arditti, whose work appears in both volumes and whose sustained encouragement has been invaluable.

Additionally, I thank Loraine Edwalds and Meta Hellman for proofreading the completed pages of volumes one and two, respectively—and Joyce Goldenstern for indexing this book. Thanks also to Loraine Edwalds for her design and production advice on this series, and on many other Third Side

Press books. Finally, thanks to my partner Jane Murtaugh, whose narrative of her personal cancer history appears in *Cancer as a Women's Issue*, whose vitality in the face of that history astounds and thrills me, and whose love and respect I treasure.

Introduction

Sandra Butler

In a very real sense, each woman's story is her own. As a feminist, I am equally aware that no woman's story is just her own.

Ellyn Kaschak, *Engendered Lives: A New Psychology of Women's Experience*

It is now 30 years since I was a 19-year-old bride. When I became pregnant, I was certain this meant I was well on my way to becoming a successful adult. In my fifth month, however, I began to spot. My obstetrician kindly and briskly explained the importance of the new drug he was ordering as he wrote a prescription for DES. I thanked him, feeling gratitude for the medical breakthrough that would help me to "hold the baby."

Now my daughter is preparing to become pregnant and is researching the information that didn't exist when I was a young woman, asking the questions I could not formulate, making the decisions I never understood I had. I watch her, feeling apologetic, angry, and impotent.

It is now five years since Barbara Rosenblum died of breast cancer. She was initially misdiagnosed, and her cancer was only discovered after her prognosis was already terminal. She lived exuberantly for three years and then died an unnecessary and iatrogenic death, a death that still fills me with rage. Together we wrote *Cancer in Two Voices*, an attempt to make the very personal experience of cancer in the life of one lesbian couple a public and, therefore, a political act.

It is now four years since my mother was diagnosed with breast cancer. It was only at my insistence that she went for a second opinion, afraid doing so would hurt her doctor's feelings. Even now she talks of her lumpectomy with relief that they did not "take her breast." Now my mother takes Tamoxifen every day. She too is grateful.

It is now three years since I was diagnosed with thyroid cancer. Like my daughter, I gathered information, friends, resources, opinions. My thyroid was surgically removed within three weeks, and I take Synthroid every day. Once a year, I am taken off the artificial thyroid, and my body scanned for microscopic traces of thyroid activity—activity that signals the possibility of further cancer. There must be no thyroid activity at those times, no metabolism, no natural energy. It is all artificially produced now. When I don't take my medication, I grow blurry, yielding, unable to think clearly, make decisions, engage in my own life. Women who love me step into the vulnerable breach. I am grateful.

Cancer has insinuated itself into my body and my life. Weekly, the name of another friend, teacher, colleague is whispered, the pause that follows accompanied by each women's fears, memories, sense of diminishment. Time has such urgency now. A sense of immediacy pervades all my choices, all my thinking. I am in a primary relationship with time, everything and everyone else secondary. I struggle toward my life. But cancer is part of my life now, part of what shapes my politics. I no longer assume the dreams that begin with the words "when I am an old woman." I have no certainty now, just the precious nature of each moment, each day. My life as a partner, a lesbian, a Jew, an activist, a writer, a mother, daughter, friend, all my worlds and all my commitments to them have become focused, intense, protective.

I have health insurance and the tenacity and education to insist on answers to my carefully researched questions with often rushed or impatient doctors. I have the access and resources to help me formulate those questions and a community of women to love and care for me through any illness that might become part of my life. But much of that is a reflection of my class, my age, my privilege. That is a relief for me, but for my mother, my daughters, and the women who love me, it is not nearly enough. It is not enough because it is just about me. And because no woman among us is untouched, does not have a story like these to tell.

▲ ▲ ▲

I find myself remembering other moments as I read these pages. It is now 27 years since my abortion. I can still see myself, frightened, lying stiffly on an orange plastic sofa in an unfamiliar room, staring fixedly at the water-stained ceiling. I was instructed brusquely that the tubing that had been placed in my body would irritate the mouth of my cervix and the fetus would pass naturally within 24 hours. Afraid to do anything but be grateful that I had found someone to help me and that I could afford the $300 that was required "up front," I left hurriedly when it was over and went home to wait. Within 48 hours I was in a hospital, near death. The fetus but not the afterbirth has "passed." I lay there, without visitors, terrified, lonely, and filled with shame when I was told that legally I needed to sign a death certificate for the afterbirth. I never told anyone I had aborted a baby. After I was released from the hospital, I never mentioned it again. To my mother. My daughter. The baby's father. No one. It was my secret. My shame. My responsibility. There were no anthologies then.

It was been 18 years since I first uttered the carefully chosen words that described my experience at a pro-choice speak-out on abortion. I can still feel the stinging tears of relief when I heard one woman haltingly parallel my story with hers, then a second and a third. Then the shared expression of outrage at the similarities of our experiences, the fears that had never been spoken aloud, the economic and emotional vulnerability. Within weeks, women began to meet to organize the first demonstrations. Feminists began to organize, to write, to lobby, to change the laws, the attitudes, the possibilities.

We began a movement with our testimony, the analysis that followed, the careful strategizing, the political savvy, and the personal courage. As I read these pages, I remember when feminists began yet another movement, when other women began hesitantly whispering other silenced memories.

Is it now 16 years since the first woman disclosed her childhood incest to me. Certain she was the only one. There were no meetings yet. No speak-outs. No anthologies. Incest, like abortion, was an isolated, terrifying, and lonely experience. But after *Conspiracy of Silence* and other feminist books and articles were published, women gathered and began to listen to each other, began to compare experiences. From those early beginnings, we gathered the heartbreaking and enraging stories of battery and incest, acquaintance rape and sibling abuse, pornography, and sexual victimization. Feminists listened and began to create both sanctuary and services and to develop both medical and legal protocols. Our analysis became more inclusive and comprehensive, incorporating the range of experiences women were reporting.

And we created choices for women who had none. Women were told that they were "asking for" their rapes, their beatings, their unwanted pregnancies, by being promiscuous or by being sexual at all, and were either ignored or vilified. But feminists created clinics, centers, counseling programs, shelters, respectful and accessible resources for women in pain, frightened, and alone.

Now we are creating choices for women with cancer. For the past 50 years, medical options for breast cancer have remained the same. Surgery. Radiation. Chemotherapy. There was, and still is, inadequate and sexist research, unconscionable patterns of funding—insistence on focusing on the personal causes, our biology, our psychology as the genesis of disease. "We cause our illnesses" we are told. Rarely is the larger world, the one in which our lives are precariously being lived, held accountable: the air that is thick with smog, the water filled with industrial wastes, the animals fattened with chemicals, the fruits and vegetables sprayed with poisons, and inevitably, our bodies absorbing it all. Removing a breast does not necessarily remove the cancer. Cancer is not a localized manifestation of errant cells. It is a disease of the entire body and the entire planet that manifests itself in our breasts, lungs, bones, ovaries. It is a systemic disease.

Similarly, sexual abuse is not a localized experience. It is not simply something one man does to one child in one family. Rather it is an inevitable expression of male power, male privilege, and male hatred of women. Removing an abuser from his home does not remove the possibility of his continuing to abuse. Or other men continuing to abuse other women. Violence against women is a systemic disease.

And in understanding the systemic nature of physical, economic, psychological, medical, sexual,

and racist violence against women, feminists expand
our analysis to incorporate international connections
and symmetries in industrialized countries, as well as
in Third World nations to include the knowledge that
forced sterilization of poor women, disabled women,
and women of color is another crucial dimension of
the abortion "rights" movement and the
understanding that sexual abuse and the particular
forms it takes in North America is but one dimension
of the malevolent shapes of international sexual
slavery. Against young virgins and old women. Brown
children and red. Yellow mothers and white sisters.
All of us.

My own life experience has been a trajectory from
silence, ignorance, and grateful acquiescence to
political engagement in a series of declared epidemics,
epidemics that have struck my mother, my daughter,
and me. Epidemics that have taken loved ones,
friends, members of my community, and valued
colleagues. I know now that none of us remains
untouched. None of us can allow herself the luxury
of thinking she is safe. These movements are all
connected in my life and my politics now. Abortion.
Sexual abuse. Cancer. I have come to see that it is
silence that kills. Disconnection. Ignorance. Isolation
from each other. It is the act of testimony that binds
us, allows us to recognize ourselves and each other,
moves us outside out own skins, our own history, our
own pain. Connects us to something beyond ourselves.

Women are insisting upon ourselves and our
experience in male-dominated disciplines, gathering
and translating the data we gather, discarding what is
patently sexist and irrelevant, listening respectfully
and carefully to the testimony of women's lives, and
organizing in our own communities all over the
world. We are fighting our way clear of the netting of
paternalistic medicine, judgmental psychology, sexist

judicial systems in small and dramatic ways. Each of us in her own way.

I attended a women's music festival in Yosemite 10 years ago. Meeting an old friend, we began to walk around the central performance area, the ground filled with the dancing and reclining bodies of shirtless women. As we talked, she pulled off her t-shirt, exposing her double mastectomy. I was startled and uneasy about what I anticipated would be her vulnerability among the hundreds of two-breasted women. But as we walked, women approached us to murmur "thank you." There were no questions, just appreciation for what I began to realize was a purposeful political act. And, after a while, I thanked her as well. This is how she looks, I thought to myself. While it was another five years before I saw first Deena Metzger, then Barbara Rosenblum with one breast, by then I saw only a woman whose body had been reshaped. Not disfigured, not amputated, not distorted. But all of who she was simply in an altered body.

It is now one year since I traveled across the United States and Canada to read from and discuss *Cancer in Two Voices*. The outpouring of women was both gratifying and moving. Women who had never before thought of themselves as political, who held tightly to the belief that cancer is something that happens to other people, who maintained the illusion of invulnerability, became politicized. They began to see the similarities in their lives, their experience of illness, and their desire to create what they needed to fight their disease. Women who were already engaged in the range of liberation movements that have occupied political women for the past decades saw at once the importance of the connections of the health of the body, of the planet, of the psyche, of the body politic. And both groups of women had a deep

longing to gather with other women to hear their
stories as well. Passing the story on. Adding to it.
Finding the particularity, the common thread.

▲ ▲ ▲

As I write these words, it is one month until my
55th birthday. I have completed menopause without
estrogen replacement therapy because of my exposure
to DES. Instead of a medical intervention, I am a part
of a political one, a consciousness-raising group. Five
years ago, eight women gathered to create The
Wandering Menstruals. Like many feminists, we
created a form, one that did not yet exist, but one
that we needed to negotiate our middle years with as
many resources as we could. We have shared medical
and psychological information over these years,
supported each other in what have been very different
choices, and enjoyed each other, as well as all the
exhilarating possibilities that are opening in our lives.
I rejoice at this collection of possibilities. Women
are continuing to speak out, to create forms, to insist
on ourselves, our experiences, our analyses, our lives.
It is in these pages that my own experience of cancer,
my fear, outrage, hesitancy, terror, resignation,
vulnerability are mirrored. Deena Metzger recorded
the psychological, medical, and political experience of
breast cancer with *Tree*, and Audre Lorde added
immeasurably to that beginning with *The Cancer
Journals*. Now other feminists are continuing their
passionate legacy. Women are taking photographs of
our one-breasted bodies, decorating them, displaying
them, enjoying them, talking about them, expanding
the choices available to heal them, challenging the
attitudes of doctors, friends, ourselves. We are no
longer invisible, silent, our voices powerful, our
example clear. This gathering of essays insists on life

and on death as a part of life. On friendship and on autonomy. On interdependence and independence. On individual choice embedded in community. On the importance of a sense of humor in the face of life as well as a sense of outrage in the face of unnecessary death. This is a chorus of voices, no political party line, but the sounds of women telling our stories to each other and listening. Listening to each other, for in our words is the information we need to live. We are again shaping a movement and taking our lives into our own hands, for they are not safe anywhere else.

Part 1

Confronting Cancer

B'Gone: My Mother's Legacy

Suzanne Joi

Uterine Fibroids . . . Fear . . . 41 years old . . . Hysterectomy. Lumps . . . Fear . . . 46 years old . . . Breast Cancer. Double Mastectomy . . . Death . . . 51 years old. My Mother's Legacy.

Uterine Fibroids . . . Fear . . . 41 years old. I am my Mother's daughter. I refuse to follow in her footsteps. Her legacy must stop here.

I am at high risk, not only because of heredity, but also because my mother took DES in order to get pregnant with me: hence my middle (and now my last) name *Joy.* She thought she would never be pregnant again, but thanks to the miracle drug, DES, there I came. And here comes "high risk."

My fibroids measure 20 centimeters. My internist, although an MD, is willing to allow me—even encourages me—to try acupuncture and Chinese medicine rather than insisting I need surgery. She makes sure I am aware that any traditional, i.e. Western, doctor would be calling the hospital arranging for a bed for me at this very moment. She tells me I must see her every month and if my fibroids—the size of a grapefruit—continue to grow, I must have surgery.

A grapefruit is lodged in my womb, growing there, disrupting my bowels, making me pee as if I am pregnant, feeling like I *am* five months pregnant, making my monthly flows angry, bright red ragings, and causing me to walk, ride, sit, or stand in constant dull lower abdominal pain. My baby kicks her feet against me in glee as I hold her to my heart and I

1

scream with sudden sharp pain. But I refuse to follow in my mother's footsteps.

I chose my acupuncturist—a doctor practicing in my chiropractor's office. She introduces me gently and calmly to the world of needles and Chinese medicine. She searches for my weakened pulses; she peers at my extended tongue; she probes my distended stomach, feeling my "grapefruit" from my pubic bone up to my belly button. My energy is blocked. My energy is weak, barely flowing.

Pulling my pants up over my knees and down under my hips, rolling up my sleeves and tucking my shirt up under my breast, she locates all the vital points and sticks me with needles I only know are in me if I raise my head and peer down over my breasts to see them. Then she turns on soft, healing, Asian music and tells me to relax for the rest of the hour. I fall into a deep, immediate sleep. When she returns, she looks at me—triumph replaces the concern I saw earlier in her face. "Yes," she announces, "if you will do this every day, I know your fibroids will shrink . . . disappear even."

My eyes fly wide open. I believe her. My MD had hoped only for containment of the rapid growth, along with my ability to withstand pain, and now my acupuncturist is talking of disappearance . . . if I see her daily. "Oh, are you moving in with me?" She laughs, thinking I am joking. I cannot afford to see her daily, so we settle for once a week.

I see my acupuncturist weekly. I must change my whole diet. My liver is sluggish. (More fearful legacies: I have a great aunt who died of liver cancer.) Try to eat beets to help the liver. No more chocolate. No more cafe mochas. No more sugar. No more chocolate. No more food food. Only roots and greens and whole grains. Roots. I must eat food that resembles the afflicted organ. Chinese medicine.

Roots. No more chocolate. Only all the vegetables I want to eat. My spleen is barely functioning. I must eat nothing cold, or even room temperature, to help my spleen. Even water I must drink hot. Try hot water next time you are thirsty!

Everything I put into my mouth must be hot. No more chocolate. I drink hot water. No more frozen yogurt. (I had already stopped eating ice cream for the most part.) I refuse to follow in my mother's footsteps even if it means no more chocolate.

Chocolate is something you eat once a year, on your birthday, or favorite holiday. I was hoping she would say once a week, expecting once a month at the very least—but once a year!! Luckily my birthday is coming very soon.

My doctor gives me herbs, 10 big pills to take three times a day on an empty stomach. $24 per week plus $40 per week to see her. I probably save at least that on my chocolate-less groceries every week. Chinese herbs made specifically to treat uterine fibroids.

My doctor I insists must change my lifestyle, to get rid of stress. This I love. Someone or something tries to stress me out, I say, "What, you want the rent today? Sorry, you can't do that, doctor's orders, no stress!" I must teach my body to relax, let my energy flow. Every afternoon I must put on soft, soothing (preferably Asian) music; I must make sure that no one or nothing interrupts me; I must relax for at least 30 minutes. I end up taking 90-minute naps daily. And no chocolate.

No fruit—fruit is cooling. Chinese medicine. Certain foods provide heat, certain foods are cooling. I can eat only watermelon on occasion, no other fruit.

I used to disdain carob as fake chocolate, as instant coffee is to grinding my own beans, as plastic is to gold, as pressed wood is to mahogany, as TV dinner is to gourmet dining, as store-bought Safeway cake is to baking from scratch. But after one chocolate-less week, and after all my close friends insist, I reluctantly ask my doctor if I can eat carob instead of chocolate. She says, "Oh, is there a special occasion?" So I eat carob on my weekly special occasions.

I tell my 22-year-old daughter I need to name my fibroid so I can talk to it and tell it to leave my womb. She names it *B'gone*. At night, I heat up a castor oil pack and apply it to B'gone. The pack is wool flannel soaked with castor oil, heated and then laid across my belly as I lie on a towel spread over plastic. I cover the pack with additional plastic and my heating pad and then wrap the towel around me and it. The first few hours of sleep I get, I wear this pack. Everyday I consume a teaspoon of extra-virgin olive oil, mixed with air-popped popcorn, a whole grain, or my favorite carrot-dill, swiss chard hot dish.

My MD is hoping my doctor can contain the growth, at least until I reach menopause—probably in ten years. After menopause, fibroids shrink on their own. I wonder if I can reach menopause sooner. I try to search my heredity in case menopause is also inherited. My mother is dead and without her womb anyway, so I cannot ask her when she would have gone through menopause. My grandmother at 89 years old cannot remember when she went through menopause exactly, but she is sure it was over by the time she was about 54. She does remember killing 12 rabbits, rushing off worriedly to the doctor, fearing pregnancy "late" in life. He finally refused to allow her to kill any more rabbits, saying she was not pregnant, it was over. (She *did* have a husband, she reminds me, knowing I have only the magic fingers of my women lovers, so I would never confuse menopause with possible pregnancy. I find it unnecessary to tell her about parthenogenesis again.)

I begin to feel great, even without chocolate. My bowels are almost normal. I only feel pain when I press my lower abdomen. My stomach shrinks to about three-months-pregnant size. My flows look regular and my bleeding is more even, less painful. I am excited because my birthday is coming up. I will make it to 42 years old without a hysterectomy. Even more exciting, I can have chocolate! My acupuncturist wants me to go see my MD. My MD squeezes me in the day I call, perhaps perturbed that I haven't been back to see her in over two months.

I lie on the examining table and she probes my belly, feeling for B'gone. She cannot feel B'gone, except very low by my pelvic bone. She examines me internally and finds that B'gone is only 10 centimeters now, lodged mainly on the right side of my womb. We are both incredulous. B'gone has shrunk in half in six weeks. She now thinks B'gone will leave totally, and she wants to see me in three months.

I am so incredibly happy, grateful to her and feeling as close to omnipotent as I have ever experienced. I rush off to my acupuncturist's office to worship the ground she walks on and to let her know the miraculous news. I owe her my life, my health, my womb.

I have chocolate from Just Deserts for my 42nd birthday, I have my womb, and I have stopped my mother's legacy here.

Better yet, I have a new legacy to pass on to her granddaughters.

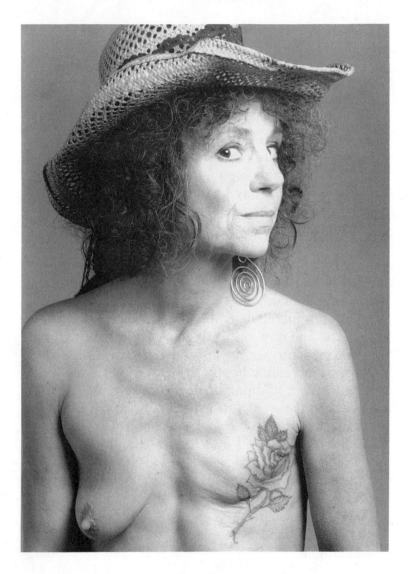

Andrée O'Connor

Tattoo by Chinchilla, Triangle Tattoo, Ft. Bragg, CA

Photo by Deirdre Lamb, 400 N. Main, Ft. Bragg, CA 95437
Copyright © 1992 Deirdre Lamb Photography

A Rose in Cancer's Thorn: Andrée O'Connor*

Beth Bosk

ANDRÉE O'CONNOR   When I came out of the recovery room with the mastectomy, I just got such a kick out of it. I realized I loved it. There's two factors here: the mastectomy and the cancer. Having cancer is not terribly funny, but having the mastectomy itself sort of delighted me. I felt like I had just been initiated into some higher sisterhood, the old Amazons, with their amputated breast, and I felt proud—as if now I had to live up to the Amazon image, functioning almost without men, leading an androgynous life.

There's an old saying, "All great minds are androgynous." In any kind of creative work that's true. You have to have an androgynous mind to create. Manifesting that physically can't be bad. It's just a symbol but keeps one on track. I've always hoped that my mind was androgynous, so to have my body like that as well suits me.

Yet you have taken a deliberate cosmetic approach to your mastectomy scar, having tattooed over and

---

* The first section of this article is from an interview with Andrée O'Connor on 4th Gate Gazette with interviewer Beth Bosk, broadcast on community radio station KZYX, Philo, California, March 10, 1992. The second section is excerpted from an interview with Andrée O'Connor on The Faith Daniels Show (NBC) on October 15, 1992. The third section is excerpted from an interview with Andrée O'Connor on 4th Gate, October 30, 1992.

7

around it the apparition of a rose. Why even deal
with a mastectomy scar cosmetically?

ANDRÉE   For me the answer would be because life is
full of agony and ecstasy, and when something
negative happens to you there usually is a way to
turn that into something positive—not always, but
usually—and I think it is well worth our trouble to
try and do that. The mastectomy was a procedure
done to save my life; without it, there was a
100-percent chance I was going to die. That was the
first step to saving my life, so it was a good thing to
do. But it did mean the loss of a breast, and a
seven-inch scar.
    And so for me, to have a tattoo of a rose put over
the scar in that area in general was partially an
aesthetic decision (because it balances my other
breast—my remaining breast—there is something now
on this side of my chest too); and partially a
statement that although something negative
happened, it turned into something beautiful. I
wouldn't have had a rose on that side of my chest
had I not had a mastectomy. It wouldn't have
occurred to me, for one thing, and it wouldn't have
had anywhere near the same meaning. So for me it
turned it into something wonderful that I am proud
to show people rather than just the loss of a breast.
    The word *mutilation* comes up so much with
mastectomy, more so than any other surgery, and it is
probably because breasts are so loaded, so symbolic
that for a woman to lose her breast is always seen as
a form of mutilation. I just don't see it that way; it
doesn't have to be that way, especially now, because
the newer surgery is called a modified radical
mastectomy, which means they leave your muscles.

You decided without question against silicone implants even before all the medical information emerged about how dangerous and damaging the implants have been to other women. Would you talk briefly about deciding against that cosmetic approach?

ANDRÉE   I guess it's personal, but it is also political—maybe it's poetic. As a writer, I'm really opposed to anything false in my life. I love things that are real and true, and I'm always searching for truth, so the last thing I would want to do is give myself a false breast and present it as real. It would be a deception, and that runs against my fur. I don't do anything to my hair. I've got curly hair on the natch—what you see is what you get—and I'm not insisting that other people do that, but I really don't like a lot of the political implications in cosmetic falsies, so I wouldn't have considered a reconstruction. It had nothing to do with the medical implications, which now, of course, have come out in all their horror.

I'm dealing with breast cancer. I have lost a breast. I want the world to see that because one out of eight women you know has breast cancer—or did have breast cancer—or will have breast cancer—and if you were to walk down the street, you wouldn't know that.

This is an invisible epidemic because everybody looks normal, because all these one-out-of-eight women are wearing prostheses so that they look okay, and that does not get the message across to the world that we are being killed off by this—we really are we are losing our young women to breast cancer.

By the time it is one out of eight, it is normal *for a woman to have one breast.*

ANDRÉE   Yes. And it is moving to one-out-of-seven and the age is getting down now into the thirties and twenties, so younger and younger women are getting it, and it really is wiping us out. Thirty percent of all women who get breast cancer will die of it. That's one-out-of-three! It may be me. I have a one-out-of-three chance of dying of breast cancer. And this is after all the treatment: the mastectomy, the chemo-therapy, the costly tests—all the other procedures they've got—still one out of three of us die. It's a flatline. There are two or three other cancers that have gotten a lot better over the years, where they've been able to have a much higher cure rate. Breast cancer is a flat line from the turn of the century to now; it's the same. More and more women have it all the time, but we are dying at the same rate.

Thank you for contributing to the transformation in awareness of breast cancer. One of the responses I've been getting is women finally dialing the telephone number to make appointments for mammograms since your portrait appeared in public.

ANDRÉE   Women have told me that too. That before the real fear was that they didn't want to find out because if it was cancer, it was going to be so ugly they didn't want to live with it. And then they realized it didn't have to be ugly, and so they are willing to save their own lives.

The rose symbol was a spiritual move on my part. The rose is sacred to the Goddess, historically, and temple priestesses—temples to the Goddess—used to carry red roses with them. So there is always this

connection between the rose and the Goddess, and
for me personally, it has that spiritual connotation.

I think with any kind of art, any time we transform
something into something more beautiful I think there
is a spiritual value to it. I really do. I mean I think art
is one of the most spiritual things anybody can do, so
even art on your body, transforming it that way, is
spiritual.

Other than that, whenever you find out you have
cancer, it hurls you into a spiritual sphere, in that you
are thinking in big terms now about life and death
and afterlife—what's really going to happen—and
that's, of course, going to effect your day-to-day life
and probably keep your priorities a lot straighter. I
think that spiritually we are all a little piece of God,
and that if we make our bodies beautiful, that can
only be sacred.

▲ ▲ ▲

One of the NBC producers saw the article about
me that appeared in *Ms.* and called to ask if I would
do the *Faith Daniels Show.* My intentions were really
two-fold: one, to get women to see themselves
differently, to not be caught up in the Barbie doll
syndrome, seeing themselves as "bodies" (a mastectomy is devastating when a woman sees herself that
way); and two, to try to bring to public attention the
fact that breast cancer is the number one killer of
women and there is no funding—none!—for
prevention or cure. Only treatment.

*There were two women on stage. You represented
two divergent and maybe even historic perspectives
about body worth. That issue emerges as the show
proceeds.*

THE FAITH DANIELS SHOW[*]

FAITH DANIELS   *Take a look at this photograph, if you will. When Andrée O'Connor lost a breast to cancer, she said No to reconstructive surgery. She refused to wear any kind of prosthetic device. Instead, she had a large rose tattooed on her chest and says she is happy living with one breast. She says she is making a personal and a political statement. She is joining us today, and so is Ronnie Calfani, she too had breast cancer, but she chose reconstructive surgery. She now counsels women with breast cancer and believes wearing a prosthesis or having reconstructive surgery is a vital part of emotional recovery. . . . I want you all to look at the picture once again, because, Andrée, you are quite proud of the decision you made, aren't you?*

ANDRÉE   I never thought of it in terms of "proud"— I don't think it is an issue of pride—but I'm certainly very content with the decision I made. I think it was the right one.

FAITH   *Why did you decide to go that route?*

ANDRÉE   Intrinsically, if something happens to me that's negative, the bottom line is this: I'm going to try to transform it into something positive. I'm at least going to live with it with dignity. That's what I hope to do.
   In this case, losing a breast was the best thing I could do to save my life, so I did it, and I got a tattoo of a rose, because it transformed it from a negative thing—an amputated breast—into what I

---

*   Broadcast Thursday, October 15, 1992

consider a beautiful thing. That lead-into-gold transformation was significant to me.

FAITH   *Did you go through a lot of angst in making that decision?*

ANDRÉE   No.

FAITH   *You never considered wearing a prosthesis?*

ANDRÉE   Never.

FAITH   *Never considered reconstructive surgery?*

ANDRÉE   No.

FAITH   *How did you know so instantly, when you were going through so much trauma, that that was not going to be a choice you would make?*

ANDRÉE   I think choices like that probably come from a very deep part in ourselves. I had never even thought about breast cancer, and one minute, at four o'clock in the afternoon, I'm told I have breast cancer and thirty-six hours later, I'm missing a breast. So it was all very quick. But decisions like that I don't think people have to think out for a very long time. It just comes from your whole philosophy of life, your whole way of doing things. That was my way of doing things.

FAITH   *At what point did you then decide that a tattoo was the appropriate way to go?*

ANDRÉE   Just about the same time. The man that I live with had seen a picture of a woman with a much smaller tattoo over her mastectomy scar and told me about it, and I said, "Yeah, that sounds like just the thing to do. That's what I want to do."

FAITH   *Did the doctor support you in this decision?*

ANDRÉE   Definitely.

FAITH   *Nobody questioned it?*

ANDRÉE   Not at all.

FAITH   *And other people are aware of your decision?*

ANDRÉE   Many. I live in northern California, and I've been quite public with it regionally—since the very first day—trying to be of some use to other women who are going through it.

FAITH   *To what degree do you go public? Do you show off your tattoo and the scar . . . ?*

ANDRÉE   Do you want to see it?

[Andrée lifts up the bottom of her t-shirt to reveal the tattooed rose. Audience applauds.]

FAITH   *So you have no problems doing that, obviously.*

ANDRÉE   None. The philosophy behind it in a nutshell is that I would rather live with something as it is, or transform it, rather than try to hide it—no matter what it is. It might be economic. I mean I would rather be overtly poor, and have everybody know it, than pretend I have more money.

   The psychological bottom line is this: "If anybody finds out the truth about me they might not like me," and I think that is maybe the unconscious thought all human beings have—they want to be liked—and "if they find out the truth about me, they won't like me" would be a terrifying thing to live with.

This way, people know the truth. And when they like me, they like me with one breast. And I never did define myself by my left breast.

▲ ▲ ▲

We have such a deficit vocabulary when it comes to breast cancer—"missing." Look at the challenge. Suddenly you have this asymmetric body situation and the stirrings of what you can do with it. I know this is a deadly disease. It means it can reoccur. It means you can die. Soon. But in terms of your life left, for those moments or months when you are just living it to the fullest, you can feel so beautiful this new way.

ANDRÉE   You just touched on it. The big deal is cancer. The big deal is not losing a breast. There is no other part of your body—my body—that I would rather lose. Not an eye, not an arm, not a leg. It is not that big a deal. I wasn't really terribly busy with my left breast anyway.

It's cancer that's the problem. It's the diagnosis. It's being told, "You have cancer. You have a 35 percent chance of cashing in within a couple of years." That's the important thing. Your life is suddenly different.

What I wished I'd said on that show is that right around the time I had my mastectomy, a year ago, within a day or two, Dave Drevecki, the great baseball pitcher, lost his pitching arm to cancer. They amputated it the same week I had the mastectomy. At the time Bruce Anderson, because we're friends, wrote me this beautiful note of sympathy. But he kind of made it seem like it was the biggest tragedy in the world, that I'd lost this particular breast. So I shot back a postcard saying, "Hey, it wasn't my pitching arm."

And that sums it up. This man lost his entire meaning of life. I didn't, it was just a breast. And we've got to keep things in proportion.

Let's talk a little erotica here. You return to your lover with one breast, and later on you add a tattoo. How does it change between you in terms of your lovemaking, really?

ANDRÉE   Actually, not at all. A lot of women have double mastectomies and have both breasts removed, either at the same time, or subsequently. That could still happen to me—it could happen to any of us—and that might be a whole other thing.

Having one breast—I mean how many breasts do you need on that level erotically—you still have all the sensations that the lover that you are dealing with (man or woman) still can get into with your breast. We've talked about it and it hasn't seemed to bother him.

Earlier, I was trying to ask Andrée if there was an erotic aspect to having a rose tattooed on her chest—the red rose itself—whether there was any kind of replacement delight that she was offering her lover.

ANDRÉE   Temple priestesses, long ago, would carry red roses. The red rose has always been associated with the Goddess. And I am only on the most casual level involved with the goddess, I'm not very good at ritual. But I do think of God as the Goddess, so that mattered to me.

I'm also of Irish descent. Red and green are the colors of the fairy, they're the colors of magic. I wanted those colors on me, on that kind of level, because I think there is power in that. So you put all

those symbols together and a red rose with green
leaves was perfect for me.

*But red also is what we do to our lips to attract
sexual attention or emulate the hue of youth. Women
blush their cheeks. Blush red is associated with
turn-on and turn-on attempts.*

ANDRÉE   Red lipstick is supposed to emulate blood—
engorged labia when a woman is turned on—if my
mother knew that, she'd never wear red lipstick
again. But I just haven't seen any sexual erotic aspects
of this—I'm sure they are there—but I've been so
aware of the Amazon aspects. The Amazons cut off
one breast in order to be better hunters and warriors,
and I suspect also to make a statement about
androgyny, that they were living as both men and
women. They were fully functional human beings in
an ancient world. I love the association of that, and
that isn't a very erotic association with men. It's more
an independent kind of association.

*Given the community we reside in, I imagine you
were deluged with suggestions for alternative ways of
treating your breast cancer. Did you even consider
anything other than the modified radical mastectomy?
Have you amended the allopathic treatment?*

ANDRÉE   A lot of people talked to me about
macrobiotics after the fact (because it all happened so
quickly). In alternative medicine, including macrobiotics, there are many claims and there's a lot of
anecdotal evidence, "This person stopped her breast
cancer. That person got cured of something else." I'm
not saying it's not true, but you have to have large
studies with large numbers of people where the
numbers are solid in order to have any cause and

effect proof. It has become a pet peeve of mine. I'm
sure it's true that somebody else stared at the sunset
every day and her breast cancer went away. There is
the possibility of remission with any disease.

*You still smoke, so I suspect you get this question
more often than you want to hear it. But what is the
connection between smoking and breast cancer?
What are you doing to yourself?*

ANDRÉE   Statistically, it is insignificant. In fact, in one
current study, the control group smoked more than
the breast cancer group, as it turned out. So I keep
smoking figuring it is probably my best shot.
[Laughs.] You tend to get lung cancer, esophagus
cancer, lip cancer. I stand to get all those cancers
from smoking. But it does not have an association,
statistically, with breast cancer. What does is the DDT
and DDE that were in our mother's milk when we
were babies and in our milk as we all grew up. And
the PCBs and the CFCs that are right now
bombarding us.

*With our demographic hump, we'll be the generation
the medical profession is going to test estrogen
replacement as a remedy for menopausal discomforts
on. Andrée, have you uncovered anything along those
lines? You mentioned estrogen before.*

ANDRÉE   Basically, some kinds of breast cancer are
more estrogen-powered than others. I have an
estrogen-powered breast cancer. Therefore, the idea
was to snuff estrogen in me. Chemotherapy throws
you into menopause no matter what your age. You
can be 25 or 30, go through chemo, and you're going
to be in menopause because it completely wipes out
your whole hormonal system, apparently.

Now I take Tamoxifen after chemo to guard against estrogen. What it does is it blocks estrogen. I was trying to talk my oncologist into giving me estrogen for menopausal symptoms and she said, "Don't *even* dream about it." So I wouldn't recommend anyone saturate herself with estrogen. Besides, menopause is not a disease. It's a natural part of life, just like when you start periods at puberty. So why not just go through it naturally and therefore protect yourself against breast cancers that would be fed by that.

All those things that are supposed to happen to women when they are deprived of estrogen are not happening to you. Your skin is not getting wrinkled and rough. You haven't become a screaming mimi. Your hair has not overnight turned white. You haven't gained weight. What has happened to your bone density?

ANDRÉE   Well Tamoxifen not only stomps (or blocks) estrogen, but for some reason, it helps your bone density, so they are now thinking of giving it to women with osteoporosis, or to women who wish to prevent it. So it's a nice adjunct, that it will help my bone density.

We have a patriarchal, male-dominated medical profession, pharmaceutical profession, and Congress that is in charge of calling the shots for women and once again, it's women who are being taken advantage of.

ANDRÉE   Congresswoman Pat Schroeder said, "Men fund what they fear. Men don't fear breast cancer." That's the problem right there. But I maintain, men do not want to live in a world without women. And as the numbers go down—now in the Western states,

one out of seven, in the rest of the country, one out
of eight women getting breast cancer—as the
numbers go down, they are going to live in a world
of one-breasted women who are dying within a few
years.

They are not going to want that to happen. I am
trying to preclude that by saying if every one took
off their pretend breasts and went around with one
breast or no breasts, we would scare the world, we
would scare men into funding us, into finding the
why and the cure for this. Because men don't want
to lose all their women. They don't want to live with
one-breasted women exclusively.

It is an invisible epidemic. No one sees anything.
Everyone looks fine. If the denial continues, then the
disease will continue. It's gone from one out of fifteen
women to one out of seven here in the Western U.S.
so swiftly. Every ten years it goes down another
number. Where does it end? In another 50 years, we
are not going to have any women without breast
cancer unless something is done, and nothing is being
done because "done" means you prevent it or you
cure it. It does not mean you go in for a $3000 shot
of chemotherapy today. This is ridiculous. They are
making a fortune off of us. And we are dying as they
are doing it.

I'm getting really mad at women who will not wake
up and deal with this. That they are sacrificing
women who don't yet have breast cancer. These
women owe it to themselves and other women to act
like adults about this, realize what we are facing, and
fight it. That's why I've gotten a little militant lately.

Coming Out As a
One-Breasted Woman

Louise Lander

"What's your bra size?" the nurse wanted to know. I answered without thinking: "I haven't worn a bra in at least ten years, and I'll be damned if I'm going to start now." This exchange was repeated three times over the course of two or three days; after the third interchange, I persuaded the nurse that I didn't require the services of a Reach to Recovery volunteer because my surgeon had already shown me the exercises for my arm.

I was in the hospital, where I had just had a mastectomy, and this little back-and-forth was my first exposure to the social pressures to which one-breasted (or no-breasted) women are subjected. This subtle coercion to pass as having two breasts seeks a total lie in more senses than one. Losing a breast means passing through a tunnel and emerging as a different person in a different world, seeing and feeling things differently from before, and being amazed that others don't seem to realize what a drastic transformation has been wrought.

Reach to Recovery, under the auspices of that august bastion of the cancer establishment, the American Cancer Society, is but a paradigm of the social coercion, subtle and not so subtle, that results in most postmastectomy women presenting themselves to the world with two more-or-less matching mounds projecting from their chests. Reach to Recovery sends a volunteer—a woman who herself has had a mastectomy and presumably has adjusted well to that fact—to visit a woman a few days after her surgery, to demonstrate exercises to increase arm movement and also to demonstrate the art of passing as two-breasted. She gives the patient, the recent amputee, the gift of a temporary prosthesis, a bit of lamb's wool to stick in her brassiere so that she may immediately begin practicing how to pass. I escaped this rite of passage myself, but Audre Lorde recounts the experience in *The Cancer Journals*:

> The next day . . . a kindly woman from Reach to Recovery came in to see me, with a very upbeat message and a little prepared packet containing a soft sleep-bra and a wad of lambswool pressed into a pale breast-shaped pad. She was . . . a woman of admirable energies who clearly would uphold and defend to the death those structures of a society that had allowed her a little niche to shine in. Her message was, you are just as good as you were before because you can look exactly the same.*

I was appreciably luckier than Lorde in my relation to the medical establishment on the subject of wearing a prosthesis. Lorde describes her first visit to her surgeon's office after leaving the hospital, how carefully she dressed for it and chose the jewelry she would wear (I knew *exactly* what she experienced!), and how devastated she was when her surgeon's nurse sternly upbraided her for not wearing a prosthesis because that was "bad for the morale of the office." In my case, when my surgeon asked if the Reach to Recovery volunteer had been to see me and I recounted my repeated refusals to consider wearing a bra, he just laughed and said, "You'll do all right," as if my stubborn self-assertion were a good sign. And later, when I asked him about the obvious hunk

---

* Audre Lorde, *The Cancer Journals* (San Francisco: Spinsters/Aunt Lute, 1980), p. 42.

missing from my right armpit, he started to say,
"Well, if you have reconstructive surgery . . ." and
when I loudly insisted that that was out of the
question, he again sounded mildly amused.[*]

In the meantime, while I was still in the hospital, I
had started thinking about what being one-breasted
out in the real world would concretely mean. For
example, I take the kind of yoga classes in which
wearing a T-shirt with special yoga shorts was my
normal way of dressing. Could I picture myself in a
class feeling comfortable in a T-shirt, showing off my
one-breastedness? I wasn't sure. I felt very much
alone and groping in the darkness; at the time I had
only a very vague memory of Lorde's *The Cancer
Journals*, which I had read many years earlier, and
didn't recall her eloquence on the "travesty of
prosthesis." My original, gut reaction wasn't really
principled—I just regarded a bra as an instrument of
torture. (Besides, in the bad old days when I wore
them, it had always been a hassle to find a bra small
enough for my diminutive breasts.)

My feeling about reconstructive surgery was also a
gut reaction. The idea of letting someone insert a pad
of silicone gel (or any foreign substance, for that
matter) in my chest made me faintly nauseous. And I
had read in Rose Kushner's *Alternatives* that a
surgically reconstructed breast "*does not* look like a
natural breast" (italics in the original). "They're
lopsided and uneven," she quotes one woman as
saying, "but I don't care what I look like when I'm
naked."[**] Meaning, to me, that if a person is

---

[*]   I often wondered if the fact that my surgeon was not an
American—he was an Israeli—made him more tolerant of such
nonconformity than most members of his profession.

[**]   Rose Kushner, *Alternatives* (New York: Warner Books, 1985), pp
297 and 293.

alienated from her body, it doesn't much matter what she allows to be done to it. After eight years of doing yoga, I felt much too close to my physicality to be that cavalier about it.

For me, one-breastedness was really the only possibility. But I felt confused and alone about the prospect, not sure how I would cope with it, not sure how other people would react to it or how I would react to their reactions. It began to occur to me that there was an analogy between the social pressures to pass as two-breasted and the social pressures to live as a heterosexual that Adrienne Rich analyzes in "Compulsory Heterosexuality and Lesbian Existence."[*] It seemed that this was another case of women shaping their appearance, despite discomfort or expense, in response to externally imposed norms of attractiveness. It also occurred to me that there was a large loss created by the fact of post-mastectomy women passing as two-breasted: it removed a way by which women who have had this searing experience could recognize each other, could be reassured that—again like lesbians—we are everywhere. (And with 180,000 new cases of breast cancer being diagnosed every year in the United States, we are.)[**] Conversely, the fact that women who have experienced breast cancer typically pass as women unscathed makes it easier for the rest of the population to avoid thinking, or feeling discomfort, about this enormous scourge.

I was mulling over such thoughts in my hospital bed, and I connected them with a recent discovery I

---

[*] Adrienne Rich, "Compulsory Heterosexuality and Lesbian Existence," in *Signs: Journal of Women in Culture and Society*, vol 5, no 4, 1980.

[**] American Cancer Society's 1992 estimate.

had made, an item I had seen in the newsletter of the National Women's Health Network announcing that a feminist press was planning to publish an anthology on women and cancer, with a deadline for submissions six months after my surgery. Surely the editor of a feminist anthology on women's experience with cancer would be interested in a feminist treatment of the pressures to pass as two-breasted, and an argument for open one-breastedness as a feminist stance, as a way to resist the pressures to conform to yet another externally imposed standard of present- ableness and as a way for postmastectomy women to connect with each other and to force the world to face the fact of their existence in enormous numbers. I was wrong. And I discovered that there was yet another layer to the coercive forces I was struggling against—the layer of feminist rationalization.

The editor—who turned out to have had a bilateral mastectomy herself, followed by reconstructive surgery—was subtle enough not to refuse to consider any type of essay on the subject of one-breastedness and not to couch her reaction in terms of siding with social coercion. Instead, she expressed a willingness to consider a personal account of my own experiences but refused to consider anything that smacked of advocacy that other women should follow my course, on the grounds that such an argument would be elitist. Claming that she would lose her job, a clerical position, if she went one-breasted, she insisted that to argue for one-breastedness amounted to "an exhortation of the correctness of a privileged position in a class society."

By the time I received this letter, I was out of the hospital and back at work. I think of myself as a writer, but I pay the rent by doing word processing part-time on the evening shift at a large accounting and management consulting firm, and my experience doing low-status office work seemed to bear no relation to the editor's. Everyone in my department knew why I had missed two weeks of work, everyone had been very supportive, and everyone could see that the right side of my chest was flat. I wasn't wearing sweaters because I couldn't bear the feel of wool against my newly healed scar, and I do own some loose-fitting tunics that I've always liked to wear, but I wasn't making a point of wearing clothes that concealed my asymmetry. I responded to the editor with what I thought was a rather mild-mannered letter describing my own work experience, and tentatively arguing that perhaps the reason her course of action was more common than mine had something to do with our society not liking to see people who are somehow different—say, mentally retarded or using wheelchairs to get around—and therefore exerting subtle but powerful pressures to conform to the norm.

This approach only provoked an even more negative reaction than the first one. The editor insisted that she refused to accept "any form of moralism" in her anthology; the fact that there existed no "socially realistic or effective" means of preventing or treating cancer meant that it was impermissible to argue "what 'should' be done" by a person with a diagnosis of cancer.

In the meantime, I had talked to other women, lesbians even, who had said things like, "well, if I had a mastectomy, I would wear a prosthesis as a matter or privacy," or "well, I think that beauty is just as valid a value as truth." I was feeling rather isolated and not up to putting myself on the front lines of a feminist war. Also in the meantime, I had started taking a poetry workshop and had gotten very involved in writing poetry. I loved the immediacy of it (my previous book had taken five years to research and write), I loved the obsession with language of it, and I found it to be marvelous cancer therapy—three months after my surgery I had come up with seven cancer poems. And the idea of taking time out from poetry to do another kind of writing was very unattractive. So my submission to the anthology became five poems in place of an essay.

Now I've reached a place in time and space when it seems appropriate to put down on paper my experience and thoughts. I've spent six months being one-breasted, and I've found myself pushing the limits bit by bit. I wore a baggy T-shirt to my first yoga class and felt extremely self-conscious, but my comfort level rapidly rose week by week (yoga classes are nothing if not supportive). Before long, I wore whatever I would have worn before my surgery. During the spring, I found that I couldn't bring myself to wear any of my tight-fitting turtleneck T-shirts to the office unless I was wearing another layer over it. Then one day I was surprised by a plumber in my at-home outfit of sweatpants and that kind of T-shirt and found that the world did not come to an end.

During a trip to Mexico in the summer, I spent a night at the home of a lesbian feminist in Tepoztlán, taking along the long silk underwear that I had been wearing as nightclothes throughout the trip—the top of which was the most revealing of my asymmetry of anything I owned—and found myself having an inner dialogue about whether I should emerge from my room to brush my teeth in my street clothes or my silks. I concluded that it should be my silks (which I would normally brush my teeth in), because my hostess should be able to cope with my obvious asymmetry.

Sometimes I think people aren't very observant. Sometimes I think you are less likely to be observed if you are over 50 and small-breasted to begin with. Sometimes I fantasize designing a public-opinion poll to test whether people notice my one-breastedness and, if so, what they think of it.

I look at other women's breasts a lot, not just because I'm a lesbian, but because I hope someday, somewhere, to find another woman with an asymmetrical chest. I fantasize about a Betty Ford or a Nancy Reagan announcing, not just that she is going to have a mastectomy, but that she is not going to wear a prosthesis or have reconstructive surgery afterwards. I think about the ugliness of an asymmetrical chest—even with clothes on to conceal the hideous scar—and wonder whether this perception of ugliness is intrinsic or only a matter of conditioning, or even perhaps a matter of clothes being designed to accommodate two mounds on the chest and not draping well when there is only one.

I think about the differences between a breast prosthesis and other kinds of prostheses: if I lose an arm or a leg, a prosthesis fulfills the functions of the lost limb, enabling me to walk or to manipulate objects as I did before; if I lose a breast, a lump of silicone inside my bra or under my pectoral muscle cannot comfort me or give pleasure to others the way the warm, cuddly mound that was amputated used to do. The only purpose of a breast prosthesis is to give me a silhouette that conforms to the norm, to engineer a lie—to myself and to others—that nothing has happened to me.

The analogy between coming out as one-breasted and coming out as lesbian seems overwhelmingly obvious. In both cases, one is "other," a freak, something that makes people uncomfortable and that therefore society would rather pretend doesn't exist.

If we can't help existing, we are coerced to pass, as
straight or as two-breasted—as not having
experienced an event as life-changing as coming out.
We are urged to engineer our appearance so as to
present an incomplete, distorted picture of ourselves
to the world. In both cases, passing means cutting off
the possibility of making connections and of showing
the world how many of us there are. In both cases,
coming out would be easier if it were a collective
phenomenon, not just an individual act. Excuses for
not coming out abound. We are everywhere, and we
can choose not to hide that fact.

Drawing Circles:
The Zen of a Mastectomy

Pamela Ferguson

My mastectomy was in October 1987. I've passed the five-year "survival" mark, but thousands of women haven't. Since my surgery, diagnoses for breast cancer in the U.S. have soared from 1 woman in 10, to 1 in 8. I first wrote about my experiences in *Sojourner*, the feminist monthly newspaper, in March 1991. This essay updates and expands that article. My story has been ignored by mainstream media and publishers, as being "too new age," "too alternative," "too feminist"—because, I suspect, I buck too many myths. I'm surviving without the usual wallop of overpriced American medicine and dehumanizing chemotherapy.

My life has had to change, but I haven't fallen apart. I've learned that breast cancer is caused by a complex of factors. Surviving it requires good teamwork: optimism, faith, exercise, diet, a sense of humor, compatible physicians or therapists, luck, a support network, and life goals. In short, involvement.

▲ ▲ ▲

On the night before my surgery I studied my breasts in the mirror and said goodbye to them, because at that time I thought I'd lose both. I thanked them for being with me on our long journey. I was 43. "Breasts," I said sadly, "this isn't your fault, but we have to part if I'm to survive." I recalled my puberty, the embarrassment of developing earlier than my friends, and my efforts—standing in front of a mirror at age 11—to flatten my breasts by folding my arms behind my back. In the next suburb, my best friend was pinching her mosquito bites and crying, "why can't they develop like Pam's?"

I thought about the time in New Orleans when the late artist Dennis Ruiz immortalized my breasts in pastels for a controversial show on female and male nudity that outraged the Catholic diocese. I thought about the day in San Francisco when my former partner Sophie photographed me topless during a difficult time in our relationship. Later, when I heard that trauma or loss some eight years prior to the discovery of cancer can be a triggering factor, I wondered if the sorrow I experienced over our breakup contributed in some way to my illness.

I thought about the past thirty years, and how society has bounced back and forth between extremes of the ideal, between flat-chested Twiggy and bosomy Jayne Mansfield. I developed the sort of bust that drew wolf whistles and catcalls in the street, and I hated it. No wonder breasts are used to sell everything from car tires to vacations in Africa.

▲ ▲ ▲

Breasts are big business. So are mastectomies. So is breast reconstruction, as we learned during the silicone implant controversy.

Such facts hit home when you have breast cancer. It's a very politicizing experience, a two-way mirror. Self. And society.

Breast cancer activism can be very healing. It gives rage a constructive outlet. I felt rage when I heard that the Bush administration spent more on one F22 bomber than on a year of breast cancer research. I felt rage when I heard that my Black sisters had been valued according to their breasts when they were sold as slaves. I felt rage when I interviewed a young Black activist in South Africa who'd had her breasts kicked shut in a drawer by police interrogators. I felt rage at the indignities women endure because of breast fetishism and sexual abuse and the possible roles these play in breast cancer. I bonded, fast, with others who've been through similar experiences. There's a massive network of us of all colors, incomes, and persuasions. Each of us has a different story to tell about the cancer industry.

Of the four doctors who examined my breasts in the months before a fast-growing tumor required immediate surgery, two found a lump and advised a mammogram; two found nothing at all and said, "don't worry." I opted to go with the latter, more comforting views. I work partly in the holistic health field as a shiatsu instructor, so I delayed having a mammogram because of the low-dose radiation scares of the time. I now realize I was wrong.

Also, I couldn't bear the thought of anyone using a scalpel or needle on my breasts, for a very common reason. I suffered from fibrocystic breasts. Not only was breast self-examination difficult because lumps increased or diminished with my menstrual cycle, but my breasts were painful, and no source of pleasure during lovemaking. I used to edge my way out of the New York subway in case anyone swung an elbow or backpack into me.

▲ ▲ ▲

I lost my right breast during surgery, and a few dozen lymph nodes, just in time too, because the cancer had leapfrogged to one of them. The cysts in my left breast turned out benign.

My friends were traumatized. "Why you?" they wailed. "You have always been our fitness role model!" My years of vegetarianism, daily exercise,

and yoga had not prevented me from getting cancer.
But such disciplines certainly had helped me prepare
for and pass through surgery without pain, helped me
survive and make informed choices.

First, I wanted to survive, and to recover quickly. I
was midway through writing a political novel set in
South Africa's state-of-emergency and couldn't wait
to return to my typewriter. The immune system needs
such a life goal as a booster. It also needs humor, as
Norman Cousins tells us so well in his classic
Anatomy of an Illness.[*]

After my surgery, friends descended with videos of
Charlie Chaplin, Whoopi Goldberg, and Jacques Tati.
People seem bothered by the fact that I wasn't
traumatized. There wasn't time. I had about five days
between diagnosis and surgery. Practical considerations loomed. I had exactly $400 in the bank and no
health insurance. But family and friends rallied
overwhelmingly. They moved into my life with gifts,
loans, and items I needed, like decent pajamas and a
robe. Without their help I would have ended up on
the streets of New York.

I concentrated on prepping myself well, drawing on
all my knowledge of yoga, meditation, shiatsu, and
tai chi, to harmonize body and mind. I went rowing
in New York's Central Park with my loved ones on
the afternoon before my surgery, to energize my
upper body. That day was a gift. It was a yellow and
golden fall with apple crisp air and a vibrancy of
light that seemed to surround me with healing energy.

As I was being wheeled into the operating room, I
sent a message to one of my friends to stop projecting
so much anxiety. "Don't give cancer any credo," I

---

[*] Norman Cousins, *Anatomy of an Illness* (New York: Bantam,
    1983).

said. "Just project light." I consciously blocked negative input from acquaintances and the media. This, coupled with a wonderful relationship with my surgeon, Dr. Idillio Noseda,[*] carried me through the experience without trauma. I joked with him about my mammogram "moonscapes" pinned up on screens in the operating room. "Be careful how you cut my muscles," I said dopily. "And give me beautiful scars."

As soon as I awoke from surgery I visualized myself doing yoga postures. Call it self-hypnosis if you like, but I also drew a lot of energy by concentrating on a photo of myself looking radiant on a beach. The next morning I started to move my hands and feet, then my legs, and gradually my arms. Apart from the discomfort of being bound like a trussed turkey, I experienced no pain and required no painkillers then, or in the days to follow. But I wasn't alone. My dearest partner gave me foot reflexology. Her nursing skills meant I could go home a day after surgery, which was a blessing and kept costs to a minimum.

Each day I did deep breathing exercises to movement until I could draw slow, graceful circles in the air with my arms, to Mozart flute and harp concerti. The circle evolved out of my exercises quite spontaneously, and appropriately, I realize now. Not only is the circle a healing concept, but it is a beautiful, whole, and very uplifting movement. I had lost a circle (my breast) and somehow, instinctively, my body wanted to create new circles for me. The circle was also a practical grid for measuring progress. My aim each day was to draw larger circles, horizontally and vertically, first with one arm, and

---

[*] A greatly loved Swiss Italian who works among the poor of New York's Greenwich Village and Little Italy.

then with both. Within a couple of weeks, I had full extension.

How well I recall the feeling of ecstasy strolling in Central Park, enjoying the dappled light and yellow leaves, and the clear, pure tones of a violinist who played daily by the pond. I was alive. Within seven weeks, I resumed my twice-weekly swimming routine.

The American Cancer Society sent me a Reach to Recovery kit of exercises. Though technically sound and helpful for many women, they lack the grace and harmony women need after such surgery. The kit includes a length of rope for pulling and stretching exercises, a good idea, but not exactly cheerful. What's this for? I wondered as I unwrapped the kit. Do I hang myself with it if I get depressed?

The illustrations are all of white, middle-class women, a point severely criticized by African American breast cancer activists like the late Audre Lorde and Salem, Massachusetts, health educator Augusta Gale, both of whom yearned for role models during their own hospitalizations.

Although the incidence of breast cancer among African American women is lower than the incidence among Caucasian women, the death rate among African American women is higher, and the American Cancer Society has done nothing to address this problem in the Reach to Recovery literature.

▲ ▲ ▲

I teach my exercises to shiatsu students, doctors, nurses, and physical therapists, to help them work with cancer patients here and in Europe. I have also taught the exercises in hospitals and been saddened to see so many women nursing their scars like frightened little birds tucked under their arms. It's equally dismaying to see how many women suffer from lymph edema, badly swollen arms and fingers, much of which, I feel, is preventable with the right exercises and scar therapy.

With vitamin E oil, scars and scar tissue soon become soft and supple, without the horrors of mutilation and disfigurement that have clung to the subject too long. Alas, too few doctors encourage patients to work on their scars in a way that is healing and loving both for themselves and their partners. Backed by a breast obsessed society that makes some women feel they aren't "women" after losing a breast, the medical emphasis is on quick cover-up, prosthesis, reconstruction or implant, without giving women the space or encouragement to work on their scars first, physically and emotionally. It's no wonder a lot of women never even touch their scars, let alone allow their partners to see them undress after a mastectomy, and it's heartbreaking when such relationships flounder as a result. NBC's Betty Rollin[*] probably helped more women than she could imagine when she appeared on a *Geraldo* show on breast cancer during October 1987. "I have the chest of an eight year old," she smiled. "It doesn't bother me. And it doesn't bother my husband."

Those of us who choose to remain one- (or no-) breasted, without prosthesis or implant, do so as a way of showing there can be life, swimming, and sunbathing, after breast cancer. A temporary prosthesis was so uncomfortable, I yanked it out of my blouse while dining with friends at a Japanese restaurant in New York a few weeks after my surgery. What a liberating experience!

---

[*] Betty Rollin is author of *First You Cry* (New York: New American Library, 1986).

But those of us who go one-breasted are often lucky enough to have supportive partners and networks. We strip in health club dressing rooms and saunas. We jog and lift weights. We rejoice in the beautiful poster of Deena Metzger of San Francisco, who, arms outstretched, head raised to the sky, celebrates her scar with a snake tattoo.*

My exercises utilize a lot of similarly joyful imagery along with the circle movements ("stretch out, make your scar smile !" or "raise your arms upward, like a flower opening to the sun"). They continue to help me, and I can tell they help other women, just from the change of expression and relief on their faces afterward. We're celebrating the joy of survival, not hiding ourselves like apologies for womanhood.

I also share my experience of creative visualization based on a knowledge of meditation, and the Simonton method outlined by oncologist Carl Simonton and psychologist Stephanie Matthews-Simonton in their book *Getting Well Again*.** Imagery works best when you choose it for yourself, relative to your own life. Each morning I would repeat affirmations like a mantra ("my body is perfect in the eyes of God") and then imagine a line of karate students high-kicking away my cancer cells.

The turning point came when I realized that cancer is a confused cell. I no longer wanted to attack it or kick it away. The word *malignant* vanished from my thoughts. I began to use a strong white light in my mind to dissolve cancer cells. I actually felt

---

* Deena Metzger, *The Women Who Slept With Men to Take the War Out of Them, and Tree* (Wingbow Press, 1983).

** Carl Simonton and Stephanie Matthews-Simonton, *Getting Well Again* (New York: Bantam, 1982).

compassion for the confused cell and tried to coax it back on course.

Sometimes I would meditate on a chart of the lymphatic system, send it light, then close my eyes and try to inhale that energy. This daily exercise made me feel more involved, more in control.

Involvement is a key to survival, as is faith in a combination of therapies based on an informed source. Few would claim that any one form of treatment is a panacea—and there is growing recognition of the power of linking conventional with alternative methods of treatment. Cancer is an individual experience. What worked for me may not work for you and vice versa. I say this to preface my reason for refusing the typically heavy-duty chemotherapy "cocktail" prescribed in cases like mine where the cancer has metastasized. I was shocked when an oncologist insisted on this cocktail for me, without even meeting me in person or outlining my options! To him I was a "premenopausal woman of 43" and the source of several breast specimens in frozen section. I was horrified to think any patient would accept a prognosis from a specialist who had never talked to her (or him) face-to-face.

After much research, I opted for the Rudolf Steiner mistletoe immunotherapy (known clinically as Iscador). Steiner was a turn-of-the-century Austrian born anthroposophist, mystic and educator, probably best known as the creator of the Waldorf school system. His anthroposophical medicine, based on natural and homeopathic remedies, is little known outside of strict Steiner circles in the United States but is widely known in Europe, especially in Germany and Switzerland, where it is used at several cancer clinics. Only MDs can prescribe Iscador. Anthroposophical medicine is a postgraduate training. Mistletoe is cultivated at the Lukas cancer clinic farm of

Arlesheim, Switzerland, where Iscador is processed, and MDs can order it through pharmacies in Europe.

I could no longer afford to live in New York or return to my previous workaholic lifestyle, so I sublet my apartment and joined my partner in Switzerland where I was fortunate to have a teaching outlet. We lived simply and cheaply in a rickety old farmhouse apartment with woodburning stoves and primitive plumbing. I cycled through forests, swam in lakes, bought organic veggies at local farms, and relished the glorious views of the snow-capped Alps. I entered the soothing, beeswax-candle-and-Birkenstock atmosphere of Dr. Verena Hablutzel's general family practice in Zurich, where treatment and options were discussed and there was no question of any belief system being imposed on me. On the contrary, Steiner MDs are usually quite reticent types. You have to convince them you've researched Iscador and don't regard it as some magic cure. Although the modern use of mistletoe for cancer was Steiner's inspiration— he recognized a similar cellular structure and growth pattern—mistletoe has been used for centuries by natural healers to boost the immune system and reduce tumors.[*]

The mistletoe essence is self-injected, and a different strain is used according to cancer type. Mistletoe from apple trees is used for breast cancer, and that appealed to me. I was encouraged by Iscador's track record, especially with breast cancer, in clinical trials done at Basel University hospital. I also knew that MDs in Europe had been using it for the prevention of breast cancer for women in

---

[*] The Christmas tradition of hanging sprigs over the door is rooted in a healing belief in Europe that mistletoe counteracts high levels of radiation occurring during December.

high-risk groups. It has none of the side-effects or
risks of either heavy-duty chemotherapy or
Tamoxifen. Moreover, being a natural remedy, it
blended with my belief system, and was affordable at
a fraction of the cost of standard chemotherapy. The
heavy-duty cocktail prescribed for me in the USA cost
more than my annual income. Iscador cost less than
$50 a month.

I took Iscador for nearly five years. Six months
after my surgery, a tiny, gritty area near my scar
revealed another malignant lymph node.* When I
heard the result, I remember sitting and crying at a
cafe outside Zurich's elegant Kunsthaus (main art
museum).

Then I walked in the mountains and meditated on
death. With a sense of fatalism, ironically, came the
knowledge that I wasn't about to die; I had too much
work, too much teaching to do. And, appropriately, I
thought about Jung quoting some ancient sage who
said a healer must pass through a life-threatening
illness in order to learn about healing. I was learning
things I'd never heard about or read anywhere in the
world. I wanted to learn more.

Hablutzel felt I needed some form of chemotherapy
in addition to Iscador, and her oncologist colleague,
Dr. Holger Japp, outlined all my options, heavy-duty,
medium, and mild, with relative side effects and
prognoses. I chose the mildest form of conventional
chemotherapy (Alkaran), even though Japp told me
there was a 67-percent chance of cancer recurring.**

The combination of Iscador and Alkaran had none
of the appalling side-effects normally associated with

---

* My surgeon had warned me this might happen.

** I didn't know Alkaran would fast-forward me into
menopause—but that's another story.

chemotherapy (destruction of immune system, hair loss, vomiting, incapacitation etc.), a vital factor in my decision. I needed to be able to continue to heal myself, write, and earn a living.

I slowed down a lot. Tiredness was overwhelming at times and brought flu-like symptoms or exhausting allergies. I had to give up my Wonderwoman image. Sometimes I used to sit and watch a spider weaving and repairing its web between the old farmhouse beams, over and over again. What a lesson in patience, endurance, and flexibility! I marvelled at the way the web withstood gale force winds and rain.

The web was a miracle to me. Spider and I became partners in our respective "circle drawing" and "circle repairing" ventures. I continued contributing to my healing through diet, exercise (yoga, cycling, swimming), and visualization. Interestingly, my decisions were ridiculed by doctors who didn't know me, but blessed by doctors who were friends and colleagues. Oncologist Dr. Japp used words we don't normally associate with the medical profession when he said I was "in tune" with my body. Another, more skeptical cancer specialist told me I was writing my own death sentence by refusing heavy-duty chemotherapy. I'm proving him wrong.

A vegetarian for years (no meat or fish since 1974), I opted to go the strict macrobiotic route for several months after my surgery, because I had heard about Michio Kushi's amazing success with a range of cancer sufferers. Because of my background in the Oriental healing arts, I respected the macrobiotic logic of high grains/low fats, beans, seasonal veggies and seaweed, to adjust the yin/yang energy imbalances in the body that cause illness and dis-ease. But then something interesting happened. Within a year I found myself bucking miso, seaweed, and lotus roots, because I associated the tastes with meals following my surgery. I craved fresh fruit, raw veggies, Earl Grey tea and cheese, and sensed intuitively when it was time to ease up. I'm still vegetarian and try to minimize my dairy and sugar—both macrobiotic taboos—but like everyone else, I enjoy an occasional binge.

Steiner MDs advise cancer fighters to avoid "nightshade" vegetables like eggplant, peppers, potatoes, and tomatoes. Six months before my surgery I can recall experiencing a sudden aversion to green and red peppers. Now I know why. Only in the past few years have I felt OK about potatoes and tomatoes.

Where breast cancer is concerned, animal fat and estrogen factors are prime considerations. Global breast cancer is highest in dairy and/or meat producing countries of North America and Northern Europe (especially Germany, Switzerland, Holland and Ireland) and in New Zealand. Is high-fat dairy or meat the culprit, or the estrogen they pump into the animals? The Orient has the lowest incidence of breast cancer—especially Japan (even post-Hiroshima) where a traditional diet is lowfat, nondairy, but high in B-complex, and favors fish over meat. However, Japanese American women suffer from the same high incidence of breast cancer as other American women, suggesting that diet is a significant contributing factor.

Generally, health practitioners and researchers advise us to avoid tobacco, alcohol, caffeine, fast foods, and chocolate. But is this enough?

Awareness of the estrogen factor cannot be overstressed. The prime time for breast cancer is just prior to menopause, when hormones are switching tracks and there's a surge of estrogen in the body, a way of saying, "Hey ladies, last chance for conception." Estrogen feeds breast cancer cells. It's the common denominator linking breast cancer with the pill and postmenopausal estrogen therapy.

Other, more subtle factors, may also link breast cancer in Western cultures to industrial pollution, breast fetishism, and sexual abuse. Of all the millions spent on breast cancer research, few programs ever bother to question those of us who've actually experienced the disease. Women on Long Island, New York, who suffer from the highest breast cancer rates in the union, are so frustrated by state officials' dismissal of environmental factors like toxic waste, they have initiated zone by zone research for themselves.

Those of us who've experienced breast cancer can help others prevent it, help raise awareness about self exams, mammograms, diet, and exercise. Upper body stretches (swimming or similar exercises) help breast health and drainage—vital factors to minimize congestion and cysts. I repeat these facts obsessively to my students—and to my nieces (one of whom has has had a benign cyst removed). We're a high-risk family. My paternal grandmother died of breast cancer, cancer runs through both sides, and my paternal cousins share my history of fibrocystic breasts.

Surviving cancer is hard work, requiring research into a whole gamut of contributing factors. We owe this to one another to personalize bald statistics. And to help the next generation of women stem the tide.

Sylvia's Reality[*]

Portia Cornell

Sylvia was born to a respectable family in the deep South. On Sundays they went to the Methodist church, after which they visited with their relatives. Often they left early when Sylvia's mother had one of her terrible migraines. Sylvia felt from an early age that she was different.

She knew she was interested in girls, not boys. At twelve years of age, she watched her friends go off on dates. She thought to herself, "If anyone knew I liked girls, they would lynch me like they do blacks."

She hid her desires. She wore lipstick and shapely pastel sweaters.

"You're getting so big, I think maybe we should switch you to a boned bra," said her mother, and took her downtown shopping.

"Let's get a sundae," said her mother, conspiratorially.

"OK," said Sylvia. She knew her mother was diabetic, but what could she do.

When she was eighteen, Sylvia married Harold as her family expected. When he kissed her at the altar, she didn't kiss back. After three years, they got a divorce. Sylvia moved to the North. She went to Divinity School where she met Rhonda and had her first affair with a woman. She knew it was a sin, but it was delicious.

Rhonda had a nervous breakdown. Sylvia transferred to Social Work School. There she felt she could learn the tricks she needed to keep herself sane.

---

[*] This is a true story, with the names and places fictionalized.

"You're not learning to read people's minds, are
you?" wrote her mother.

Sylvia's grandmother had been a psychic, who drew
her curtains and invited people in to speak with the
dead. Sylvia wanted to be a psychotherapist, but she
didn't tell her mother.

Sylvia's mother died. She had been blind for two
years. Sylvia went to her first Encounter Group and
learned that her mother had never "seen" her. For
four years after this Sylvia was manic depressive.
During her recuperation, she read women's science
fiction. She yearned to live the life of those heroines
of outer space.

Then Sylvia found feminism. Her moods evened.
She was able to work. She ran a Women's Center. She
was an excellent administrator. And she dreamed of
starting a women's community that would be like a
little village with a post office, a library, a hospital,
everything the town she grew up in had, only for
lesbians. She would feel safe there.

"You have to start small, something like a
bookstore," her best friend, Julie, told her. Julie was
practical-minded. Sylvia bought a share in a newly
formed feminist bookstore.

"You have to organize it collectively," said her
lover, Andrea. "I'll help."

But that was not Sylvia's dream. Her dream was
that she would direct the village. She saw women's
collectives folding like tents in the night. She didn't
believe in them.

She announced the first meeting of her project. It
was called "Women's Reality."

"I'll come," said Andrea, even though it wasn't
exactly her style.

Lots of women came to the first meeting. They
thought it was a terrific idea.

"We need a Health Food Store," said a lesbian nutritionist.

"We need a common entertainment space," said another woman.

The room was bursting with ideas.

Most of the women who came to the first meeting were not present at the second one. There were new people then and not so many. Sylvia knew how to run a meeting. She wrote everyone's ideas on the chalkboard. By the third meeting, there were only five women present, again all new ones.

Andrea said, "Women don't have the follow-through they used to."

Sylvia kept holding meetings. Sometimes only one or two women came.

Sylvia couldn't face the fact that she couldn't make her dream of a safe little town, like the one she grew up in, only for lesbians, become a reality.

Sylvia's doctor said Sylvia had a lump in her breast that needed investigation. Sylvia told the small group of women who showed up to the "Women's Reality" meeting, and they formed a circle around her and sang: "Listen to my heart's song. I will never forsake you." Sylvia cried. Andrea held her.

The report from the doctor was "invasive breast cancer with lymph node involvement." Sylvia lay in her bed after the mastectomy, staring at the cracks running into each other in the white ceiling above.

"I want to die," she thought. "I want to go home."

But she didn't tell Andrea when she came to visit. She never told anyone. She was used to not saying what she was thinking. That was her way.

Sylvia went throught chemotherapy and radiation. Her friends did a shamanic healing ritual for her. Sylvia located her totem animal. She flew around the room, gently raising and lowering her arms. She was an owl.

Sylvia listened to healing tapes every afternoon. She lay on her bed and floated away to soft music and gentle voices. She learned astrology, channeling, and how to read akashik records.

Sylvia wasn't working, so she ran out of money. She cashed in her IRA, the bonds from her father, and her share in the bookstore. When this ran out, she wrote a letter to all the women she had ever known asking for money. She received $10,000 in gifts.

Finally, she moved back South with her brother and his family. She cooked dinner for them, listened to tapes and read books. Andrea called often.

"You must be trying to support the phone company," said Sylvia's brother's wife. She wasn't used to lengthy phone conversations.

"They don't know who I am," complained Sylvia.

"Can't you just tell them?" asked Andrea.

"They don't want to know."

"Tell them anyway."

Sylvia was silent.

"Sylvia can't come to the phone. She's down with the flu," Sylvia's brother told Andrea on Christmas day. A month later Sylvia went to the hospital.

"Don't come to visit," she told Andrea. "I can't entertain."

Andrea didn't know what to do. She knew that Sylvia was very ill. She wanted to be with her.

Julie called. "I think we should drive down. I think she's dying."

"She said she didn't want me to come," said Andrea.

"You mean, you still believe she knows what she wants?" asked Julie.

"Yes, I think I do," said Andrea.

Julie hung up, angry. She was afraid to drive down alone. She felt abandoned by Andrea. But she had promised Sylvia something and she wanted to fulfill her promise. For thirteen hours, she raced through the darkness of winter night.

She walked into the hospital room at 11 p.m. Sylvia's brother, his wife, and Sylvia's two nephews were sitting silently watching Sylvia lying in the bed. Her face was pale and her eyes closed.

"She's been like this since yesterday," said her brother.

Julie pulled a chair close to Sylvia's bed and took her hand. "It's all right, Sylvia," she whispered. "You can go."

Sylvia opened her eyes, looked at Julie and squeezed her hand. Her eyes closed, and she sighed peacefully.

The nurse came in, to check Sylvia's vital signs. "She's gone," she said. "I'm so sorry."

Everyone in the room was crying softly.

The family invited Julie to spend the night at the house. She slept in Sylvia's room surrounded by her books and tapes.

They talked at breakfast the next day.

"She never told us anything," said her brother. "We had no idea she was so sick."

"I know," said Julie. "Sylvia was a very private person."

Later they went through Sylvia's things. They found that she had no assets or life insurance.

"Oh my God," said her brother's wife. "That means we have to pay for her funeral. Well it's going to be real simple."

"Is there anything of hers you would like me to take?" asked Julie.

"Yes. Take the tapes and all the books," said her brother.

"You know she went crazy this past year."

Julie didn't say anything as she gathered up the books and tapes.

A month later Andrea held a Memorial Service for Sylvia at her house by the river. About 30 women came. They sat in silence listening to Sylvia's favorite healing tape. Then ony by one, with tears in their eyes, they spoke of how they felt about Sylvia's death. Each woman had a different perception of who Sylvia was and how her illness had affected them.

"I respected her vision," said the owner of the bookstore.

"She never told me what was going on," someone sitting beside her said.

"I left her alone. I respected her privacy," said a colleague.

"She lived in a world of her own," said Andrea, staring out the window.

A breast cancer survivor said, "I look at that beautiful river and think about us sitting here today with Sylvia gone. And I know that 'life flows on.'"

Julie didn't say anything. She just cried.

Facing Death as an Alternative

Elissa Raffa

Lou was a 60-year-old separatist dyke, a fiery, often demanding and extremely loving friend. She spent the fall of 1990—almost three months—in various hospitals and rehab centers, first being treated for and then dying of metastatic breast cancer. In spite of the many terrific lesbians who gathered around Lou during these months, in spite of our loyalty to Lou and our belief in the possibility of finding alternatives, what could have been a positive dying process was perverted by three conditions. First, the very real threat of Lou becoming homeless, of her being discharged from the hospital with no place to go. Next, the ever-present question: what will Medical Assistance pay for? What treatment could Lou submit to in exchange for another night or another week in her hospital bed? Finally, the unwillingness of the oncology staff at the hospital to admit that Lou was in fact dying.

Lou herself had a hard time with the idea of dying. From where I stand, I imagine that she could have been more prepared. I believe that, by being better prepared, she could have more successfully withstood the pressure from the medical and welfare systems, that she could have been spared some pain. I imagine women with cancer learning to face death as an alternative, a source of strength in dealing with the frequently abusive health care system we live with right now. Whether women choose or refuse mainstream treatment; live for many years after a cancer diagnosis or not; die at home, in a hospice, or in a hospital, we could—as individuals and in

communities—become prepared for death. Develop
our beliefs about what happens after we die. Develop
our rituals for taking care of the dead and each other.
Know that our medical decisions are not based on
fear of the unknown. Become willing to admit when
treatments are no longer working.

Health care is a business. The bottom line is that
no one, neither Medical Assistance nor insurance
companies, will pay for a person to die in the
hospital. To stay in a hospital, you have to receive
billable treatments. It's not MA's concern, nor the
insurance company's, if a person has nowhere to go
when they're discharged. Quite literally, it's not their
business. On the other hand, if a person consents to
treatments—whether or not the treatments are
needed, or working—they can put off the question of
where to go next. Although welfare recipients are
often treated like criminals in our society, the real
welfare fraud is perfectly legal: for example, a
hospital selling expensive and unnecessary treatments
to dying people.

In Lou's case she was sold hip repair surgery three
weeks before her death. She had already been in the
hospital for two months, had already been through
the radiation and other treatments prescribed by the
oncologist. The doctors gave her this choice: sign up
for the surgery or get out. Yes, Lou had a fractured
hip, but she also had breast cancer which had
metastasized to her spine, her bones and her lungs.
And she'd had rheumatoid arthritis for ten years.
Because of the pain from both diseases, she had
hardly walked more than a few steps for several
months. A perfectly repaired hip would not change
the effects of the arthritis and cancer: brittle bones,
severe pain, muscles out of tone from disuse.

I knew this, and Lou's other friends—smart,
competent, radical, lesbian-feminist and separatist

women—knew this, yet we watched her get
railroaded into the surgery and were ineffective in our
attempts to intervene. We reacted with politeness
when outrage might have been better. We didn't want
to take away her hope or her power. We guessed that
she had, at most, a month or two to live but the
professionals were telling her—selling her—eighteen
months. What did we look like in contrast? Like
unsupportive friends who wanted her to die sooner?
Lou was understandably scared. The medical
professionals preyed on that. Unable to admit that
their treatments would not "work"—would not
extend Lou's life—they pushed her to give consent to
a treatment that was invasive, useless and that
diminished the quality of Lou's last weeks with us.

In our city there is one alternative to dying on the
street—available to a very few poor people with
cancer—Our Lady of Good Counsel Home, run by
the Hawthorne Dominican Sisters in Saint Paul. The
hospital social worker told us about this hospice, but
he ruled it out as an option, claiming untruthfully
that Lou needed to accept that her death was
imminent before the hospice would admit her. Lou
wasn't ready to talk about dying. We didn't learn
what a good choice the hospice could have been until
it was too late. There may have been even more
options. She was too sick to seek them out, and
I—like her other friends—was busy providing her
with healthy food and companionship. I'm sorry I
didn't question the information we got from the
hospital staff more thoroughly, express my doubts
more insistently, and check out the hospice more
quickly. Most of all I'm sorry that I didn't know how
to help Lou embrace death as a welcome transition.

▲ ▲ ▲

In the eight years before Lou learned she had cancer, she went to work every day cleaning people's houses, scrubbing their toilets and floors on her hands and knees, in spite of the intense pain in her swollen joints. She didn't want to go through the ordeal of applying for disability and being turned down several times, standard practice when people first apply. Although the rheumatoid arthritis got worse, Lou pushed herself to work until one day in August 1988, when she sat down and cried in the middle of scrubbing someone's kitchen floor. That was the day she decided to quit working. Her application for disability was approved on the first try.

At home, although her apartment building did have an elevator, Lou had to struggle with the step up to the bathroom and the slippery tile in the shower. Sometimes I nudged her to get on the waiting list for subsidized accessible housing, but Lou always said, "I'm not ready to face another change." Her other friends and I tried to help to ease her pain by driving her to get groceries every week and out for rides in the country.

A year after Lou stopped working, her doctor found a lump in her left breast. Lou was terrified of hospitals and medical procedures, but the first few months were smooth sailing. The family practice doctor who discovered the lump, the mammography technician, the surgeon who removed her breast—all were competent women who provided her with respectful care. Lou even arranged to have her good friend Leslie, a registered nurse, stay with her in the pre-op room and walk alongside her as she was wheeled into surgery. Given the limitations of a hospital, the mastectomy happened under the most loving conditions. And Lou was optimistic about the cancer being gone.

In April 1990, six months after the mastectomy, we celebrated Lou's sixtieth birthday. She put weeks into organizing the event—designing invitations; mailing them to more than a hundred women; and arranging for the right potluck food, the right decorations, even the right lesbian chamber musicians. I canvassed Lou's friends for contributions to an inexpensive one-piece stereo system. We thought it was a big step up from the little portable headset Lou listened to.

She didn't get much use out of the stereo. The remote control device that came with it could rewind a tape or change the radio station, but it couldn't turn the power on. In order to do that, Lou had to struggle out of her seat on her saggy green couch and take five or six steps across her living room, a task that became more difficult each week. She adapted to the increasing pain from the arthritis—and probably the cancer, although we didn't know it—by spending more and more time on that couch. She rebuked her friends for even mentioning that she might get a wheelchair or wheelchair-accessible housing, so we adapted along with her. We signed up for weekly shopping trips without Lou, delivering groceries, spring water and kitty litter right to her door. Eventually, she gave away her bed and slept on the couch. She rarely left the house.

Toward the middle of that summer, Lou complained of a new pain in her chest and shoulder, behind her now-healed incision. She tried to get a diagnosis—was it arthritis or more cancer?—but the technician who was assigned to take a diagnostic x-ray hurt her. He was rough, and not understanding about her arthritis when he tried to get her up on the high stainless steel table and position her body under the camera. Lou stormed out in a rage. "I'm never going back to the hospital," she swore.

She decided to put the thought of cancer out of her mind, and to assume or pretend that the pain she felt was a new symptom of the arthritis. She tried to manage that pain with careful dietary plans, homeopathic remedies and frequent prescription changes. Her rheumatologist called in a new prescription for a different painkiller every few days. Friends added stops at the neighborhood pharmacy and cooking meals to the list of chores we did for Lou. Nothing helped much, but she was always gambling on the future, always wanting to hit the right combination.

When she finally hit a crisis that even she couldn't deny, Lou waited two days to let anyone know. She called on the Sunday of Labor Day weekend to say that she hadn't eaten since Friday night. The pain of just standing up from her seat on the couch had grown unbearable. I raced over to her house to put some food into her hands. I sat with her while she ate, and until she fell asleep. Then I went home to call for help from women who were just getting back into town. Four more days passed before anyone could convince Lou to go to the hospital.

▲ ▲ ▲

She spent her first few days back in the hospital resting and eating, and trying to gather the courage to go through a new round of diagnostic tests. Her other friends and I organized to visit frequently—to feed her cat; to bring her mail, books and music from home, and good food (hummus, deviled eggs, lentil soup and fresh kale)—so that she could ignore the mushy food sent up from the hospital kitchen.

A CAT scan revealed two tumors on Lou's spine. Lou was beating me at Scrabble the evening the oncologist breezed into her room with this news. "We'll start you on radiation right away," Dr. Alice Monroe said, "that way the Utilization Review Committee won't make you move."

This was the first time we heard of the hospital Utilization Review Committee, and almost immediately it became a staple phrase in our vocabulary. The Committee is the body responsible for making sure that all patients in the hospital receive billable treatments. They had approved Lou's stay so far, but now that a diagnosis was in, she needed to choose a course of treatment. "Immediately," the busy Dr. Monroe urged, "Before Medical Assistance limits you to outpatient treatment."

Dr. Monroe could see that Lou was in no position to go home. According to the rules, if Lou was already undergoing treatment, she couldn't be moved out of the hospital. So the doctor offered Lou this friendly deal: start the radiation right away and put off thinking about where to go next.

I was already worried about where Lou would go next. I had seen the way hospitals discharge people who are totally unable to take care of themselves, send people home to places where no one can care for them. "I don't want you to be discharged without a plan," I warned her.

When Lou's two weeks of radiation neared an end, she set up a late afternoon meeting with Jack, her hospital social worker, and a few friends. The discharge plan presented by Jack was to move Lou to a rehab center for physical therapy. From there, she would go home, when the rehab staff decided she was ready. Jack had already filled out Lou's applications for subsidized accessible housing and

home attendant care. He assured us that a better
living situation could be waiting for Lou by the time
she was done with rehab. He neglected to tell us that
Lou would never be rented an apartment unless she
applied at each building in person. And he didn't
mention that the county was virtually out of funds
for attendant care. By the time we knew how hard it
would be for Lou to be taken care of at home, she
was already moved to rehab and no longer Jack's
client.

On the other hand, Jack went out of his way to say
that Lou couldn't be certified for hospice until she
had, in the doctor's best estimate, six months or less
to live. "I don't need that yet," Lou snapped at him.
He agreed that it was too soon to talk about dying,
but suggested that we keep the information about
hospice programs for the future. That brief
conversation closed the door in our minds to the one
place that could have taken Lou in.

It says it right in the brochure from Our Lady of
Good Counsel: all a person needs to be eligible for
that hospice is to be financially unable to pay for
nursing home care and to have a definite diagnosis of
incurable cancer. Some people live there for two
years. Some leave the hospice when they go into
remission, and then come back when they aren't well
enough to live at home. But we didn't have the
hospice brochure yet. All we had was the word of the
hospital social worker, and we were still in the habit
of thinking of social workers as more trustworthy
than doctors. Jack tied the idea of hospice to a
number—six months. Lou didn't like the number.
More importantly, there was no doctor around who
would say that her cancer was incurable. They had
not given up the fantasy of fixing Lou, or at least
keeping her going for a year or two. It was their
business to believe in medical solutions.

▲ ▲ ▲

Lou hated rehab. Most of the other rooms on her floor were occupied by nursing home residents, and she hated the sight of them. Normally, the nursing home residents and rehab patients lived on separate floors in the same building, but a reassignment of rooms was taking place just when Lou arrived. "They're sitting around waiting for their deaths," Lou said.

For Lou, the rehab program was supposed to be a temporary stop on her way to something better, independent living at home. She made up her mind to get through rehab as quickly as possible. Every morning, she worked hard in physical therapy, even though walking just a few steps made her cry out in pain. Every afternoon in her room, she worked hard on the phone, trying to set up housing and attendant care.

It was the policy of all the subsidized accessible buildings to have the applicant meet with the manager in person. No, she couldn't be interviewed over the phone. If she wasn't well enough to meet with them, how could she be well enough to live independently? They were right, of course. Lou needed a hospice more than an accessible apartment. But the hospital and rehab staff still wouldn't discuss hospice with us, and Lou needed an accessible apartment more than she needed to be sent to her old apartment with the shag carpeting and the step up to the bathroom. The housing people stood their ground.

Lou had a bit more success with the home health care system. They, too, wanted to wait until she was home to interview her about her needs. "But who will attend to my needs while I am going through your process?" she asked them. "That's right," I coached her, "Don't agree to go home without a plan." They bent their rules, interviewed her at the rehab center, and approved two hours per day of attendant services. Not enough, but the county had made huge budget cuts and that was all they could afford. Lou counted it as a success.

At first Lou made steady progress in physical therapy, and then she experienced a sudden setback. She neither demanded nor received an explanation for the setback. Looking back at this juncture, I can see that Lou had given up on medical professionals. She was willing to suffer pain as long as she could suffer at home. No one on the rehab staff intervened on Lou's behalf. They were running out of billable time.

On October 21, my friend Nancy and I were summoned to come pack Lou's bags at the rehab center. My throat was tight with fear and anger. How could they send someone home in this condition? Lou could hardly move. She could transfer from her bed to a wheelchair to the front seat of my car only with great difficulty, and she never stood up completely. I asked Lou if she was sure, and if she had talked about what would happen next with the rehab staff. No, there hadn't been much talking. Everyone was working off the plan that had been put in place at the hospital: hospital to rehab to home, an inevitable sequence, dictated by Medical Assistance. Why should Lou's needs stand in the way of progress?

▲ ▲ ▲

Lou lasted only two days at home. The walker with wheels issued by the rehab center was useless; it couldn't plow through the shag carpeting. Lou instructed Nancy and me to put an extra cushion under her, and place the portable commode right next to the couch so she could transfer without having to walk at all. She slept sitting up. On Monday, the personal care attendant came and cooked for her. On Tuesday, she cooked and helped Lou with a sponge bath. Friends filled in here and there. After everyone left on Tuesday and Lou was alone, the pain outgrew her capacity for suffering. She called 911 for an ambulance to take her back to the hospital.

X-rays showed that a broken hip was the cause of Lou's inability to walk. The fracture could have been the cause of her setback in rehab—frightening, but not hard to believe that she could have been sent home with a fracture—or it could have happened in her two excruciating days at home. On top of the news about the fracture, Lou was told that the breast cancer had now metastasized to her ribs and leg bones.

Although we took the cancer's spread to be the most significant news, the doctors zeroed in on her hip. It was too soon to prescribe more radiation, so they worked on selling her some hip surgery. Her hip, unlike the rest of Lou's body, presented a technical problem that could be solved. An orthopedic surgeon visited her bedside to talk about the options of hip repair and hip replacement. "I need time to think," Lou told him.

While Dr. Monroe, Lou's regular oncologist, had always been somewhat brusque, the oncologist who was on duty when Lou was admitted was like a Stepford wife who had gone to medical school. She talked at Lou mechanically, evading every question we asked by repeating the diagnosis and the recommendation for hip surgery without a trace of compassion in her voice.

Lou was frustrated by this circular discussion, and more afraid than she had ever let herself be. The more her questions were evaded, the more Lou's voice had an angry edge.

"Calm down," the Stepford oncologist ordered her.

"Why should I calm down?" Lou asked her, "I just figured out I'm dying." This was the first time Lou said it. An opportunity to deal with it. But the doctor blew it.

"We're all dying," the doctor responded in a chilling metallic voice. And that was the end of her visit.

Oncologists won't talk about death. I was surprised by this, but probably shouldn't have been. Somewhere along the line, I ingested TV images of kindly doctors having earnest conversations with the spouses and children of cancer patients. "Three months," those Hollywood doctors say with deep concern and then leave it up to dad and the kids to break the news to mom. But the dykes who stayed by Lou's side were never confided in by the hospital staff. We were tolerated, but never treated as a woman's daughters or sisters would be. And I, having grown up with a real-life controlling surgeon for a father, knew how he hated to admit defeat.

Oncologists are interested in treating the different forms of cancer, not in talking about the effectiveness of treatment or the impact a particular treatment will have on a person's prognosis. All along, the oncologists efficiently sidestepped questions of Lou's prognosis.

"The future is brighter with the treatment."

"How much brighter? You must have some statistics."

"The treatment we recommend can control the spread of cancer."

"For how long?"

"You have to be positive." Translation: we will sell you any treatment that is technically feasible until you refuse consent, or you die, whichever comes first.

▲ ▲ ▲

Leslie, who was in a graduate program in nursing, did a library search for the statistics we wanted. She found that even medical researchers shy away from the subject of breast cancer in its advanced stages. The reports she read discussed early diagnosis, breast self exam, mammography, lumpectomy, mastectomy, and lymph node involvement. Every report ended with a statement about the importance of keeping the breast cancer from metastasizing to the bones.

But Lou had breast cancer in her bones and, before she would consent to major surgery, we wanted information about what kind of difference it would make. Would she be all right in bed with a broken hip? Yes, they could probably keep her still enough to keep the fracture from getting worse. And her pain was being controlled with IV morphine. Still, the oncologists pushed her to agree to the hip surgery. It was the only billable treatment they could recommend.

When Dr. Monroe came back on duty, we pressed her for a guess at Lou's prognosis. "You have a good eighteen months ahead of you," she assured Lou. "The hip surgery will make a big difference."

None of Lou's friends believed that she had eighteen months. It was hard for us to talk to Lou about it, because she became immediately sold on the idea. She took it as news; we took it as an empty promise. Unlike the doctors, we acknowledged that no one can see the future, and we tempered our protests with kindness. Rather than telling Lou, "You're going to die soon, and the hospital is using you to train a new orthopedic surgeon," we suggested calmly that she postpone the surgery. The orthopedic surgeon promised that he would have Lou up and walking in three days. He didn't mention the fact that she hadn't walked in five months, or that she had both cancer and rheumatoid arthritis in every bone in her body. He just saw a broken hip, and broken hips are repairable.

Lou was in terror of being cut open again. We advised her to wait, to see whether the cancer treatments would help enough to make walking again a realistic goal. But waiting wasn't an option, unless she was discharged from the hospital. No one—not Lou, not her friends, and certainly not the hospital staff—forced a confrontation about the issue of homelessness. We should have, because it was bound to come up again, but we didn't. Lou vacillated in her decision. When her friends visited, she would talk about her doubts. When her friends were at work or en route to the hospital, the orthopedic surgeon would pay her a visit and push just a little bit. She signed the consent form when no friends were around.

▲ ▲ ▲

Once Lou consented to the hip surgery, she became cheerful and started to make plans for protecting herself. This time, Leslie was unavailable to escort Lou all the way to the operating room. Instead, Lou arranged to have friends in her room when she was wheeled down to surgery and to welcome her when she came back: two friends at 1:00 p.m.; the surgery at 1:30; five to twelve hours, depending on whether the surgeon opted for hip repair or hip replacement; and then time for Lou to wake up from the anesthesia.

No one was there when the orderlies came at 10:30 a.m.—three hours early—to take Lou down to surgery. "We changed the schedule," they told her, and no matter how strongly she protested that she needed her friends, her bed was wheeled out of her room against her will. She had, after all, signed a consent form, and if she was a little scared, she should calm down, it would make things go so much more smoothly. Lou was taken down to the operating room screaming in protest. By the time she came back with a repaired hip, she was no longer herself.

When I called to check in at 5:30, Lou was already waking up from anesthesia. I raced to the hospital. "Was she alright?" I asked Nancy who was already there. "Did she have anyone with her?"

"She couldn't reach anyone on such short notice. But the surgeon said it was a simple procedure."

Technically, it went like a charm.

We thought Lou was just groggy from the anesthesia when they pushed her bed back into the room. "Hi honey, you're safe now," we told her. We even applauded, but Lou started to cry. We stepped back, and tried to be less rowdy while the nurse dabbed at Lou's parched lips with a little wet sponge on a stick. Then Lou started to talk. The way she told it, she had gone kicking and screaming under the knife itself.

"You know that's not true," the nurse said to Lou, apparently for our benefit. "You were asleep, under anesthesia, before the surgery began."

Lou was in a panic now, crying and screaming. "They hurt me. They forced me." She was talking about the surgery, the way it felt to her—anesthetized or not—but she was also talking about something else, something that happened to her a long time ago, when she was four. Lou came back from the hip surgery talking in bits and pieces about a story which we friends recognised as a childhood abuse memory. Something—probably the anesthesia, which is known to bring up such memories, but maybe the experience of being forced into surgery itself—triggered Lou's memory of being sexually forced at the age of four.

The next day, Lou was even more anxious, and less coherent. She spent the next three weeks—the last three of her life—going in and out of a delirious state. The oncologist called in a psychiatrist, who prescribed Haldol, a major anti-psychotic drug. The oncologist said, eventually, that the cancer was probably affecting Lou's brain. Why, I asked, repeatedly, did this effect on her brain appear so suddenly on the day of the hip surgery? No one at the hospital would go near that question.

Lou spent days alternating between being focused inward, and then suddenly bursting with anxiety. "Help me," she screamed. Questions about how to help only made her scream louder. The help she needed was not of a physical nature. She was afraid to die. Even in her delirium this made sense. Her friends gave her as much reassurance as we could. Some women talked with Lou about staying connected to one another in the spirit, about making a journey, and seeing people and fires and animals along the way. They helped her seek peace with the things we can not see. They helped her move her joints so that they didn't freeze. They held her hands up to let the fluid drain out.

I had another focus. I wanted to get Lou out of the hospital. Now that she was a psychiatric patient, there was no more talk of Utilization Review. But if her mind cleared, there was always the chance that they would discharge her again, with a prescription for take-out psychiatric drugs. I wanted to see Lou resting someplace safe, someplace where she could just be. Where, eventually, she could die in peace. I wanted to see her cared for with respect. I made an appointment to visit Our Lady of Good Counsel Home with two other friends.

▲ ▲ ▲

I liked the hospice. I liked the calm smell of baking bread and the sweet sound of water in a little fountain. I liked our tour guide, a solid woman who described herself as a fallen Catholic. To my surprise, having long ago rejected Catholicism, I liked the nuns in white habits and black veils. Most of them were old women; a couple were younger. They talked comfortably about death, and not at all about Jesus.

Only two things stood in the way of Lou moving to the hospice: they had no empty beds for women, and Lou still thought she had to agree to die within six months in order to make the move. "That's nonsense," one of the younger nuns said indignantly. "That hospital social worker is always getting it wrong." As a matter of fact, she explained, that was why there were so few beds for women. Men usually came to the hospice ready to die, after having been nursed as long as possible by their wives, mothers, and daughters. Their beds opened up frequently. But women usually came because there was no one at home to take care of them. They often arrived in relatively good health. Because women give but do not receive the unpaid health care in this society, beds for women at the hospice are always in demand.

"You don't set dates for people's deaths," the hospice director told us. "Accepting death is a process. Lou doesn't have to accept a date for her death before she even gets here. She just has to be done with radiation and chemotherapy." Lou had been ready to give up cancer treatments for quite some time; she just hadn't known it was an option. The hospice looked like a nice, caring, clean, wheelchair accessible, free home where Lou could have rested and said her goodbyes in her own way.

By the time we figured that out, Lou was hardly coherent.

The nuns at the hospice pushed Lou's name to the top of their waiting list. One week, they estimated, until the next opening. But before she could go, Lou had to give informed consent. In the middle of a dying process that was scaring the hell out of her, Lou had to give informed consent to a move she still equated with death. Lou's friends knew she was dying anyway, but she still didn't want to hear it. Not directly. Slowly, whenever she was willing to listen, I told her the good things about the hospice.

It was a community of women. They would take good care of her there. It was quiet, pretty, and sunny. Calm and clean. It smelled good, like baking bread, not like a hospital. They would take care of her if she was sick, but it would also be a nice place to live if she started to feel better. It was more like being at home than being in the hospital. They had Fourth of July parties. In spite of my political disapproval, Lou had always loved the Fourth of July. Now I encouraged her to love it. She was worried about moving to a Catholic place. I repeated to Lou what the hospice director had said to me. "We don't pray over people. We're not that kind of nuns."

Sometimes she was interested in the hospice, but other times she didn't want to know. "No, no, no, no, no," she would scream. "I can't. You're hurting me." I rubbed her forehead and told her not to worry about it. I tried to calm myself, to stop thinking about this as a race. I hoped that Lou would be willing to go to the hospice by the time there was an opening. And I hoped there was an opening before the hospital Utilization Review Committee reared its ugly head.

As the week passed, Lou was still afraid, but she seemed more willing to consider the move. "Tell me," she would say, and I would repeat the same simple list from the top. Women's community. Fountain. Fourth of July. One day she woke up smiling. She had dreamed about the hospice, she told me. In her dream, it looked like a Japanese temple. I didn't tell her that it looked more like a Catholic school.

The peaceful times alternated with more screams of "help me," and refusals to eat. Lou was scared, but she was no fool. She spit out spoonfuls of jelly with pills hidden inside. We sat with her when she slept, and talked softly when she woke up screaming. While her other friends helped her to make peace with a spirit realm, I tried to give her hope for whatever time she had left on earth.

▲ ▲ ▲

It was snowing hard the night Lou began to die in earnest, and her friends kept a vigil around her. I myself almost didn't make it to the vigil. It was Tuesday night, the night I always took a break from hospital visits. I had no inkling, no premonition at all that Lou's time was so near. As I made my way home from my university class on unplowed city streets, I was preoccupied with the death of another woman, a stranger who would soon die and leave an open bed at the hospice for Lou. What a relief that Lou would finally be free of the hospital, free of the pressure to accept more medical treatments just to keep a roof over her head. And just last night she had said, with the oncologist as a witness, that yes she wanted to go.

I came home to one short answering machine message. "Call me, it's Nancy." I thought about not calling, about turning down the thermostat and climbing into bed and letting Nancy wait until morning, but my desire to cross something off my list got the better of me.

"You have to go tonight," Nancy told me, "if you want to see Lou alive."

Apparently, Lou's kidneys were failing and the only real question was whether she would let go Tuesday night or the next day. I decided to brave the snow drifts to see Lou alive. Or to watch her die.

Eight women were gathered in her room when I got there. Lou had not spoken for several hours, they told me. We took turns holding her hand and looking into her face to wish her a good journey. We promised to remember her. We read from her all-time favorite book, *The Member of the Wedding*, and from a book of winter haiku. The room was dark, except for a string of red plastic chili pepper lights around her window. We would have lit candles, but it was against hospital rules. Outside, the snow fell as fast as rain.

One by one the women left to drive home in the blizzard and get some sleep in case they were needed to continue the vigil the next day. I decided to stay for the overnight shift, based in large part on who else was staying and who was leaving. The one woman in the bunch whose unshakable faith in doctors irritated me was going. Janet and Irena were both staying. I hardly knew them, but I knew I trusted them.

With just three of us there, we drew our circle closer around Lou's bed. We touched Lou's strained, pale face and watched the breath rattle through the 'o' of her tightly stretched mouth. Every once in a while Lou startled, like someone who catches herself dreaming of falling, and gave a deep wordless cry. "It's okay," we told her, "It's okay."

The hour from midnight to one moved slowly, and I struggled hard to keep my eyes open. I finally decided to take a nap in the eighth floor lounge, just a few minutes to tide me over. I took my sweater and pants off and shivered on the hard plastic cushions under the thin hospital blanket. I had barely dozed off when I woke to Janet hovering over me. "I think this is it," she said.

I threw on my clothes and followed Janet back to Lou's room. Janet, Irena, and I watched Lou take her last three breaths. After the first breath I thought: there's no one there. Just twenty minutes before, Lou had been inside her body. Now the body, still breathing, looked like an empty husk. After the third breath, we sat in silence, holding back our own to listen carefully for the next. It never came. We sat a while longer and then, in one smooth motion, pulled our gaze away from Lou's face. All three of us turned to the clock and then to each other. Ten minutes to two. "I think she's gone," Irena said, and the vigil we kept now became a vigil for ourselves.

There were people to notify and decisions to make, but we stepped slowly—not with caution, but with a heightened kind of love and care I had never experienced before, allowing the right moves to become apparent. We sat a while longer with Lou's body, then talked to the nurse at the desk who had to get the resident on duty to come up and verify that a death had occurred. Irena asked right away to have the IV's removed from Lou's arm, but the nurse told us that we needed to make a no-autopsy decision before they could do that. We made a few calls to some of the women who had left only two hours ago. No one argued in favor of an autopsy.

Deciding against an autopsy meant closing the door on the possibility of taking legal action against the hospital. I knew that Lou, and all of us, had been wronged when they sold her that hip surgery, but I could not imagine trying to right this wrong through litigation. What would I do, quit my job to organize a lawsuit? I hadn't quit my job to organize home care for Lou. "No autopsy," we said, and the nurse freed Lou's body from the beeping IV machine and left us alone in her room.

More women showed up, some bringing squash and apples and sweet potato pie. We touched Lou's face as the warmth drained out of it, and talked quietly about necessary tasks like contacting the cremation society and Lou's out-of-town friends.

The care we took with each other was, luckily, mirrored by the nurses on duty that night. Each time we needed to make a decision, they explained what was customary, and then left the room while we figured out what we wanted. What we wanted was never customary, but the nurses didn't question or criticize. They did set one limit: that our impromptu wake in Lou's hospital room be over in time for them to dress Lou's body and send it down to the hospital morgue before the day shift nurses arrived.

Some women left as the sun rose, to go to work or to sleep. Three of us, Irena, Diana, and I, stayed to witness this last hospital procedure. Most families, the nurses told us, didn't stay to watch, but we were welcome. Most people in the U.S. leave their dead in bed and see them next all made up, with powdered face and styled hair, at the funeral home. They miss the part when the dead look really dead: wrapped in a sheet from head to toe, face covered, the sheet tied around ankles and waist and neck as no living person would ever allow. That's when a body looks like a body, but before we knew it, the men from the morgue arrived with a gurney which seemed designed to hide the fact that a death has occurred. They slid Lou's wrapped body onto a metal cart with wheels. It could have looked like the ordinary carts they use to wheel people into surgery, only this one was fitted with a rigid top frame which held a white fabric lid at sharp right angles. Instead of draping Lou's body with a simple, suspicion arousing, form-fitting sheet, they whisked her away under cover. That way, people paying their early morning visits to patients on the oncology unit could be spared (or denied, depending on your point of view) the sight of death.

When the nurses wrapped Lou and the men from the morgue wheeled her away, I cried for the first time that morning. I cried small, hot tears—not about death, but about the denial of death. The nurses were gentle, almost reverent, as they rolled Lou's body from side to side to get the sheet around it. Lou's body looked wasted and fragile, her skin as white and translucent as porcelain. Irena, Diana, and I stood pressed against the wall to keep out of the nurses' way. We stared in amazement as Lou's hip came into view: flawless, perfectly healed, the scar a pale brushstroke on the surface of her pale skin. "Her hip," said Irena who had, several times that morning, managed to give speech to my thoughts. And then my tears started falling: tears of anger and despair at the twisted priorities that led to sending a fallen-apart body with a perfectly functional hip down to the morgue and on to the cremation society.

Cancer Action Guide

Ann Mari Buitrago

If your doctor has just told you that you have cancer or that you may have cancer, the best thing to do is to get into action.

You may first want to cry, scream, and yell that you are afraid and besides, it is not fair. It's better to rant and rave a bit than to pretend nothing unusual is going on.

But then you need to start learning everything you can about your situation. You'll want to know what tests you will be taking to help find out if you actually have cancer. If cancer is confirmed, you'll want to know what choices you have in treatments. How effective are the treatments? What are the side effects? You may want to request a second opinion. What have other cancer patients in your area learned about these matters?

If you don't get informed and get into action, you'll just sit there immobilized by fears, choking with panic from being and feeling out of control of this critical event in your life.

You don't have to let that happen.

Here's how to start getting into action:

STEP 1

As soon as you leave the office of the first doctor who uses the word *cancer*, go to the nearest store and buy a notebook that will fit in your pocket or bag. Write down everything you can remember that you were told about your condition and what tests are going to be done and what they are for.

Don't be surprised if you can't remember anything you were told at the first appointment. You've had a big shock and your brain may have temporarily tuned out. If you can't remember anything your doctor told you, make a list of questions to ask at your next appointment—one question per page to leave room to write the answer. Here are some questions you might want to ask:

- What is the name of the form of cancer?
- How do you spell that?
- Where is it?
- What does it look like?
- What stage is the growth?

If you are to have blood tests or other procedures, ask these questions:

- What are the names of the tests?
- How do you spell that?
- How are they carried out?
- What is each of them for?
- What will the results indicate?

Now each time you see a doctor, take your notebook and write down what she/he tells you. When the doctor sees you are determined to know what is happening to you, she/he will take the time to explain and may be happy to write down the things you want to know for you. Afterward, at home, you can read over your notes, think about what you have learned so far, and make a list of things you want to discuss with the doctor at the next appointment.

You have a right to know everything the doctors know about your condition. It is your body and your life. So speak up, ask questions, request explanations. You also have a right to a copy of your medical records. All of them. Doctors are more than willing to make copies for you if you ask. (There may be a small charge for copying costs.) Just tell your doctor that you would like to have a copy of all her/his reports and those from other doctors she/he sends you to and all the reports from the tests: blood tests, ultrasound, CATscan, MRI, D&C, etc. If surgery is done and a pathologist examines the tissue to see if it is malignant, ask for those reports, too.

If anything at all is done to you, someone has to write a report. Ask for a copy.

Ask your doctor to explain anything you don't understand in any of these reports.

STEP 2

As soon as you know for sure that you have cancer and know the particular type, start collecting information. Or, if you are not feeling well enough physically, ask family members and friends to help. (The rule is, if you really cannot do it yourself, ask for help. Don't forget to call on your children for help, if they are old enough. Being left out of a family crisis can be very scary.)

Here's what to do to get more information:

- Tell your doctors (your primary care doctor and any specialists you are referred to) that you want to learn as much as you can about the type of cancer your have. Ask them if they have any articles or books you could read. If they tell you that reading about your cancer will just upset you, tell them nothing is more upsetting than having a disease you don't know anything about.

- Your local cancer support group can offer a variety of kinds of help. Even if you are not ready to go to meetings, the group will have collected useful literature and can put you in touch with people who have struggled with your kind of cancer. It's good to talk things over with someone who has been through what you are going through.

- Call the American Cancer Society hotline, 1-800-4-CANCER. The researcher who answers can send you free literature and will check the ACS data banks for the latest research information on the diagnosis and treatment of your particular cancer. (Have your notebook handy. By this time you may want to have a larger one for use at home; the smaller one is still best for taking notes on your knee in a doctor's office or hospital room.)

- Call or write World Research Foundation (15300 Ventura Blvd., Suite 405, Sherman Oaks, CA 91403, 818-907-LIVE). This is a privately run library with a large world-wide computer data bank of articles on both standard Western medicine and alternative treatments. Tell them your diagnosis and whether you want literature on just standard medical treatments or also on alternative therapies. (Alternative therapies are commonly non-toxic, homeopathic approaches.) Each search costs about $60. A large pile of reading material will arrive in the mail. For a bit more you can have the search expedited and mailed Federal Express.

- Another service in Seattle, Washington, CAN HELP (3111 Paradise Bay Road, Port Ludlow, WA 98365-9771, 206-437-2291) will help you search for organizations, private clinics, and private MDs that practice traditional and alternative medicine. After seven days of analyzing your medical records and consulting with its specialists, this group writes an evaluative and detailed report on the alternative, orthodox, and experimental therapies that appear most promising for your diagnosis. With the report, you get background articles and computer printouts of relevant studies. Call first; they are open seven days a week, 24 hours a day. $400 for a 7-day personal report; $150 extra for a 2-day report. Patrick M. McGrady, Jr., director, is a medical writer not a doctor.

- Write or call the Cancer Control Society (2043 N. Berendo St., Los Angeles, CA 90027, 213-663-7801). This group holds conferences and publishes literature on non-toxic cancer therapies. One useful service is their list of individuals (names, addresses and phone numbers) who have survived ten years or more on nontoxic therapies. You can call and talk to people who had the same kind of cancer you have.

- Contact International Health Information Institute (14417 Chase Street, Suite 432, Panorama City, CA 91402). This is primarily a telephone consultation service. The director, Jack Tropp, a freelance writer and consultant, was a correspondent for *Prevention Magazine* and research director for various cancer centers. He helps inquirers sort the wheat from the chaff among alternative/holistic therapies. Thirty-minute phone consultation costs $50; thirty- to sixty-minute call costs $75. Sliding scale available.

- Request information from the Foundation for Advancement in Cancer Therapy (FACT) (P.O. Box 1242, Old Chelsea Station, New York, NY 10113, 212-741-2790), a non-profit educational organization that distributes information on nontoxic therapies for cancer. Books, articles, and cassette tapes are available.

- A book that lists and describes many alternative, non-toxic therapies is John Fink's *Third Opinion* (Garden City Park, NY: Avery Publishing Group, 1992). It has many subtitles: An International Directory to Alternative Therapy Centers for the Treatment and Prevention of Cancer and Other Degenerative Diseases. For People Who Want to Make Informed Decisions About Alternative Cancer Care Programs, Support Groups and Informational Services. This book also includes "Guidelines for Choosing a Therapy," a glossary of commonly used terms, a bibliography, and a region-by-region listing of treatment centers.

STEP 3

Read and think about all this information. Discuss it with your doctors, your family and friends. Little by little, decide what to do.

STEP 4

Eating a healthier diet is another measure many cancer patients take even before other medical questions have been settled. A healthier diet will make your body as strong as possible to withstand or intensify the effect of whatever treatment is chosen. A better diet may not cure the cancer, but it will enable your body to fight whatever cancer is around after surgery or treatment. It will also make you feel better.

Eating better is something you can do for yourself long before all the tests results are in or you've decided on a treatment plan. You don't have to sit passively and wait. You can get into action right away. You can start helping your immune system get into its best fighting shape.

There are many books to get you started thinking about how to eat better. A good place to locate them is the local health food store and the local support group. Among the better known books are these:

Michio Kushi, *The Cancer Prevention Diet*. New York: St. Martin's Press.
Aveline Kushi & Wendy Esko, *The Changing Seasons*. Wayne, NJ: Avery Publishing Group. (Cookbook.)

These books set out the basic principles of a traditional macrobiotic diet, which recommends avoiding all dairy products, sugar and all nightshade plants (tomatoes, potatoes, eggplant, peppers and tobacco) and centering the diet on organic food, primarily grains and vegetables, cooked with only small amounts of fat. The cookbook's menu plan is organized around a seven day plan for each season. The dishes rely heavily on food familiar to the Japanese palate.

Annemarie Colbin, *Food and Healing*. New York: Ballantine Books.
Annemarie Colbin, *The Book of Whole Meals*. New York: Ballantine Books. (Cookbook.)

These books set out a modified macrobiotic eating system, centered on grains and vegetables but with menus and recipes adapted to American tastes. The cookbook is organized around a seven day meal plan for each growing season and step by step instructions on how to cook each dish. Organic food is preferred. Sugar, fat, dairy and nightshade plants should be avoided or eaten infrequently. Colbin's eating regimen is less strict, principally because the book is not directed at cancer patients but at the general public and has the added benefit that it is food that tastes good to Americans and is good for the whole family, sick or well.

STEP 5

Remember to keep on doing things for fun and, as much as possible, continue to live the kind of life you enjoy. That's part of getting in action, too. And as soon as you are stabilized and feeling better, start helping someone else get into action. Share the material you've collected and pass on what you've learned. However long we live, there is no need for our lives to be dull and boring and useless.

"Here's How Things Are Going" Bulletin*

Ann Mari Buitrago

Part 1

I hope that everyone who receives this bulletin knows that a year ago I was discovered to have a rare form of ovarian cancer. If not, now you do.

I have initiated this bulletin and those to follow at the urging of my more far-flung friends who want to know how I'm doing and generally what's up. This first one is long in order to catch everyone up. I expect successors to be one pagers.

SYNOPSIS

I've been feeling and doing fine all year except for a few weeks last month when there was a brief but big scare that I might have developed a second primary cancer. "No, no, no," I said, stamping my feet. "That is totally unacceptable, completely out of the question." And that's what the breast specialist said, too, after he poked and prodded and studied the pictures. "Nothing here but a little thickening of the breast tissue brought on by aging," he said. Lovely man. And so smart, too.

So I spent the weekend in Portland celebrating—movies, dinner out, coffee shops, art exhibits, helping take care of a friend's baby, dancing to a live

---

* This article is an abridged version of three bulletins the author wrote to inform her friends and family of her progress in dealing with ovarian cancer.

performance by Flor de Caña at Zoots, and picking
up my new computer from Chip Berlet in Boston.

Treatment began with six chemotherapy sessions in
Portland following surgery. Then I researched
standard and alternative regimens and last fall
decided on a homeopathic immune-system-building
therapy, centered on Iscador (mistletoe), in addition
to my macrobiotic, organic diet and daily yoga. In
November I spent a month at a Swiss clinic, home
base of the Iscador treatment, and will continue this
treatment by self-injection indefinitely. I am
monitored by my oncologist every three months
(physical exam) and by my homeopathic doctor
rather more frequently (blood tests).

I have enclosed a copy of "Cancer Action Guide,"
a pamphlet I am developing to suggest ways for
people to get into action once they have been
diagnosed.*

If you stop reading now you will not have missed
anything except details and a few funny stories. Suit
yourself.

DIAGNOSIS

A few days before Christmas 1990, off I went for
my routine annual physical at the health center in
Eastport. I had no symptoms or complaints. Home I
came with a diagnosed tumor of unknown character
and a string of appointments for further testing
arranged by my primary physician, David Austin:
CATscan, D&C, MRI. Rob and other dear friends
drove me to these trysts, each of which began with
digging the car out, in the midst of horrendous
snowstorms. The results of the D&C and the MRI

---

* Ann Mari Buitrago's "Cancer Action Guide" appears on pages
  75-82 in this book.

simultaneously confirmed in early January that the tumor was malignant. By that time I was looking about six months pregnant. Nonetheless, Rob and I stacked five cords of wood on the side deck without any difficulty on my part. His either.

The gynecologist in Bangor arranged for an emergency appointment with a gynecological oncologist in Portland. There are only two in the whole state and they are in partnership in Portland. One is Puerto Rican. I got the other one, Gary Smith.

"May I call you Ann Mari?"

"That depends entirely on what I am to call you."

"Call me Gary."

"Fine. You may call me Ann Mari. Otherwise you would have to call me Dr. Buitrago."

After examining me and my records, Gary pronounced that there was a 99 percent chance that the tumor was malignant.

"Why isn't it 100 percent?"

"Because there is an extremely rare tumor that produces the same symptoms but is benign.

"Oh, I vote for that one! My kind of tumor."

AS BUSH WENT TO WAR, I WENT TO SURGERY

Rob and I drove to Portland on a snowy Monday morning and checked into a Suisse Chalet near the hospital, borrowed scissors for Victoria to give me a snappy haircut, and a vase for Jason's gorgeous red roses. The Szatkowski-Eckhardt support system radiated me with love, fun, service, and chicken soup from that day until this.

Surgery, inelegantly called "debulking," was to occur on Wednesday, January 16. "Don't let them start the war until I'm ready to protest again," I muttered slurrily as I rattled along to the operating room. The surgery was a success in the sense that all

the visible cancer could be removed and there were
no indications of cancer in the lymph nodes.

But the report from pathology indicated that the
tumor was not the benign tumor I had voted for. It
was not even your garden variety ovarian cancer (not
that that is any great bargain). It was instead a rare
sarcomal tumor of the mixed mesodermal type. Only
one percent of all ovarian cancers are of this type,
i.e., 17 new cases each year. It is an extremely
virulent tumor and not dependably responsive to
chemotherapy and/or radiation.

Because this tumor is so rarely seen, my case was
presented to a hospital staff conference. The
conference report recommended throwing the kitchen
sink at it—massive doses of multiple chemotherapy
and radiation. Gary Smith recommended against such
treatment on the grounds that research had failed to
show any connection between such treatment and a
longer life and that, long or short, that life would be
miserable. He proposed instead a short course of
rather mild chemotherapy (carboplatin) followed by
daily maintenance doses of Lukeran by tablet forever.
He argued that he had several patients live for several
years on this regimen and, of course, the quality of
their life was superior to one that involved massive
chemotherapy with all its disagreeable side effects.

Gary wanted to start the chemotherapy before I left
the hospital. I refused on the grounds that I wasn't
even fit to sign a contract. Rob, my major and much
loved support system, brought me home to recover
from the surgery and decide what to do about
treatment. If not chemo, then which of the many
alternative therapies? How to find out about them?
But first, an easier decision: what kind of food should
I be eating to get strong and to prepare to help my
immune system fight the cancer and to withstand
chemo if I decided to accept it?

FOOD: WHAT TO EAT AND WHERE TO GET IT

Within a week or two, having read a dozen diet and nutrition books brought and mailed to me by friends, I decided to go on a modified macrobiotic diet. The American Cancer Society's recommended eating plan assumed you were addicted to junk food so they recommended augmenting your hot dog with a serving of frozen vegetable. Michio Kushi's *Cancer Prevention Diet* and Anne Marie Colbin's *Food and Healing* and *The Book of Whole Meals* made enough sense to me that I felt a macrobiotic diet could only do me good, whether or not it prevented cancer. The rules are simple in concept: no dairy, no nightshade plants, no sugar, and only small amounts of fat and fish. My first modification was to add small amounts of organic meat, particularly chicken. How could I get well without chicken soup?

I found two local organic farming couples nearby. Bonnie and Arnold Pearlman (Crossroads Farm in Jonesboro) had beets, carrots, and squash in their root cellar. Bunny and Susan (Yellow Birch Farm in Pembroke) had a supply of onions and free range chicken, goat, and lamb in their freezer. Fresh ocean fish and seafood was readily available. The local health food store and my food coop group had organic beans, brown rice, pasta, sea vegetables, tofu, miso, tempeh, and the requisite oils, teas, vinegar, soy sauce, and sea salt. The country is not as isolated as it used to be.

Rounding up a supply of green leafy vegetables during the winter months was not so simple. Our local health food stores do not carry produce. So, on each trip to Portland for chemo I stuffed two picnic coolers full of organic greens from the health food stores there. Friends often returned from trips to Bangor with a prize organic broccoli found at a supermarket. When that ran out I could order fruits and veggies from a mail order organic distributor in California.* It cost the earth, but they arrived in good shape two days later.

Step by step Rob and I learned to cook and eat a macrobiotic diet, modified to include small amounts of animal protein. We discarded dishes that were simply unpalatable. I threw my entire supper in the garbage one night, while Rob, good farm boy that he is, plowed through about half of his before following suit.

The most difficult part of being on such an eating regimen outside a big city is the destruction of most spontaneous social life. You cannot eat in restaurants or drop in on friends for a meal. Once you've left home without food you can never accept an unplanned invitation that involves eating. For the most part friends do not eat organic food, much less eschew dairy and nightshades (tomatoes, potatoes, peppers, eggplant), so they cannot invite you for a meal unless they are prepared to restock their pantry and acquire a few recipes that do not require any forbidden food. It is easy enough, however, to cook so there will always be leftovers to pack up, and friends and even restaurants are pretty understanding in letting you bring your own food along. What can they say when you tell them you have to eat special food because you have cancer? Poor dears. But I always leave a nice tip for their kindness. One waitress told me, "Cancer? Geez, my father had cancer and he never ate any special food." After a thoughtful pause she continued, "Of course, he died." Then she heated my soup for me.

For someone whose idea of the good life is eating out five or six days and nights a week, undertaking

---

* You can reach Diamond Organics by phone at 800-922-2396.

this new gastronomic order indicated a serious commitment to taking care of my body.

SEARCH FOR A HOMEOPATHIC DOCTOR AND NUTRITIONIST

A frustrating search for a homeopathic doctor and a nutritionist gave me my only period of anxiety. While initiating the diet described above helped allay some of the panic, still for this brief period I felt the cancer might come back and kill me before I got my troops and battle plan ready to fight.

Part of the difficulty in finding the right source of help lay in the remoteness of where I live, my insistence on a homeopath who was also an MD and my temporarily reduced physical capacity as I recovered from surgery. There are no homeopathic doctors in my county and none that appealed to me in the state. I located a naturopathic doctor only three hours away. She had tried to build a practice like the one I was looking for but could not sustain it in this area. She was a wonderful person and did me the great favor of suggesting I stop taking mevacor (to combat high cholesterol) since it put a big strain on the liver. When I brought it up to my other esteemed doctors, they said "Oh, what a good idea." But I doubt if it would ever have occurred to them on their own.

Many other leads led to dead ends but none funnier than the hunt for Ann Wigmore and the Hippocrates Institute in Boston.* No answer for several days at the number Mae started me out with. Information produced two related "800" numbers. The Ann Wigmore Foundation number connected with a message that the number had been

---

* This suggestion came via my friend Mae Churchill in Santa Monica.

disconnected. A pleasant-voiced man answered the Hippocrates Health Institute number. I told him briefly my situation and my need for nutritional guidance during this period while I would be taking chemotherapy. He went right to pieces, exclaiming over and over that I should not consider taking chemotherapy. "No one ever lives more than three years if they take chemo," he kept repeating. I also got treated to a full description of his struggle with prostate cancer: no chemo and Hippocrates care and no cancer. I asked, "For how long?"

"One year."

"Fine, good for you, but I don't have prostate cancer so I'm not inclined to generalize from your situation to mine. Do you have a description of the nutritional regimen the Institute recommends?"

"Oh no, it's not like that. You come for a good long stay and eat and exercise and take classes if you like. It's a 21-day program at a lovely facility by the beach."

"And how much does it cost?"

"For 21 days it will cost between $2,500 and $3,800, depending on the room arrangement you choose. When would you like to come?"

"Listen, what beach? Are you in Boston?"

"Oh no, we're in West Palm Beach."

"Florida?"

"Yes."

"So what is the relationship between your Institute and Ann Wigmore?"

This brought on a lot of mumbling and false starts and finally something about the raw food diet principles being based on her research.

"Is she still alive?"

"Oh yes. She is quite old, but she is still alive."

"And where is she?"

"She lives in Boston."

Quick as a fish I figured out what had probably happened here. This talented and nationally known nutritionist trained the next generation to carry on her work in helping people heal by eating better. Two of these disciples turned out to be sharpies who saw how to turn this program into a real money-maker. All that was required was to move the operation to Florida. So there they are basking in the sun, raking in money while the woman whose work made it all possible is doing who knows what in Boston. Never would I put my body in their hands. Besides, their literature features only strappingly healthy white couples and families frolicking in the sun and has a whole lot too much about high colonics, my litmus test for quackery.

The search for a winning doctor/nutritionist combination came to a successful conclusion when Ellen Ray got Zack Sklar, who edited Jim Garrison's book on the Kennedy assassination and co-wrote the screenplay for Oliver Stone's *JFK*, to persuade his doctor to take me on as a new patient. Dr. Jesse Stoff, an MD and homeopathic doctor, ran The Solstice Center in Great Barrington, Massachusetts, at the time.[*]

The Center had a staff of nutritionists, eurythmy and visualization instructors, and an acupuncturist. My first conversation with Jesse went like this:

"What did Zack tell you to make you agree to take me as a patient when you are not taking new patients?"

"Oh, he's such a nice person. Um. Um. He said it was important," said Jesse, not meeting my eyes.

---

[*] He has since moved Solstice to Tucson, Arizona where he is opening a clinic. You can reach him at 2550 E. Fort Lowell, Tucson, AZ 85719, 602-323-2244.

"What did he say precisely, Jesse?"

"Well, he said it was important. Um. Um . . ."

"Did he tell you that the revolution would fail if you didn't help me get better?"

"Well, yes, that's more or less what he said."

"And you went for that shit?"

"Yep, I went for that shit."

By the time I got to see Jesse in early March, I had already decided to accept my oncologist's recommendation that I begin chemotherapy and had had one treatment. Jesse was initially puzzled over why I would decide on chemotherapy and then come to him. He felt that if I didn't have confidence in chemotherapy I should not be doing it. I explained the grounds for my decision: that I needed some time to investigate alternative treatments and I was uneasy doing nothing while research proceeded. So I just made it up in my head that a well-trained doctor and nutritionist could put me on a regimen that would make my body as strong as it could be made both to help it fight the cancer and to withstand the little dose of poison I would be giving it each month.

"Can you do that?" I asked Jesse.

"Yes," he said, "we can put you on a detoxification regime."

He and Sarah Bingham, the nutritionist, and Jeffrey Rossman, the psychologist-visualization instructor, had a big consultation and produced my detox program the next week. I am on it to this day.

Meanwhile, Jesse and I agreed that at the end of the six months of chemo, I would return for evaluation, by which time I would have decided whether to continue with maintenance chemo or switch to an alternative treatment. He gave me help in seeking out information on alternative therapies and silently tolerated my rough comments on "bloody infusions in Switzerland." Although I knew that the underlying principles of the work at Solstice grew out of anthroposophy, a philosophy developed by Rudolf Steiner, I was not aware that the clinic in Switzerland that gave those "bloody infusions" was the center of anthroposophical medical work of which Jesse was a part.

Friends had also been talking to me about the Lukas Clinic where Audre Lorde was treated, urging me to go there rather than start chemo. Too pigheaded am I. I knew nothing about the clinics or their method of treatment. Not until I investigated it myself would I consider undertaking a treatment. I didn't even agree to chemo until I'd read all the articles from traditional medical journals and got information from the American Cancer Society.

DETOX PROGRAM

The program worked out by Dr. Stoff and my nutritionist, Sarah Bingham,[*] left my modified macrobiotic diet in place but added many new potions: herbal melange (refined mud, guaranteed 100 percent Austrian Moor mud by the government of Liechtenstein!), clay and psyllium, carrot and beet juice, dandelion root tea, horsetail tea, lots of magnesium and special forms of vitamins C and E. The dosages of most of these preparations increased just before, during and after each chemo treatment. I checked in with Sarah after every chemo to see if any changes were needed and to assess whether we were making headway on reducing the side effects. We were successful in reducing the amount of time I felt wonky to one day.

_____

[*] You can reach Sarah Bingham, M.S., at 77 Church Street, Lenox, MA 01240, 413-528-1980.

Even though I am through with chemo, I continue
on this program, minus the clay and psyllium and
with a greatly reduced amount of meat. After I have
been cancer-free for two years, the team will
re-evaluate.

The Solstice program I failed at completely was
visualization. I liked their visualization psychologist,
Jeff Rossman, very much. He talked to me in a
normal voice, gave me useful information, listened to
me and gave me a lot of encouragement. When I told
him that, although I liked hearing his voice because I
liked him, I was bloody sick of his tape because, first
of all, it took up time I wanted to be out looking at
the ducks in the river and secondly because, "You go
on and on telling me to recall the thrill of riding a
bike when I was a kid. I never had a bike when I was
a kid so that part made me cry and besides, not
having had the experience, your description of all the
energizing thrills rang no bells in my psyche. Even if
it had I wouldn't have noticed because I was too busy
crying. And how could I follow your instructions to
relax my face muscles when I had them all screwed
up crying? So you know what I did? I went out and
bought a bike that I ride up and down the road by
the river."

"Perfect, perfect, perfect," Jeff shrieked with
laughter. "Throw the damn tape away. The day you
bought yourself the bike you got all the benefit you're
likely to get from it."

Jeff suggested other tapes and I did give them a
good try but I hated their condescending voices—even
if I am an idiot child I don't like being talked to as if
I am—and I hated their premise that I was sick
because I had a terrible self-image and I should work
to change it. So I abandoned tapes, rode my bike
with the five-year-old neighbor girl, Emma, and
watched the ducks. Much better.

Jeff also gave me instruction in visualization, some
books to read and some tapes. That was no good
either. Oh, I was first rate at thinking up a fighting
image. In it swooping eagles scoured my body,
snatching up odd bits of limp grey cancer strands,
piling them up on the bank of a river where a band
of coyotes dashed out of the woods, tore them to
bits, and kicked them into the fast running river with
their hind legs. Down the river and out to sea. This
image made a big hit with psychologists. Why
shouldn't it? I designed it for them. I'm clever that
way—me and prisoners and other confined persons.
We catch on fast to what those in charge want to
hear. I read all those books—Bernie Siegel, Carl
Simonton, and their ilk. A good image has cancer
weak, its destroyers strong. But the image came from
my mind. I didn't "see" it. How can that help? I still
think about it from time to time, usually while resting
after yoga.

And as to Bernie Siegel, Carl Simonton, and their
ilk, I hate those books. They drove me into a fury
and I threw them across the room. Maybe they help
some people, but I'm not one of them. According to
these books, not only are you responsible for having
gotten cancer in the first place, but if you don't get
good at their kind of stress management, diet,
visualization, fulfilling work, and other life-style
changes it'll be your own fault for not getting better.
The only book that didn't make me rant and rave
was Larry LeShan's *Cancer As A Turning Point*. Nice
man. Nice attitude.

I'm no good at meditating either, although I start
each day sitting quietly in a chair looking at my river,
drinking a cup of miso soup, thinking of nothing in
particular. Maybe that's meditating. That is followed
by a half hour of yoga, the Hittleman version, which
is in turn followed by breakfast of organic oatmeal

and raisins with a tad of maple syrup. On days when
I give myself an injection I have a nice half-hour
lie-down with a hot water bottle on my stomach—
again looking at my river and any passing eagles,
coyotes, foxes, or otters.

On most days, while dinner is finishing and I'm
waiting for Rob to get home, I do half an hour of
eurythmy (explained below).

Those are my regular routines. They seem to suit
me fine.

THE BIG RESEARCH PROJECT

I set up research as a two-step affair. The first step
was to accept the offer of friends and acquaintances
who were librarians and researchers in medical
facilities to run computer searches for all information
and articles on my tumor. This gave me a large stack
of current establishment research literature. My
oncologist reluctantly agreed to give me a few articles
from his files—reluctantly, because he thought the
discouraging outcomes would depress me. But I
persuaded him that nothing could be more depressing
than having the tumor and remaining in ignorance as
to its nature. "If you're planning to spit in the devil's
eye," I told him, "you have to be prepared to take
very careful aim because you are not likely to get a
second chance."

I also called the American Cancer Society Hotline
(1-800-4-CANCER) and some additional numbers
they supplied. This is a fine service. The Society will
send you free literature on your type of cancer. The
person taking your call will check their data banks to
tell you what the most up-to-date treatment
recommendation is for that cancer and where
experimental trials on new treatments are being
conducted. (It's important to know your precise
diagnosis and stage before making this call.) Doctors

use these data banks, too, so what your oncologist tells you and what the ACS researcher tells you *should* be the same. If not, discuss it with your doctor and keep searching.

This service enabled me to confirm what Gary Smith and my early reading had told me: that my tumor was rare and there was no recommended treatment. But the knowledgeable woman who handled my call offered to get out all the textbooks in her reference library and read me the chapters on mixed mesodermal sarcomas. As she read along, I heard her hesitating, so I interrupted to reassure her I knew how dismal the reported outcomes were, that most people died in pretty short order, and that I would not be upset to hear more of the same. By this time, the dismal reports had become a friend, presenting the concrete reality I must deal with, leaving no room for some generalized free floating anxiety over cancer in the abstract. Opponents with names and form and texture are much easier for me to organize against than an elusive fear of death.

For six weeks I poured over the information from all these sources, ordering additional articles after scanning the footnotes, including a recent one in Russian that I have not to this day succeeded in getting translated. Gary Smith was right; this material paints a dreary picture. The tumor is rare, it is virulent and it does not respond well to any standard treatment. Survival time runs from eight months to eight years or so, but controlled research indicates that length of survival is unrelated to type of treatment administered. Therefore, there is no recommended protocol for treatment.

In light of these facts my oncologist had recommended a short course of moderate chemotherapy— even though he was not certain that it would have much impact—rather than the massive doses plus

radiation recommended by the hospital's oncology
department when my case was discussed at staff. His
view was that massive doses of chemotherapy would
make my life miserable without improving my
chances for survival. I thought his view had the best
evidence and logic behind it. Accordingly, I undertook
a short course of moderate chemotherapy, beginning
late in February 1991 and finishing Labor Day
weekend. Gary had originally said eight treatments
but during a later conversation he said "six or eight."
"Okay, six then," I said.

Rob and Lorry Foster, respectively, drove me to
and from my first two treatments. After that I drove
myself to Portland, a five-hour journey, every five or
six weeks so that I didn't have to make the trip back
right after the treatment. I found I felt better faster if
I didn't travel for a few days. The Szatkowski-
Eckhardt support system made that possible. Rick
offered his apartment, which provided the most
privacy, as home base. I took over his fridge with my
special foods and his kitchen while preparing meals
to take to the hospital along with my mud and
carrot-beet juice. I became well known at the hospital
for my big red basket of mysterious goods.

Chauffeur service to and from the hospital was
provided usually by Victoria, sometimes by Chris.
The chemo was administered overnight by IV drip
and I was home by mid-day. The vague nausea I felt
the first morning following chemo, despite the
prescribed medication to combat it, compazine, was
gone by noon. The remainder of the first day I slept,
awaking only at suppertime to down a large bowl of
chicken soup. On succeeding days, I spent the
mornings alone, taking walks and trying to read *The
New York Times*. This was usually unsuccessful until
day 3; I felt so weird and uneasy inside my body that
I could not concentrate sufficiently to read, and

though I persisted in walking, it did not reduce the strange tension. These symptoms, not unbearable but unpleasant, persisted until the effect of the homeopathic medicines took hold at the fourth treatment. Thereafter, the only noticeable symptom was a desire to sleep most of the day after I came out of the hospital. However, even that symptom disappeared along with the first morning nausea at the final treatment when I was given a new medication for nausea, Zofran (ondansetron). I woke up in the hospital full of piss and vinegar, skipping up and down the hall and reading the morning paper while waiting for Victoria. We went straight from the hospital to an outdoor concert where we danced away the afternoon.

Victoria was my faithful afternoon companion on walks, errands, lunch, and raids on the capuccino haunts. (Sarah, my nutritionist, suggested that the rule against coffee could be broken occasionally for mental health reasons.) I only fully realized what a major contribution Victoria's company made to my well-being when she was out of town during the fifth chemo. Being alone away from home with no one to talk to all day was extremely difficult. So I called her up every afternoon!

The rest of the support system—Daniel and Trisha, Michael and Barbara, Rebecca and occasionally Philadelphia-based Elizabeth and Oran Suta—wandered in for talks, meals or video movies. A talented healing community.

After a few days I stocked my car with organic veggies, including organic decaffeinated coffee, and drove myself back to Pembroke where I was welcomed enthusiastically by the animals, sweet Rob, and a shining clean house. Another talented healing community.

During this treatment period, the next step in the Great Cancer Research Project involved locating coherent information about alternative therapies. I read a book entitled *Third Opinion*,* a sizeable compendium with names, addresses, and brief descriptions. I wanted to know more, however: have you ever treated my kind of cancer and, if so, with what effect? What is the claimed efficacy, beyond selected cases? What is the scientific basis underlying the claimed efficacy of the treatment?

I was able to shortcut what might have been a lengthy search for this information via extended correspondence, thanks to an article my West Virginia friend Jeanne Walton clipped from *East/West* magazine (now called *Natural Health*) on an archival data bank service in California, World Research Foundation.** I wrote to World Research, enclosing a check for $43, requesting a search of their archives for alternative treatments for ovarian cancer.*** By and by a large stack of paper arrived and I sat for many weeks reading, taking notes, and sorting articles into piles and thinking.

In the end I decided that the most promising was a treatment based on mistletoe developed by the anthroposophic medical community, headquartered in Arlesheim, Switzerland, near Basel. I corresponded

---

*   John M. Fink, *Third Opinion* (Garden City Park, NY: Avery Publishing Group, 1992).

**   World Research Foundation, 15300 Ventura Blvd., Suite 405, Sherman Oaks, CA 91403. 818-907-LIVE.

*** They can also do a computer search for standard medical articles in case your friends don't include medical librarians and researchers. Another such service is CAN HELP in Seattle, WA. 206-437-2291.

with the clinic directly about their experience with this sarcoma and ordered all the literature concerning ovarian cancer published by their Cancer Research Foundation.*

This second batch of reading convinced me that these were the most scientifically systematic researchers and practioners. Research and clinical testing they have been conducting since the 1920s has consistently indicated that their main medicament, made from mistletoe (trade name, Iscador) does not attack cancer directly. Rather, it is effective against cancer because it acts to strengthen the immune system. I was also impressed by their reported results. They do not have a 100 percent success rate; I do not trust therapies that report 100 percent success.

So after six months of chemotherapy and study, I chose the alternative treatment that was first recommended by my friends and my homeopathic doctor. Never mind, I always have to learn these things for myself.

THE IMPORTANCE OF RESEARCH AND RECORD-KEEPING

For me all this research and decision-making was itself therapeutic and healing. The panic and immobilizing fear that most of us feel when confronted with a life-threatening disease probably comes from a variety of sources. But a major source is the fact and feeling that we are out of control of a critical event in our lives; that we are suddenly being led or pushed around by doctors, nurses, and other health care workers. Worse, if panic gets more than a momentary hold, we cease to be able to understand or remember what little information doctors and others have given us about our situations. And, of

---

* Cancer Research Foundation, 4144 Arlesheim, Switzerland.

course, with so little information we are completely unable to formulate any questions or ask for clearer explanations.

I think I have been so little troubled with panic because I went straight from the doctor's office, when the tumor was first discovered, to the 5&10 and bought a notebook. I wrote down everything I had been told and I have continued to take notes at each meeting with anyone providing care. When I read over those notes later, I draw up lists of questions (including "How do you spell that?") and explanations I want to discuss at the next meeting, or by phone if it seems urgent. Whenever tests are ordered, I get out my notebook to write down the answer to these questions:

- What are the names of the tests?
- Why are you having them done?
- What will they tell us?
- What will we do then?

And I request a copy of all my medical records on a continuing basis: reports on the results of blood tests, X-ray, MRI, CATscan, mammogram, pathology tests, surgery, consultations, and second opinions—absolutely everything. I read them and I ask about anything I don't understand.

I don't know if all this careful record-keeping and systematic search for information would have the same panic-reducing effect on others, but it has kept me walking with composure, hand-in-hand with reality. These humble tasks have kept me from any tendency I might have had to hide from the possibility of an early death, and they have allowed me to face and deal with that possibility while in an active rather than a passive mode, armed with concrete information, not phantasmagoric fears. As a consequence I was able to get the idea of death to occupy a different and more comfortable nitch in my life. At first, it sat on my shoulder all the time. Every time I turned my head sideways, it stared into my face. This seemed healthy for a while; I needed to stare it in the face until it was an old familiar and not a frightening stranger. But you can't get much else done if you spend the whole day and night staring at death. Before long, after I got into action, it receded into a more respectful and manageable ten paces behind. There it remains except that every once in a while I beckon it to my shoulder. We have a good look at each other to be sure we understand our deal: because you are real, I must make a place for you in my thinking and feeling, but you are not allowed to dominate my life. I know very well that despite my best efforts and those of my health care workers, this cancer may kill me. But it is not going to get my life by making me so obsessed with the possibility of death that I cannot enjoy living the life I have.

Part 2

Once I had decided on Iscador, Dr. Stoff referred me to Sister Rosemarie, the admissions nurse at the Ita Wegman clinic in Arlesheim, Switzerland. I called her directly, we picked a date, I made plane reservations, I arrived, she brought me to my room, I met my roommate and my doctors, I ate dinner, I slept to erase the jetlag.

The Ita Wegman Clinic is a sister clinic to the Lukas Clinic, located a street or two away. Unlike the Lukas Clinic, which is devoted exclusively to cancer patients, the Ita Wegman Clinic accepts patients of various diagnoses. Dr. Stoff chose Ita Wegman over Lukas for just that reason, feeling that the atmosphere is more felicitous. The treatment is the same at both clinics.

I spent four weeks at the clinic. It cost about $7,000 which included daily medical consultations, nursing care, daily medicines, ordinary blood tests, room, board, painting and eurythmy instructions, and my private telephone calls to friends and family.

THE DOCTORS

My doctors—two women, Drs. Hoffman and Roozen, from Germany and Holland, respectively—spent many hours studying my records, my medical and personal history, and my blood. Based on this systematic study, they set a course of medicaments (Iscador, Christmas rose, cetraria, formica by injection and others by mouth), and a course of daily activities (water color painting and curative eurythmy).

The doctors were quite extraordinary. They came to my room every day, shook my hand, and smiled into my eyes, asking how I felt and what questions I had. Then they sat down. No hands on the doorknob, making fast breezy quips and attempting a fast getaway. I started keeping a list of "discussion topics" on a tablet. After that, following the initial greeting, one of the doctors would head for the tablet. They stayed as long as it took us to go through the relevant items. Once when I asked them what story the blood tests told, Dr. Roozen checked the figures and said "They do not tell a story, they sing a joyful song!" Dr. Hoffman said, "Aren't you lucky to have a poet for a doctor? She could have just said, 'All positive.'"

The first Saturday night of my stay, Dr. Hoffman, the senior doctor on my case, came for a three-hour visit. We talked about our lives, our views of life and death, events that made a difference in the course we chose—like that. It was a case of materialist meets scientific spiritualist. We both enjoyed exploring the differences which, while not great, are crucial. My convictions that (1) I am a part of the natural order in exactly the same way as an eagle or a tree: I am born, I live, I die and dissolve back into my component parts, and that (2) I am the author of the significance, meaning, and values by which I conduct and judge that one life, seem as self-evident to me as Dr. Hoffman's beliefs to the contrary—(1) that we live multiple lives, (2) that a super-sense spirituality guides each life, and (3) that we differ from the rest of the natural world in our possession of a spiritual life—seem to her.

Dr. Hoffman is, not surprisingly, far more knowledgeable about the names and properties of plants and flowers than me; most of the medicines she uses derive from plants. Near the end of this wonderful Saturday evening conversation focusing on our shared interest and love of the natural world, Dr. Hoffman asked me if I knew of a flower called Christmas rose.

"Yes, of course," I said. "It grows under the snow, simple five petals, red, or white or pink."

"Well," she said, "all yesterday afternoon and evening I was thinking about you, pondering your records and your situation. While sleeping that night I had a dream about you and a Christmas rose. I think you are very much like a Christmas rose. All kinds of stuff can be dumped on your head, but if you brush it away, underneath there you are growing and blooming."

"I hope that's true," I said.

"Yes, I think it is," she said. "Now, we make a cancer medicine out of that plant and I think I should give it to you. What do you think? "

I laughed my assent. Why not? My doctor has a dream and I get a certain medicine. But this is a well-trained and disciplined dreamer who studied me and my medical records carefully for a week before she had that dream. I trust it. So my basic program became mistletoe and Christmas rose with a bit of the poison taken from a big red ant that lives in the woods, formica.

While I was at the clinic, the nurses administered all the medications. Just before I left, I was taught to give myself injections and was given a month's supply of vials. Some of the injections were converted to drops to swill down before meals, but mistletoe and Christmas rose I continue to inject. This regimen will go on indefinitely with changes in dosage and intervals depending on my reaction over time. There are no unpleasant side effects.

THE SISTERS

The nursing functions were carried out by an equally well trained and dedicated staff of "sisters," the title given a registered nurse and having nothing to do with a religious order. In this system of titles, doctors are addressed as Doctor Last Name but sisters are Sister First Name. I was a little puzzled about what to call the one male nurse, Gernot.

"What is your title, Gernot? Am I to call you Brother Gernot?"

"No. In Germany we are called brothers, but here there is no title."

"Not acceptable," I said. "Everyone in Switzerland has a title. If you don't have a title, you don't exist. I'll think of one for you."

"That would be nice."

"I have it. It's a Spanish title. Compañero. It means comrade. Compañero Gernot. How's that?"

"Too long."

"No problem. The short version is Compa."

"Compa Gernot. I love it."

And thereafter I became Compa Buitrago because Gernot knew I hated the title "Frau." Fraus are either fascists or dumpy persons or both, I told him one day.

The sisters and compas were extraordinary. As with all the anthroposophic medical personnel, they were fully educated and trained in mainstream medical standards and practice. After that they learned anthroposophic medicaments and practice. Some of the sisters were Swiss; others came from Germany, Austria, Holland, and Sweden. Many had worked in Ireland, England (with a resulting delightful cockney accent), South Africa, and the United States.

The floor ran itself on the best anarchic principles. No charge nurse. Tasks and patients were assigned at a group meeting. Care was taken that the sisters had several hours off during a shift (and a week off after the taxing night shift) so that they would be fresh enough to play a healing role in the patients' care.

Before leaving on these breaks or at the end of shifts, the sisters would announce their departure and time of return to each of their patients and tell them who was replacing them. No one ever just disappeared. They always came to say "I'm leaving now. I'll be back at such and such a time. Sister Ulrike is replacing me. Be well until I return." We were not left to puzzle out for ourselves who was taking care of us. This simple act also silently communicated to us that we were important and occupied a recognized place in the system of accountability.

The two basic principles of the nursing work style were relaxed quiet and playful joy. Room doors were kept shut, the halls were quiet. Of course, the absence of television and radio contributed enormously to an undisturbed atmosphere. The sisters talked to each other and to us in natural voices. There was no false and forced jollity, although there was plenty of jollity

and larking about in rooms where the patients were
so inclined. For instance, Sister Dagmar, the sister I
came to know best and love very much, gave me
excellent haircuts, took me on a long walk up to a
crumbling castle, told us wonderful stories, fed me
dinner one night in her room, and often reported, at
our request, on her flute lessons and musical group
rehearsals. Each Sunday morning, the sisters would
gather at one end of the long hall and sing their way
down to the other end—beautiful, closely harmonized
hymns and folk songs.

Rubbings, massages, waking, and goodnight
routines were carried out in unhurried silence or, at
most, with minimal communication. It was the sisters
who instructed us in these quiet healing ways.

Every day after lunch, a sister applied a hot herbal
compress to the area near my liver, wrapped me
round with a strip of wool, placed a hot water bottle
on top and my down poof on top of that. Signs were
put on the door and roommates were instructed that
for the next hour it "would be better" if there was no
talking, no phone calls, no reading or writing or
listening to walk-persons. The end of the hour was
marked by the arrival of a pot of fresh hot coffee.
The same instructions for inactive quiet time
accompanied the every other morning whole body
rub with lavender lotion and hot water bottles. The
chiming clock in the nearby church steeple allowed
me to keep track of the hour without even reaching
my hand out from under my down poof.

HEALING ACTIVITIES

At the end of the hour I would trot off to my
eurythmy lesson with Jan Fountain, or Carolyn and I
would walk together to watercolor class with Frau
Kraan, stopping along the way for a quick pet with
the goats.

Frau Kraan, who spent her first 11 years in Madison, N.J., was a skillful and sunny teacher. By assigning exercises and uttering helpful words, she made it possible for me to make fewer unfixable mistakes and eventually paint a rather nice-looking peony. I came to see that Dr. Hoffman's choice of painting rather than sculpture or music was perfectly suited to let me combat my tendency to put everything into a recognizable form right away. With watercolors, you must go slowly, carefully building up colors and letting the forms evolve from them. I liked the discipline and, although it took great concentration, I found it very relaxing to be cut off from reading, writing and thinking for a few hours at a stretch.

Herr Fountain is as tall as I am short. We must have looked a funny pair, but our personalities suited each other quite well. In order to teach me the right feel of the eurythmy exercises, Herr Fountain told me stories of elephants (who move with the same feeling as the motion for the letter *M*), horses, the moon, cherry trees. In turn, to test whether I had caught the meaning of what he had explained, I would tell stories of eagles, the river in front of my house, the dying elms in my yard.

Sometimes these reciprocal descriptions of our observations of the natural world would lead us to more general philosophical discussions during which Jan Fountain would quote Goethe, Schiller, Hegel, and Rudolph Steiner. I would counter quote Marx, Engels, and John Locke. One day Herr Fountain was expressing his view that we all carry bits of the same characteristics that result in some people committing mass murders, ghastly tortures, child abuse, and drug addiction, embellishing the point with a quote from Rudolph Steiner. I expressed my agreement and embellished it with a quote from Engels: "Nothing human is foreign to me." Herr Fountain looked delighted and surprised. "I never thought I would have to agree with anything a Marxist said," he laughed. We eventually got to the stage, as with my long discussion with Dr. Hoffman, where we had thoroughly explicated our differences. So we just smiled at each other and let it alone, each knowing we would proceed in friendship down our different paths.

FOOD

Morning and evening meals were taken in my room; lunch in the dining room with the fun of meeting new people. The food was delicious. All organic, bio-dynamic and pure, pure, pure. Cancer patients were restricted from eating tomatoes, potatoes and sugar. But much to my surprise, the diet was not strictly vegetarian and it was loaded with dairy products—cheese, milk, yogurt, quark, butter, milk pudding desserts and more cheese, cheese, cheese. The three Yankee cancer patients wallowed and enjoyed all these forbidden foods for about a week and a half and then asked Dr. Hoffman, "Do you know what the word *strike* means?"

"Yes, of course. What's the matter?"

"Too much dairy in our diet. Too much animal fat. We're going on strike."

"Yes, you're right. It is a bit unbalanced. But it is quite pure."

"We know. And it is quite delicious, but eventually we go home and it isn't pure there. Besides, to eat so much dairy, I think you have to have Swiss genes. All mine are Puerto Rican or Irish. No good. Can't we just have vegetables and grains, like we're used to?"

"Yes, of course. I'll arrange it with the cook."

And she did.

Part 3

I am giving pride of place to a finger-shaking word to friends and family of people with cancer. Don't tell them tales about people who put up magnificent battles and survived cancer. When you're struggling to get a grip on yourself and figure out what course of action to follow, news about these people, who always sound like bloody saints, is very irritating. "I don't intend to be a good sport about this," I remember saying—shouting, really—at a friend who was only trying to encourage me, I know. "I'm doing the best I can. You want to help, find me a nutritionist but spare me tales of the perfect ones."

To prevent this account of my first year from sounding saintly, I want to stress all the incredible advantages and good luck I have encountered. Even so, it was not always a piece of pie.

1. I have never felt unwell. Except for the six weeks after surgery, I have felt my usual energetic self. No pain, no nausea, no weakness, no lethargy, no food aversion. Much easier to fight and think and do when you're feeling just fine. For a few weeks after surgery I could not concentrate enough to read, even fiction. After the first chemo treatments I also could not deal with the printed page. I was a bit worried that I had lost my ability to do sustained reading, analysis and writing, but it all came back as the effects of the anesthetic wore off and the detox program kicked in.

2. Even with my general good health, I could not have organized the food regimen, the hunt for doctor, nutritionist, and the information research without the most enormous amount of help from friends and family recounted earlier. When I needed help, I asked for it. Because they could rely

on my asking, friends otherwise provided help only when they saw that I didn't recognize that I needed a hand. ("You need to get out of the house," said Barb and Dot. "Come, hold on to our arms. We'll get you over the ice, into the car and into town for a cup of coffee.") Otherwise they let me run my life even if I had to stretch to do it. For instance, although it was obviously a chore I detested, I never asked and no one ever offered to make my carrot-beet juice. I'm sure I would have said yes if anyone had asked. Similarly, I never asked and the Portland support group never offered to do my cooking or juicing either. In each instance it was obvious that I could do the task, so unless I asked, no one was going to let me drift into being more of a patient than I was. This has worked out very well. I don't feel smothered and my friends don't feel unnecessarily put upon. I hope.

3. I had no serious financial worries. During the months I had no income, Medicaid picked up the portion of my medical bills not covered by my Blue Cross/Blue Shield policy and continues to pay a portion, though smaller, since I took early social security retirement. In addition, my mother stood steadfastly beside me, ready to keep me from sinking. She and she alone made the trip to Switzerland possible, trusting my decision that, although it sounded a little weird, it was the best course to follow.

   The minute I went into the hospital a big bunch of money arrived from our dearest friends and Brooklyn housemates to help Rob cover the added expenses of staying in Portland and putting our dog in a kennel. During the same period, a local family handed Rob $100, saying "Don't pay us back. Just pass it on when you can to someone else who needs a hand." We got the chance to do that this winter when another local family got burned out.

4. In addition to what I wrote earlier about my relatively low level of short-lived panic and the relative ease with which I dealt with the possibility of death, many factors in my life have produced a calm and peaceable foundation on which to ride out storms. For example, I am 63 not 20 or 30. And I have a lovely partner who was himself able to come to terms with the panic and fear the possibility of my death brought to his life. He dealt with his panic and I dealt with mine—a wonderful gift we gave to ourselves and each other.

5. By the time I got cancer I had sorted out a lot of basic questions about my life. This is not the first hard blow in my life, and I am reaping the benefits of not having avoided dealing with the earlier ones. Many years ago I decided that, ephemeral as life was, the basic rule to live by was "To the maximum extent possible do only what is important and fun. Do not plan on getting to something important later." Accordingly, I have done the kind of work I thought suited me and I thought was important to do, and I gladly accepted the consequences—low income, mainly, no big deal. I have lived with whom and in the way I found to be both fun and nurturing. Every step of the way I have been aware of the enormous pleasure these decisions brought me. I can't tell you how many times I have said (internally, because it sounds so corny), "Oh boy, am I ever glad I lived long enough to do this." I'm still saying it.

Not everyone is so lucky to meet cancer with these advantages—a powerful healthy body, few financial worries, the big issues in life sorted out, and family and friends who became part of the solution instead of part of the problem.

Because these factors are not always present and also because we're all wired up differently, one person's experience cannot be a sure guide to another. We each have to find or build our own paths. But sometimes telling and listening to other stories helps us find the strength to get on with the search for our own.

Part 4

This is the long-promised short bulletin. It is full of good news.

Since the last bulletin the quarterly blood tests (Jesse Stoff, homeopathic MD) and quarterly physical exams (Gary Smith, gynecological oncologist) have found no evidence of recurrence of my vicious little cancer.

Best of all, the results of the most recent battery of blood tests (August–September), according to Jesse, "are not just very good but actually beautiful!" For several of the cancer tests, my blood contains no detectable evidence of the marker at all and there has been a big increase in killer cells and the like. What this suggests to me is that my morning pre-yoga ritual of shouting at my body—"Listen, if there are any of you cancer guys still in there, just pack it up and get out! You're not wanted and won't be tolerated here!"—has worked. Jesse says the test results show that my immune system has shifted into a higher gear and has now gone on the offensive. Same thing, right?

There was much joy and jubilation over these results as it bodes well for making it past the two-year anniversary in January—a big event for a cancer that is almost guaranteed to return in 8 to 14 months. Everyone should claim her/his part of the credit: the successful surgery, the early chemo, the homeopathic regimens, four weeks of complete care at the Ita Wegman Clinic, the macrobiotic diet, yoga and eurythmy, the prayers and good vibes of friends and family, a quiet and happy life in a beautiful place with a beautiful person. Thanks to all of you for two good years. And thanks to me for figuring out what to do and doing it.

My long range goal is something like 30 more cancer-free years but the short-range goal is 3 more years. The significance of the short goal is that it will allow my two doctors and me to write an article reporting to the medical community that a person with a cancer for which no efficacious treatment is known has lived five years in the pink of health. I hope they'll both agree to such a project and that we can get it published in one of the prestigious journals that has been reporting all the grim failures at treating mixed mesodermal sarcomas.

What I've come to accept this year is that this period of relative inactivity is a necessary healing balance for the many years of working flat out for 18 hours a day. I no longer growl at myself because I am not fully productive. I am healing and I'll be ready if faster-paced work comes along in the future.

Part 5

We have hit a bit of a rough patch. A CATscan revealed that the cancer has metasticized to my liver; that is, there is a mixed mesodermal ovarian sarcomal tumor on my liver and bits and pieces scattered around the pelvis. This is a very invasive (so inoperable) and fast-growing tumor, so treatment must begin post-haste.

It is hard to decide whether to accept my oncologist's recommendation of two courses of heavy-duty chemo six weeks apart or my homeopathic doctor's recommendation to stay with a stronger version of my mistletoe treatment. I'm also investigating an immunologic therapy developed by the NCI and a metabolic treatment developed by Dr. Micholas Gonzales in New York City. Soon I will decide.

Here is what I told the reporter who interviewed me for a story in the local paper:

> January, 16, 1993, will be the second anniversary of Buitrago's surgery, and although she now is asymptomatic, she has no illusions.
> "If on January 17 this cancer recurs, I still will feel good that with two years of this combined conventional and unconventional regime, I have had an absolutely 'pink of health' life. . . . The reality is that no matter what type of treatment is involved, it only works for some people. . . . The trick is to find the kind of treatment that works on your body."

Once again I'm trying to find that combination. The only thing I know for sure is that the change for a long, gray braid is gone for this winter if I do chemo. The struggle continues, mine and the world's. If I were in a bit better shape I would apply for the Attorney General job; I have the major qualification—no children!

I feel your love and touch, and I hope you feel mine.

Living with Ovarian Cancer

Beth Kupper-Herr

I am an ovarian cancer patient . . . survivor . . .
fighter. I've just finished fighting off ovarian cancer
for the second time. While my experience with this
disease may not be typical (if indeed there is a
"typical" cancer experience), the ways that ovarian
cancer has affected my life highlight some of the
harsh realities of the disease. Anyone concerned with
changing these realities needs to know what it means
to live with them. Beyond fear and the discomfort of
treatment lie further troubles—cost, impact on
intimate relationships, and potential discrimination in
employment and by society.

I've been lucky—twice. It seems strange to state
this in connection with being visited by a potentially
deadly disease—but, in the context of the "usual"
course of ovarian cancer, I have been fortunate.

The first occurrence of the disease, almost four
years ago, was palpated during a pelvic examination.
Finding ovarian tumors in this way is extremely
unlikely, particularly because the tumors on my
ovaries were relatively small and the cancer was not
very advanced. (It was early Stage III when found,
meaning it had spread a bit beyond the immediate
"neighborhood" of the ovaries.) Because I was
relatively young—37—and had no other overt
symptoms, the masses were thought to be cysts; when
I learned, after the surgery, that I'd had a complete
hysterectomy, it came as a total surprise. It also
eliminated any possibility of having a child, an option
I had not ruled out at the time.

117

While adjusting to the shock of a hysterectomy, I found myself depressed and angry at the twin prospects of experiencing immediate menopause (which was postponed via estrogen replacement) and undergoing chemotherapy. I was determined to defeat the cancer—but afraid of chemotherapy's often harrowing side effects.

Many horror stories about chemotherapy are justified. The drugs kill not only cancer, but also other fast-growing cells, including hair and blood cells. That's why chemotherapy patients often go bald during treatment and have greater risk of illness when their infection-fighting white blood cells are low. Sometimes it's hard to remember that chemotherapy does good, because the obvious effects are so unpleasant, so disruptive to everyday life. The most traumatic change for me was the temporary loss of more than half of my hair. Want to find out how vain you are? How self-conscious? Try a few months of chemotherapy! I also permanently lost hearing (at the top end of the pitch range) and had some tinnitus (ringing or buzzing in the ears), which caused my doctor to change my treatment.

Chemotherapy disrupts and restricts the patient's daily life. I was told to avoid large groups of people when my "counts" were low, but I was a teacher who worked with dozens of students every day. I didn't want to miss work, so I took my chances.

Chemotherapy for ovarian cancer also involved me in various annoying routines, such as having to drink large quantities of water, collecting urine for 24 hours before a treatment, having blood drawn every week, and watching a nurse try—again—to insert an IV in my worn-out vein.

Nausea is the curse of many chemotherapy patients, but it was a minor problem for me. Although my vomiting increased after each month's treatment as the drugs built up in my system, I wasn't really miserable, and the nausea was gone by the next day.

After undergoing chemotherapy, I was cancer-free for 2½ years, until the fall of 1991. The only indication that the problem had returned was a very slight abdominal bloating and weight gain of a few pounds. I noticed this, not my doctor (I am not being critical; the change was too slight to be noticeable to my husband, either). Diagnostic tests—pelvic exam, ultrasound, CATscan—either revealed nothing or were inconclusive. Even during surgery, my oncologist found no sign of this subtle disease. It was only after the pathology lab finished its work that the presence of cancer cells (visible only under the microscope) was verified. Even the much-relied-upon CA-125, the blood marker that is elevated in many women when ovarian cancer is present, is of no use for me. Fortunately, two other blood markers have since been found to be of potential value in ongoing monitoring of my disease; however, they are by no means certain indicators.

I was even more fortunate the second time: by the time my cancer recurred 2½ years later, a new anti-nausea drug was available which worked like a charm for me; and a change in my medication meant that I lost no hair at all.

However, I have endured numerous frustrating delays in treatment and a feeling of increasing vulnerability due to the long-term impact of chemotherapy on my bone marrow, where blood cells are manufactured. I try not to worry, but wonder, what if I need treatment again? How much punishment can these sensitive cells take?

Still, I've been luckier than many. Because I remained strong and active—going to work every day and exercising regularly—I could hold onto my view

of myself as a vital, essentially healthy person. I had
cancer, but I still had some control over my life.

For many ovarian cancer patients, though,
treatment brings terrible suffering and makes a
normal life impossible.

The anti-nausea drug that was so effective for me
has had absolutely no effect on some women I know,
who cannot keep any food down for as long as ten
days each time they are treated.

Chemotherapy can also result in other miserable,
hard-to-ignore symptoms like constipation and
intense cramping or painful sores inside the mouth.
Some women lose *all* of their hair—including body
hair, eyebrows and eyelashes. Under such circumstances, remaining positive is a real challenge.

Even worse, sometimes a medication is found to be
ineffective (if the CA-125 remains elevated or a tumor
still is evident) and the treatment plan must be
changed. This may mean another half a year or more
of chemotherapy.

Grimmer still, women who have had several
surgeries sometimes develop adhesions (internal scar
tissue) that can create partial-to-total intestinal
blockages. These can make eating impossible and
require the patient to be fed through a tube in the
stomach.

Of course, if there were a proven way to prevent
ovarian cancer or an effective means of detecting it at
its earliest stage, thousands of women could be saved
from the physical and emotional suffering that are
too often a part of treatment.

▲ ▲ ▲

In addition to its physical and emotional costs,
ovarian cancer costs a lot of money! Just keeping

track of the bills, the varying insurance rates for different services, the major medical payments, and my share of the costs (insurance doesn't cover it all) is extremely time-consuming and often confusing.

A single medical procedure can easily generate bills from two or three sources. While writing this piece, I tried to calculate the total cost, to both the insurance company and myself, of my latest bout with cancer.

Over a period of 8½ months, involving one surgery with a week of hospitalization, six chemotherapy treatments, numerous diagnostic and lab tests, office visits, and injections to boost my bone marrow output, I came up with $23,000. And this for a relatively "smooth" course!

For women whose treatment is halted and started from scratch with a different medication; for those who require procedures such as MRIs or bone marrow extractions; when there are repeated and extended hospitalizations, the cost is truly astronomical.

This cost is passed on to all of us in ever-increasing insurance rates. And, even worse—something that has distressed me greatly, ever since my initial diagnosis—is that who-knows-how-many women, who are not fortunate enough to have comprehensive health coverage and access to quality care, simply cannot get the treatment on which their lives depend. Because of the overwhelming financial cost of fighting this disease, and the inequity of our health care system, these women die.

I don't use the word "victim" when discussing my own cancer experience, because I don't feel like one; but these women left to die are true victims of ovarian cancer.

▲ ▲ ▲

I've been lucky—twice. But not lucky enough to feel safe in telling the world my true identity. When I first wrote this article, for the newsletter of Ovarian Cancer Prevention & Early Detection Foundation, I chose to publish it anonymously. Publication in this book is my first completely public coming out as a woman with a cancer history.

Although I am apparently "cancer-free," I'm still living with ovarian cancer. Its absence of symptoms makes ovarian cancer an especially frightening form of cancer, and with a five-year survival rate around 25 percent, it's also an especially deadly one.

The first time I "beat" cancer, I believed that it was gone for good; since its return, I am more cynical.

I have learned enough about ovarian cancer to temper my optimism. I know now that it causes more deaths than all other gynecological cancers: in 1993, more than 21,000 women will be diagnosed with ovarian cancer, and 13,500 will die. This high mortality rate stems from the absence or vagueness of symptoms in most women until the disease is advanced and a cure is unlikely. There is no known way to prevent ovarian cancer, and no reliable means of detecting it early. (Pap smears don't test for ovarian, only for cervical cancer.) Recurrences are common.

Like other women who have had ovarian cancer, I find it hard to dismiss my ongoing fear of recurrence. The slightest ache, pain, "funny feeling," weight gain or loss, or more-than-usual tiredness, raises questions: Does this mean something? Should I be concerned? Is this worth another visit to the doctor?

It's easy to imagine cancer as an ever-present villain, lurking in the wings, and to wonder if—or when—this dark figure might decide to sneak subtly on stage again to disrupt the scene. I fight my fear by trying to stay mentally positive and physically strong and by trying to feel that I'm in control of my life. Still, the anxiety remains. Other ovarian cancer survivors I know feel it, too.

The burden of living with cancer is not mine alone. Those close to me—my husband, my mother, close friends—are also anxious, and they have even less control than I do. At least I can be alert for symptoms, watch my diet, and continue to exercise. All they can do is worry.

It's painful for women like me to see the stress that this fear puts on our loved ones. And, because most women act as nurturers or caregivers, we also worry about the effect on these significant others—children, spouses, aging parents—should the cancer return and not be found in time.

There can be a positive side to living with cancer. If one is lucky—like me—this ordeal can strengthen existing relationships, and even give rise to new ones. I have seen my family and close friends "come through" for me during this crisis, and I share with them the credit for my recovery and health. I've also been fortunate to know some wonderful women through my support group.

Cancer also affects the patient's connections to the larger society. Soon after my first diagnosis, my oncologist recommended that I tell as few people about the cancer as possible because, as she said, "Many people don't know what to do with it." And "going public" with a cancer diagnosis can be not only socially awkward but also professionally risky.

Some employers who know that an employee is being treated for cancer may "see" a decline in productivity where none exists, or may be reluctant to offer challenging assignments or promotions.*

The cancer survivor whose job is at risk experiences a double jeopardy. Stigmatized by the cancer label, she may have difficulty finding another position; if she is able to make a job change, it can lead to a lapse or loss of health insurance. Lack of coverage means trouble even if the cancer does not recur, for ongoing monitoring is a must, and, like treatment, this costs money.

While the social aspects of acknowledging one's cancer are less dangerous, they are, nonetheless, uncomfortable. Many people still regard the disease as a virtual death sentence, and ovarian cancer—which is neither well-known nor well-publicized, and is hidden away, deep in the body—sounds particularly mysterious and scary.

How people respond when I tell them I have cancer varies. Many are falsely cheery, exclaiming "You look so WELL!" in a slightly surprised tone. Others act as if I will fall suddenly ill before their eyes. While well-intentioned, such behavior naturally reminds the recipient of the unwelcome element in her life. Thus, I am careful who I tell. My current coworkers and many of my friends don't yet know that I've had ovarian cancer.

Ovarian cancer is a terrible disease. It shortens the lives of thousands of women every year and greatly impairs the quality of life for many thousands more. Ovarian cancer research is grossly underfunded and must compete for limited funding dollars with better-known and more visible women's cancers.

---

* CNN recently reported that one in five people who have had cancer suffer some form of job discrimination.

There is hope, and I believe that change is on the horizon. The Clinton Administration seems more sympathetic than previous administrations to women's health concerns. Public pressure on those who control the millions of dollars needed for ovarian cancer research can help bring about a life-saving discovery—reliable methods for detecting and preventing this deadly disease.

My own struggle continues. Recently, I've felt some twinges in my pelvic region, and I'm uneasy. Tomorrow I'll visit my doctor. I wonder if he'll find anything amiss—if the blood test will show a change—if the cancer has returned. If it recurs, will it once again be found in time? Even if my own luck holds, I'll continue to speak out about this disease. I may have been lucky, but I can't forget that many women are not.

Tree Juice

Candice Hepler

With no strong formal educational background, I decided to go to college to better my future job prospects. It was the spring semester of junior college, and academic classes were picking up speed. My concentration was all on my classwork. One day in January, I went to the school nurse and had my annual Pap smear, which proved normal. It wasn't until the beginning of February that I noticed a soreness in my lower back. I had had kidney stones ten years prior and feared a flare-up. I went back to the school nurse to have a more thorough exam, although the prospect of another pelvic put me off. This visit was on a Thursday afternoon and the end of my school week, so I headed home looking forward to a restful weekend.

As I look back now and remember, my body temperature had been dropping and I had had trouble keeping warm even during my many activity classes. I dismissed my fatigue because when I wasn't in school, I was doing side jobs—housecleaning, painting, etc. The nurse couldn't find anything wrong except that I looked fatter in the tummy than she did (and she was three months pregnant). I thought I was bloating and getting fatter. I remorsefully considered it a premenopausal condition.

By the following Sunday evening, my abdomen had enlarged to the point where I couldn't bend over to tie my shoes. I knew then that I had to take action.

I felt extremely uncomfortable behind the wheel of my RX-7 as I drove to the emergency room of a nearby hospital. I didn't know what was going on.

Upon undergoing another pelvic exam, I insisted on the use of the smallest speculum available. The good nurse came up with a baby-sized instrument (much to the amazement of an efficient young male doctor). It was now midnight. An early morning appointment was made for me with a female gynecologist. I was relieved she would be female. The emergency doctor's words were, "I think you are going to be surprised!"

I went to my next appointment with anxiety. I now looked like I was nine months pregnant. I was met by a woman physician whose stature made me feel quite tall. I towered over this doctor, and I am only 5'2"! (I was later to find out that she used a step stool in the surgical arena.) Yes, indeed, she confirmed that I was in trouble. She scheduled surgery for me as soon as she could. It was to be on Valentine's Day. I found this to be morbidly befitting my nonexistent lovelife.

In surgery, they found grapefruit-sized tumors on each ovary. Twins. I had given birth on Valentine's Day, via Caesarian section, to the malignant twins, Valentin and Valentina!

I learned later that the cancer had spread to the outer surfaces of my diapraghm, kidneys, liver, and bowel. Quite soon after this information became known, I was approached by another woman doctor, an oncologist, who brought with her a blessing. She wanted me to try an experimental new chemotherapy being offered through a nationwide study. I gave myself to her without question. I liked feeling like I was volunteering to do a good deed and could possibly live to tell the tale. I didn't hesitate long in signing the papers.

This gynecological study involved the use of a drug called Taxol. It is derived from the bark of the Yew Tree. During a wide screening of plants and animals by the National Cancer Institute, Susan Horowitz, a scientist at Albert Einstein College of Medicine, analyzed the crude extract of bark from the Pacific Yew and found that it killed tumors in mice. The bark is literally stripped off of the slow-growing evergreen, and about six 100-year-old trees are sacrificed to treat just one cancer patient. It is the ultimate confrontation between medicine and the environment.* The tree is found mainly in Washington and Northeastern Oregon; it is home to a rare owl and other wildlife. The Indians seemed to know its magical powers, chewing on the bark to heal their lung ailments.

I had a 50-50 chance of getting the Taxol; the study was split with another seemingly effective treatment using Cytoxin. Of the 360 women involved in the study, 180 would receive the Taxol. Luck was on my side, and in a matter of a few days, I was to be number 120 of the group receiving the "tree juice."

I began the chemotherapy as soon as it was safe after my hysterectomy. I went to the hospital every three weeks for a total of six IV applications. I stayed overnight, so the hospital could monitor my heart rate.

Another timely piece of good fortune: two weeks prior to my diagnosis, the new anti-nausea drug Zofran had been released. It was thought to be the best and most effective drug yet discovered for use by chemotherapy patients. I truly felt at times like the golden child being carried around on a pillow of love. My life had undergone a drastic swing, and all I had to do was hold on to the ropes!

My ex-lover, involved in homecare work, was able to become my caregiver and be paid by the state. As

---

* Attempts to synthesize Taxol have been unsuccessful so far because it is structually complex, but the needles of the Yew tree have been found as the answer in extracting the precious substance, thus allowing the bark harvesting to halt.

a home health aide, her duties to me were to include
assistance with personal care, such as bathing,
grooming, and dressing; assistance in getting me in
and out of bed, with prescribed exercises, and with
walking; assistance in meal planning and preparation,
and light housekeeping chores, such as dusting, light
laundry, washing dishes, and tidying. This service is
covered by Medicare, MediCal, and most private
insurances. During this fragile time, having her as my
aide was a blessing and a boon. But the tough
emotional ride for us was worse than the scariest
roller-coaster ride. She found a funky two-bedroom
duplex for us to move into. It wasn't easy finding
places to live affordably in Mill Valley, California,
and this one fell right out of the Goddess' hand!

The two women living above us were also lesbians,
and they were overjoyed to have kindred spirits move
in below. There was a good-sized yard for my cocker
spaniel and even a working fireplace! The downside
was that my roommate and I would constantly clash
on issues about communication. I was not only
dealing with a weakened physical and mental
condition, but also with our dysfunctional emotional
problems. She felt resentful that I didn't talk to her
about my feelings, and I felt totally misunderstood by
her. We were a mismatch from the beginning, but
bravely tried to hang in there for the benefits our
relationship did provide.

After the second IV, we decided to celebrate my
birthday by going on a weekend trip to Mendocino.
It was a rainy weekend predicted by me, as it seems
I've had most birthdays with this inclement condition.
I felt pensive about going but needed a change of
scenery. I wanted to get as far away as possible from
medicine and hospital things.

On the morning of the second day, clumps of my
head hair began falling out. Until then I had been

extremely lucky in that I hadn't been affected by this side effect of chemotherapy. That afternoon, we strolled hurriedly into the only barber shop in that small town. It was crowded with men and boys, no chairs available, and the wait looked endless. My roommate stood in the middle of the room and declared that I needed an emergency haircut, that I was a cancer patient and my hair was falling out in clumps. I pulled her out of the place, seeing that her hysterics were falling on an alarmed but unmoved male bastion.

At my birthday dinner that evening, my roommate told me that I had been given six months to live by the gynecologist who had operated on me. I didn't hear her and to this day have no memory of her telling me that news.

The next day I bought the first of many caps to cover my balding head. By the end of that month, I was totally hairless, even losing the minute hairs on my fingers. The hairless condition made me feel ill at ease among others. I felt like a weakened animal being pushed out toward the edge of the pack. I thought if strangers saw me bald they might wrongly assume I had AIDS, and I was fearful of being shunned.

During my chemotherapy, I had another friend come to my rescue with a machine called a Brain Balancer.* She brought this compact unit to the hospital. A software system computer-directed audio/visual component that uses rhythmic pulsing light and sound to guide the mind into a state of deep relaxation, the Brain Balancer gave a healing

---

* Relaxation Dream Medium is a hand-held control unit, directing twelve different preset programs with a choice of sounds that match actual patterns of brainwave activity. It is sold through the Hammacher/Schlemmer catalog (1-800-543-3366) for about $200.

subliminal message that would play under the sound
of breaking waves. I relaxed noticeably, and my
mental state would brighten after each use.

The gentle one-on-one sessions with this friend
helped persuade me to reach out to my many friends
and family. Since the age of three, I had tried not to
ask for anyone's help. My line was, "Leave me alone!
I'm doing something." But now I let my friends help
me by asking them for money to go on an exotic trip
somewhere. I put together a letter that brought a
great return of love and money to me. This certainly
improved my day-to-day outlook. I had something
tangible to look forward to after my follow-up
operation that July.

The operation proved that Taxol was a successful
drug in obliterating the cancer. The surgeons could
find no trace of the cancer anywhere. I only go every
three months for a checkup now as a promise to the
study. My hair has not only grown fully back onto
my head and elsewhere, it is thicker and curlier than
ever before.

I try not to think that the cancer will come back. I
like to think I was aware of what was happening in
my body, but the truth was I didn't have a clue. Now,
I look at my stomach and say, "It looks like a butt."
School no longer holds any future job enrichment for
me. My roommate and I lived together for almost
two years in total, but I have moved on to another
state where I am living with old friends. I'm learning
to talk about what's going on inside me. A
personality type such as mine deeply buries its
feelings. Who knows what really saved my life.
Taxol? Indian intuition, female gentleness, and the
support of those around me? A little denial on my
part still helped as far as I can see.

Cancer as a Chronic Illness: Lesbians Speak Out[*]

Victoria A. Brownworth

The year I was 25, I went to Manhattan for the 50th birthday bash of a lesbian artist friend. The party in her West End Avenue co-op was *intime* and lively—30-odd members of the New York lesbian intelligentsia, debating and dancing.

I had been staring at a woman seated on the end of my friend's sofa. She was striking, dressed in a dashiki-style shirt and tight pants. And she only had one breast. Like a small child seeing a handicap for the first time, I was mesmerized. What had happened to her breast?

As I contemplated the possibilities, she caught my eye and came to ask me for a dance, leaving a coterie of women behind. I was terminally embarrassed, and to cover my awkwardness I blurted out a joke about always having been attracted to Amazons. As we danced, she told me she had lost her breast to cancer. Then she laughed a big laugh and said that she had been an Amazon long before her breast was removed.

Audre Lorde was the first lesbian I had ever met who had breast cancer. She was the only woman I had ever met who had chosen not to wear a prosthesis to disguise her missing breast. She sat

---

[*] Kincaid and Parker, two women who were interviewed for this article, are referred to by pseudonyms to protect them from cancer-phobia on the job. All other aspects of their stories are accurate.

133

down with me and took my hand, saying, "I have
breast cancer, why should I hide it? All my life people
have wanted me to hide something—being black,
being a lesbian. I didn't hide then; I won't now."
Lorde said that people know that women get breast
cancer, that women should know that *lesbians* get
breast cancer.

Three years later, I was reminded of her words as I
lay on an examining table in a doctor's office. He
took a plastic card from his lab-coat pocket. The card
had graduated-size holes cut in it. He placed the card
over my right breast and then he held it up for me to
see. "You have a mass this size," he said
perfunctorily, pointing to the largest hole on the card.
"You need to see a surgeon."

By the end of the week, I was in an operating
room, a green surgical drape separating me from my
breast. Eighteen months later, the lump had grown
back, and I was once again in the operating room,
my surgeon cutting into the old scar.

Breast cancer rarely ends with the first cut of the
surgeon's knife. Audre Lorde is dead now. She fought
her cancer for 14 years as it spread from her breast
to her lymph nodes to her neck to her liver. Lorde
was a model for lesbians—for all women—with
cancer: she wrote about it, spoke about it, was an
activist against the silence that surrounds it. She often
said that there were thousands of lesbians with breast
cancer. It wasn't the hyperbole of the writer or the
activist; it was in fact a low estimate.

It is quite an expedition from that West End
apartment where I was first enlightened about
lesbians and cancer to the imposing edifice that is the
National Cancer Institute (NCI) in Bethesda,
Maryland, where Dr. Suzanne Haynes is chief of
Health Education for Cancer control. Audre Lorde
started lesbians on that expedition by breaking the

silence about breast cancer. Haynes has delved yet deeper, analyzing diverse clinical and behavioral studies to estimate the specific risks lesbian women face.

According to her projections—the first ever done for lesbians and any kind of cancer—one in three lesbians is likely to get breast cancer in her lifetime. This is three times the national average for all women, which the Centers for Disease Control (CDC) terms a pandemic. In 1992, the NCI released the latest statistics on breast cancer in the United States: one in eight women will get the disease in her lifetime. In 1991, the number was one in nine; in 1989, the number was one in ten—up from one in 14 in 1960 and one in 20 in 1940. NCI data show that about 48,000 women die of breast cancer each year; in 1992, an estimated 180,000 women were diagnosed with the disease. It is the leading cause of death for African-American women between the ages of 45 and 65.

Haynes speaks with the directness of a scientist and the concerns of a lesbian when she says, "There has to be a kind of wake-up call in the country about the high risks we face as lesbians—the special risks we face as lesbians." The first researcher to speak out on the heightened dangers for lesbians, Haynes compiled her epidemiological data for a lecture she was asked to give at the 1992 Lesbian and Gay Health Conference in Los Angeles.

Haynes' data are pioneering: There has been no documentation of breast cancer risk factors for lesbians to date. Caitlin Ryan, one of the authors of the 1985 National Lesbian Health Care Survey, was one of the first to recognize links between lesbians and high cancer risk. Not only did her data show higher risk, but 28 percent of the lesbians she surveyed had experienced some breast abnormality,

including masses and discharge. That data remain
unpublished in medical or scientific journals.

What Haynes and Ryan's data emphasize is the
dramatic number of lesbians affected by cancer,
breast cancer in particular, in their lifetimes. Yet with
all these cancer cases within the lesbian community,
only a handful of agencies or organizations in the
entire country deal specifically with cancer among
lesbians. And few have the resources or even the raw
materials to deal with one wholly unexplored area of
cancer care: treating cancer as a chronic illness.

Cancer is largely treated as a one-time event by the
medical establishment and the social service agencies
that provide support services for women with the
disease. But any woman who has had cancer—
whether it is breast cancer or some other form of the
disease—knows that this perceived medical "event"
will last her entire life however long that is.

Audre Lorde recognized that fact and tried to share
with other women the benefit of her insight into her
own illness. Susan Sontag, in her essay *Illness as
Metaphor*, also discusses the impact of cancer over a
lifetime.

Yet remarkably, doctors and other health
professionals continue to approach cancer in women
as if it happens, is treated, and is over. Nothing could
be further from the reality of the disease and its own
particular half-life. Particularly for lesbians.

As data from Haynes, Ryan, and other researchers
are beginning to indicate, lesbians have a high
recurrence rate for various cancers. Different theories
are posited for this, but the most likely is lack of
regular medical and/or gynecological care. Haynes'
data showed, for example, that 45 percent of lesbians
don't have regular obstetric-gynecological care and
another 25 percent have only sporadic care; less than
one third of lesbians regularly get essential gynecolog-

ical care. Many women can't afford treatment, and Haynes notes that the majority of lesbians, wary of the medical establishment, frequently treat themselves.

A San Diego-based study surveying levels of homophobia among California physicians showed a whopping 31 percent of obstetricians and gyne-cologists said they were "uncomfortable" dealing with lesbians. The bottom line, according to Haynes, "is scary. Lesbians should be worried, because if they don't get screened, their cancers are less likely to be diagnosed early, when they can be most effectively treated. And late diagnoses are much more likely to result in death."

▲ ▲ ▲

Even with an early diagnosis, "cure" is not always the end result for lesbians with cancer. Recurrences, new forms of cancer, and after-effects of the first cancer and its treatment all play a significant role in the life-time health of any woman who has had cancer. The key points about living with the disease, made by lesbians interviewed for this article who have survived cancers, all relate to how others perceive them—from medical professionals to friends, family, and partners.

"I am forever an outsider," said Jill Kincaid, a Philadelphia psychologist who was diagnosed with colon cancer eight years ago at the age of 38. "I am sick—a lot. No one understands what that means. Either people think it means I am dying, which I am not, or they think I am just malingering—which I *certainly* am not. But either way I am left isolated by my illness and its after-effects."

Kincaid has frequent intestinal blockages, her intestines friable from several bouts of radiation and chemotherapy and full of adhesions from surgeries.

Her weight fluctuates wildly; at certain times she is bloated and heavy-seeming, while at others she is anorexically thin. And she is always tired and often depressed.

"These are not characteristics that most people want to engage with," she points out with a touch of wryness. "There is the person I was before cancer and the person I am now with cancer—and I will never go back to being that earlier person, so people who knew me then and are constantly comparing me to who I once was are often the most damaging to be around."

Kincaid lost her lover of five years as well: "She's not dead, but I certainly lost her to cancer," she said. "The constant up and down of this disease and the lack of support for lesbians with cancer and their partners, the way the medical establishment cuts off your partner's input and need-to-know—all of that takes its toll. And it is much harder to face this disease alone than with someone."

Leanne Bryan agrees. She was diagnosed with breast cancer three years ago at 39. She and her lover parted during the course of her treatment, although she says her former partner remains supportive. "It is very difficult to maintain a relationship through an illness like this," she said. Bryan is co-facilitator of a San Francisco support group for lesbians with cancer sponsored by the Women's Cancer Resource Center in Berkeley, the nation's first feminist service organization for women with cancer. A lesbian educator and activist, Bryan tries to bring the various problems faced by lesbians with cancer into her educational process, emphasizing the need for long-term support networks and recognition of the fact that cancer is *not* a one-time event.

"There are so many different things that happen when you are diagnosed," Bryan notes. "First there is the immediacy of dealing with doctors and treatments, surgery, and chemotherapy. But even those choices, which seem so clear-cut, are going to affect you for the rest of your life. Then there is all that comes after."

Bryan, who underwent a modified radical mastectomy of her left breast and chemotherapy but no radiation ("I was slashed and poisoned but not burned"), says that her personal experiences were "actually ideal. I had good insurance, doctors I trusted, a lover to help support me emotionally and I was white. I had a flexible job and didn't have to face any outright homophobia in any of the processes I went through. But that's the exception, not the rule. And if any single one of those factors had been different for me, I don't know how I could have gotten through it all."

What women like Bryan and Kincaid emphasize is that the disease of cancer is actually chronic; few doctors, for example, consider cancer "cured" before five years has elapsed without a recurrence of any sort.

"But waiting for that five-year point can be devastating in itself," said Allissa Green, a 48-year-old lesbian who was diagnosed with cervical cancer at 39, and three years later developed an unrelated breast cancer. "I am allegedly 'cancer-free' now," she said. "But I live in New York, a cancer city, and I've lived here all my life. What kinds of carcinogens have I breathed, drunk in the water, eaten in my food, absorbed through my skin? These are things you think about when your body starts to turn on you. You ask yourself what has happened in your life to make this cancer, to grow this malignancy. And one of the most brutal aspects of the so-called cures is that they either are bombarding your body with more poisons or they are telling you you have somehow brought this on yourself."

Green says simply that she "lost everything" to cancer and had to start a whole new life after surgery and chemotherapy finally ended. "I no sooner got over the trauma of the first cancer and having all that surgery and radiation, than I had to face the breast cancer. And forever in my mind will be the question of whether or not all the after-effects of the first cancer didn't just bring on the second," she says. Green adds that because she had no savings, a small income as an artist and art-instructor, and was estranged from her family because of her lesbianism, "Cancer pretty much put me out on the street. I was too debilitated to do any kind of work for over three years. My lover supported us but she was really struggling and she had no supports. I am truly amazed that she stayed with me for the whole ordeal—in fact we are still together and have been for almost 18 years. But I understand better than anyone what *she* went through during my illness and that is one aspect of cancer and lesbians that gets very little attention. Judy had to face the fact that I might die, and all the while she was facing that, she had to take care of me, take care of herself, and take care of all of our finances. *And* she had to face the homophobia of the doctors and nurses, *and* she had to face our friends and family—all of whom wanted all this to be over with."

▲ ▲ ▲

Society equates cancer with death. Most of us have that perception, whether we have been touched by the disease or lucky enough to have been passed by. The reality of cancer is that even when death is the result, it is not a swift and neat process, it is not the sword

of Damocles cutting fast through a life. Rather it is
an agonizing process, usually at least two years of
surgery, chemotherapy, radiation, and metastacization
before death actually takes over. That time can seem
both frighteningly swift and agonizingly slow. But for
those not immediately within the cancer circle,
impatience can, and does, supersede concern.

"When my friends thought I was dying," said
Violet Parker, who was diagnosed with leukemia at
27, "they were sad but they were supportive. I had
been given about six months time. I was on
chemotherapy, and I was terrified and very, very
angry. You were not supposed to get well with what I
was diagnosed with. But then I started getting better.
And it turned out that I had been misdiagnosed. But
my friends were pretty furious that I hadn't died. Of
course no one said that, but my lover left me, two of
my close friends became very distant, and there was
really a very real sense that they resented having put
all this energy into my being sick and dying. Now I'm
sick again, and I have a lot of fears about being
abandoned."

Parker's current illness, she believes, is the result of
the massive chemotherapy she received ten years ago.
"These drugs are poisons—they are the only things
that are strong enough to kill the cancer. But what do
they do if you don't have the disease they thought
you had? Can they influence tumors? Can they *cause*
cancer? We just don't know."

Some women are now raising concerns that there
are long-term side-effects from cancer therapies that
can cause other health problems in so-called "cured"
patients. Parker has been diagnosed with auto-
immune dysfunction, which may have been triggered
by her chemotherapy. Kincaid also has an auto-
immune disease of her intestines that has intensified
since her latest round of radiation. Other auto-

immune diseases, like severe arthritis, also plague a large number of lesbians who have received cancer therapies.

"I'm not saying don't have the treatments," said Parker. "My case was a mistake, but I certainly would want treatment if it might save my life. I just think that part of the big problem for lesbians with cancer is that they don't have the same resources, either medically or in terms of other support. Who do we ask questions of? Doctors are uncomfortable with us. Straight women's cancer groups don't address our particular needs. We're fighting cancer and we're fighting sexism and we're fighting homophobia. It's a tough, tough fight—too much for one person, really. And I think that we get a lot of wrong information, or not enough information, because we are struggling with all these other issues. When you see a movie-of-the-week on television that deals with a woman with cancer, everyone rallies around her. She gets time to think about things like finding a new wife for her husband so he won't be alone and the kids won't be motherless. But lesbians have to spend all their time being concerned about whether or not bills can get paid, whether or not they can bring their partner to the emergency room or into the doctor's office or if the surgeon will be rude to her. Most often the families of lesbians," said Parker, "are not responsive. They can't overcome their homophobia, even when their child is terribly ill and might die. Or there is a struggle between the lesbian's partner and her family. These kinds of stresses are unique to the lesbian experience of cancer. And if you survive, they are still there to be dealt with."

For Green, her two bouts with cancer meant starting life over—at 48. "I have to always ask myself how long I am going to be well," Bryan notes. "Because I thought I was getting well from the cervical cancer when the breast cancer cropped up. Now in the back of my mind is always the thought— what next? I get a stitch in my side and I think liver cancer, while other women might just think they are walking too fast. The cancer *process* never ends. I've been told I'm cured because my five years have passed and no recurrence. But how do I *know*, how does my lover *know*? We don't. And that shadow never leaves you. That's a part of life they don't explain for you in the surgeon's office or the radiologist's office. How do you live with the shadows?"

Bryan lives with them by talking about cancer, by being an educator. But she said that there's no going back to one's pre-cancer life.

"You are forever a survivor," Bryan said. "Even if your cancer never comes back, it *was* there. You have a scar, or scars, a missing breast, radiation burns, something that will not let you forget it happened. And the medical establishment and the insurance companies don't let you forget either."

For Parker, the one bill that must always be paid is her health insurance. "Because I have a 'preexisting condition,' if I let my health insurance lapse, I'll never get it again—I'll never be approved. And the amount of medical bills I've had over ten years of three kinds of cancer have been astronomical. Without health insurance, I would be living on a grate, there's no question."

▲ ▲ ▲

As a psychologist, Kincaid believes that the attitude toward cancer has to change within the lesbian community, on a wide range of levels. "There are so many issues that we think we can ignore because we are lesbians," Kincaid said. "One is that having cancer or surviving cancer changes you, just like surviving incest or some other terrible trauma changes you. Cancer is a life-threatening illness; it can come back, it can scar you, maim you, make you very, very sick. How can we pretend that doesn't have a fundamental impact on those of us who have it or have had it and those of us who are close to someone with cancer?"

Other concerns Kincaid and Bryan voiced have to do with body image. Kincaid has numerous scars and a permanent colostomy. Bryan had a mastectomy. Both women are currently single and unsure how to approach potential partners with their altered bodies.

"I am proud of what I have survived," said Bryan of her mastectomy scars, "but we are so geared by this society to think of our women's bodies in a certain way. And the lesbian community tries to pretend that it isn't body-conscious. But that's just not true. In order to deal with what has happened to us, we have to be able to talk about our bodies and how they are different. There's some grief attached to losing a part of your body, and some partners of women with cancer can't cope with the physical changes in their lovers. So when are we going to address this issue?"

Parker notes that body image is a particularly vulnerable area for lesbians with cancer: "I have always been pretty. My hair has always been long and blonde—I'm a lipstick lesbian, I guess," she said. "When my hair began to fall out from chemotherapy, I was terrified. Somehow this one constant of my life, my beautiful hair, was a metaphor for the disease and my possible death. Then I lost a breast—I have an implant now. Then I had major abdominal surgery so I have an eighteen-inch scar from my sternum to my navel. My body is not the body I had. My skin is different; my hair grew back darker and straighter.

Cancer changes what you look like. And as a
consequence, it changes how you relate to other
women. We've been taught in our society that certain
things are *ugly*. Scars are *ugly*. Being bald is *ugly*.
You are visibly different from other women. That
isolates you. So how do we deal with that?"

Bryan believes that talking about cancer more and
forming support groups like her own is a big part of
the answer. Having more information about cancer
and therapies and individual experiences can only
help. And sharing their unique cancer experiences
helps lesbians break the isolation that is the most
damaging side-effect of the disease.

▲ ▲ ▲

Deborah Silberberg was diagnosed with Hodgkin's
Disease eleven years ago, while still in her twenties.
Today she considers herself a survivor—she's had no
recurrences—and facilitates a cancer support group
for lesbians. But there is no question for Silberberg
that her cancer experience was a defining element in
her life. Her work as a cancer educator reflects that
fact. She believes that being a lesbian with cancer
makes having the disease much more difficult to cope
with both in immediate terms and over time.

"Secrecy about our cancer has been one big
problem," she said. "And that secrecy comes out of
our shame about our bodies. There's still a great deal
of shame attached to women's bodies, and it's hard
for women to talk about their cancer experiences.
Women are the nurturers, the health care *providers*
for families. But who provides for these women?"

Silberberg notes that the invisibility of lesbians with
cancer and lesbian survivors of cancer contributes to
the epidemic of cancer among lesbians because "lack
of awareness and lack of education about how the

various forms of this disease affect us as lesbians
mean that we are not seeking out the kind of care we
need."

The stresses posed by cancer on lesbians are
unique, as well, and need to be addressed by the
lesbian community *and* the medical community *and*
the cancer-advocacy community. "The stress on
lesbian relationships when one partner gets cancer
can end relationships and often does," says
Silberberg. "As women, we connect with each other
through our bodies, at least on one level. And when
one of us gets cancer, it is often too close for comfort.
Partners feel out of control. We don't get enough
support as lesbians—there's much more support for a
heterosexual partner. We don't know what it is like
for a lesbian partner to look at her lover ill or dying
and cope with it. There's nothing for us to read, no
literature even on breast cancer for lesbians, let alone
other cancer. You don't know how to react to
anything—if this is 'normal' or not—because there
are no models, no guidelines."

On the ten-year anniversary of her diagnosis,
Silberberg wrote an essay on surviving for her cancer
support group's newsletter. "I don't feel like
celebrating," she said. "It's been very tough. It's
changed me in a way I'd never have chosen."
Silberberg went into menopause right after her
treatments for Hodgkin's; she's had other health
problems brought on by the cancer treatments and
the cancer itself. "Healing is not a straight line," she
notes. "Western medicine is not a straight line. I don't
know what will happen to me another few years
from now, but you are certainly never *free* from
cancer, even if you do survive it, even if Western
medicine says you are cured."

Support groups, fundamentally, says Silberberg,
need to address the varied points of the healing

process. The key question every woman with cancer has is, "'Am I ever going to feel good again?' And that is in a range of ways, not just in terms of your body. For anyone who is sick, you are always balancing, always dealing with the resentment of your body that has failed you and your separation from that body and then the separation of mind from body. You have to work at reattaching your body and mind and making them whole again. You spend a lot of time asking yourself, 'If I just take care of *this*, will I be okay?'"

Knowing that other women have been ill and survived is an essential part of coping with the reality of cancer as on on-going illness, a chronic illness. Silberberg says, "It's not easy, but it *is* doable. There *are* women out there surviving and thriving through illness."

What lesbians who have survived cancer or who are living with cancer all agree on is the need for recognition of what they have experienced—both as acknowledgment of their struggle and as help for other lesbians who might be experiencing the same trauma.

Kincaid has a list of what she wants to see happen in the lesbian community at large. "I want cancer recognized as being the same threat to our community as AIDS has been to gay men," she says. "There are so many lesbians working on AIDS issues—and while that's important, cancers are killing a huge number of lesbians each year, really decimating our community, and it is *still* perceived as a non-event. It's still the invisible epidemic. Even with one in three lesbians at risk for breast cancer—a full third of our community!"

Other essential changes Kincaid wants made include "absolutely massive numbers of support groups for lesbians with cancer, for their partners, and for lesbians who have 'survived' cancer. None of our specific issues is addressed in the larger context of the cancer-advocacy movement and that has to happen, and we have to make it happen by demanding it, demanding money for research and for facilitation and for education."

Finally, the need for an attitudinal change from within the community must be facilitated. "I don't know, even as a therapist, how we are going to manage this, but gay men did it with AIDS—and lesbians were in the forefront of that movement—so I think that we have the *capability*. There is a really potential for disaster here in our community with this invisible epidemic," says Kincaid. "Not just in terms of women lost, like Audre Lorde or Pat Parker or Jane Chambers or a host of other women who aren't famous. But in terms of how we view our own dedication to *survival*. As women and as lesbians we are really under threat from this society, and as gay men saw with AIDS, no one is real eager to run out and help a group they believe is unworthy. So we have to make the changes ourselves, force the issues, demand difference. I and other women shouldn't have to face so many obstacles just to stay alive. And we damn well shouldn't have to face them from within our own borders, from women like ourselves."

Parker is equally adamant. "Having cancer is like being a lesbian—there is no *one* 'coming out' process. You are always having to declare your disease anew, always having to explain yourself. It is such a burden, and it doesn't have to be so hard. It really doesn't. It just requires that the well members of our community acknowledge that being sick isn't a privilege that we are manipulating, but rather a dreadful struggle that we hope to survive. I hate like hell being sick. I will myself every day to be well. But that isn't always enough, no matter what the crystal-lovers tell you.

You can do all the creative imagery you want and still have a big fat cancer eating away at you. We have to stop blaming women for being sick and start asking what we can do to help, to support, to help them to survive."

▲ ▲ ▲

Surviving can be as difficult as preparing to die. Cancer changes you irrevocably, and not always for the better. It can make you fearful, even terrified. It can make you angry, rage-filled. It can make you appreciate every moment more but fear losing those moments in a way well people never do.

There is no leaving cancer behind. Whether it is in scar tissue or the aftershock of radiation and chemotherapy, it comes back to haunt you. It never fully lets you out of its shadow. And then there is always the peril of recurrences; did one survive only to face death again a few years or even months later?

There are many tests put to the lesbian who lives with cancer. She must always recognize it and acknowledge it—either because she must explain to a new lover that she has only one breast, or to a new employer that she needs a flexible work schedule or to a community whose ignorance unfortunately makes it insensitive, that chronic illness is a disability that must be acknowledged, even if it cannot readily be seen.

Some of us seem well, function in our individual worlds, move on as if the hand of death has not been planted firmly and irrevocably on our shoulder. But others of us may not recover—though maybe we won't die either—and there has to be a place for us within our community. Cancer is not a one-time medical crisis with a single outcome—death or cure. It is a long, lifetime process. And as more and more lesbians are attacked by breast and other cancers, we are obligated as a community to find ways and means to cope with that epidemic.

One essential is to follow in the steps of Audre Lorde and other courageous women who have lived with cancer over long periods of time: speak out about the epidemic, acknowledge that cancer is a threat to our women, ourselves. Speaking out, acknowledging the epidemic, is the first step toward educating lesbians that we are at risk, that many of us are already—knowingly or unknowingly—affected.

As women, as lesbians, as a community, we have tremendous potential for creating change. It was lesbians who forged the women's health and reproductive rights movements, who were in the forefront of the AIDS movement; now it is time to turn our attention to our own lives, our own survival.

Cancer begins before diagnosis and never ends until you finally die—regardless of how many years you might be "cancer-free." As a community, we need to "come out" about cancer and its affect on lesbian women. As a community, we need to rededicate ourselves to life and survival. And one of the first steps toward that process is acknowledging how close many of us are or have been to death.

Part 2

Constructing Change

The Politics of Cancer[*]

Jackie Winnow

Everything about cancer is political, and that's the way we have to look at it. As lesbians and feminists, we need to be making connections and analyzing what the media presents to us, what the media tells us, about cancer and how then we react to it. And we have to know what the realities in our lives are, rather than what the media or the American Cancer Society tells us about what the realities of our lives are once we get cancer. That's the only way we can change things.

All of these centers, every one of these centers, is political. The fact that we as feminists, the fact that we as lesbians, have created these centers as a consumer-feminist movement is so political. Somebody who was putting together a politics of cancer anthology once asked me why she should include the Mautner Project because it was direct services to lesbians. I said, "If you don't understand why a direct service agency to lesbians is political, you don't really understand anything—you've just put together the anthology."

I think it's really important for us to look at the fact that cancer is being controlled from the top to

---

[*] This article is a transcription of a talk given by Jackie Winnow at the first meeting of representatives of the first four grassroots women's/feminist/lesbian community cancer projects (in Oakland, Boston, Washington DC, and Chicago; see listing on pages 265–66) at the National Lesbian Conference in Atlanta, Georgia, in April 1991.

153

the bottom. It's been controlled by professionals, by the American Cancer Society, by the petroleum companies, by the chemical companies, by the Rockefellers. The fact that we have taken control, once again, as feminists and lesbians, is a really political act and has been very threatening to the cancer establishment, and there is a tremendous cancer establishment in this country that profits from it.

I'd like to give you a little bit of a personal background on me before I go on, so you can get a small understanding of where I'm coming from. I'm making my part of this as brief as I can. I usually talk endlessly. Maybe it has something to do with cancer. Anyway, in 1985 I was diagnosed with breast cancer, in Oakland, California. In the period of a weekend between my biopsy and my diagnosis, my lover Teya and I realized that we had to become cancer experts. So we did become cancer experts over the weekend. The day I got my diagnosis of breast cancer, I had been in a meeting. I was the coordinator of Lesbian/Gay and AIDS Unit of the San Francisco Human Rights Commission. We just had spent five or six hours at a meeting on AIDS, and all I was thinking about in this meeting was "my biopsy results, my biopsy results." When my surgeon called me at ten o'clock that night, I knew it was bad news. I had negative nodes, which was supposed to be a good diagnosis. I had a lumpectomy followed by radiation, and what happened to me in the reality of the situation was there was no place to go to empower myself. There was no central information source to empower myself to become an informed consumer for my own health care. And that was stunning to me.

We had feminist health centers, if I had a yeast infection, and we had AIDS centers, if I had AIDS, but we had nothing established for ourselves as far as cancer was concerned. So it was catch as catch can. Another woman, named Carla Dalton, and myself became known as "the cancer mavens." And everybody just started calling us all the time. We decided that really we needed to do was create a center [the Women's Cancer Resource Center in Berkeley]. The center was to be a central resource center, so that people could come and get support and information, and come and agitate about cancer. But the basic underlying point of the center is empowerment: so that women become empowered to make the decisions they need to make to live the lives that they need to live. . . . We started in late 1986 planning it. Before we knew it, we had to have a support group, because the idea of it became so—there was such a need. It was unbelievable. It all blossomed before we could really do our proper planning.

The American Cancer Society let us use their kitchen. We started our support groups, and they sent people to us. That's how our support group was started, so that as we were organizing we kept something going to meet people's needs. But people kept on thinking—because we got all this media attention too—that there was this big center, and really it was just part of the study in my house. The phone was in there, and that's how we started. We needed to start before we started, so it all just became this big circle.

In 1988 I was diagnosed with metastatic breast cancer to my lungs and bones, and that's why it's hard to me to talk loud, because of the cancer in my lungs, and it's hard for me to sit, because of the cancer in my bones. But in taking care of my own business and becoming weaker than I had been, the leadership of the center is falling apart, so Susan

Liroff, who is now director, stepped in there and took it off, and it's been really wonderful. We have our own place. It's as environmentally safe as we can get it, and we have a library. We have information referral. We have many different kinds of support groups. We have an educational program. We have a speaker's bureau, and we just have a lot of different kinds of activities. We wish we could have more, but there's just so much we can do at a time. We're just moving along in that direction.

Now, with the history of all that behind us, I think it's so exciting to see what's happening to women's programs, to see that we have created this movement, that there are now centers, that there are political action groups that are agitating on our behalf. It's very exciting that people are seeing cancer as a political issue in a society that tries to keep cancer as a personal issue. People get cancer, and it's this personal issue, and you take care of it yourself. Louis Sullivan, U.S. Secretary of Health, came out with a 600-page report about how Americans can take care of their own health care, and it was basically a 600-page report about pulling yourself up by your own bootstraps. There was no mention of national health care; there was no mention of what the corporations could do to clean up the environment or change their behavior as far as cancer was concerned. I think that we have incorporated very much the idea of individual responsibility for cancer, and we in the feminist community have done the same thing because we live in this world. It is not incidental that Louis Sullivan talks about cancer in a private way or health care in a private way. When you have Louise Hay who talks about cancer as being a personal, emotional problem, you've got Bernie Seigel asking you why you need to have it, and you've got a lot of psychobabble about why people have cancer, because there is no cure for cancer and they don't really know the causes of cancer. So here it is: people have their personal problems and that's why they have cancer, rather than the fact that there are biological and molecular things going on in the body that are being promoted by a noxious world.

We see it in our own community: if I have positive thinking, I won't get cancer; if I run, I won't get cancer; if I eat properly, I won't get cancer. So what did you do to get cancer?

We're going to have to look at that. There's this whole thing that we create our own reality, so if you sit and you visualize, you can visualize away your cancer and if you don't do it, then there's something wrong with you. You've got fear. People get cancer because they fear love, and if you didn't fear love, then you wouldn't have cancer. Love has nothing to do with it. Give me a break. And then we've got karma. Karma comes back again. This is big stuff, you know. People make a lot of money out of it. We incorporate it into ourselves too. And when you hold the individuals accountable for this disease, then the culprits go scott-free.

We've got an incredible epidemic happening in our country, and I'm going to give you some of those statistics, so that you get a handle on how incredible this epidemic really is. One in three Americans now gets cancer in their lifetime. In 1950, it was one in ten. That's an incredible jump in a very short period of time. So when we talk about people living longer, etc., etc., we're talking in 1950 it was one in ten and now it's one in three. There are five million people in the United States who have cancer. One million people are going to be diagnosed with this disease this year, and half a million people are going to die. Half a million people. And if we say that a million people are going to get cancer this year, and we're ten percent of the population, then we're talking about 100,000 lesbians being diagnosed with cancer this year. One-hundred years ago, cancer caused less than three percent of the deaths in the United States. Today it kills one in four men. When I was diagnosed with breast cancer in 1985, one in eleven women got breast cancer, and now it's one in nine.*

The rate for breast cancer for women between the ages 30 and 35 has tripled since 1977 and quadrupled for women between the ages of 35 and 39. That's amazing. It was once considered an "old lady's" disease. It is no longer considered an old lady's disease. 175,000 women will get breast cancer this year, and 45,000 will die from this disease. The thing that's really startling about this is that we have a lot of positive stuff coming out from the American Cancer Society about all that's been done for cancer. And breast cancer, the statistics for breast cancer have not changed since 1930: it's been the same amount of women dying from breast cancer now as they did in 1930.** They may live longer, but they die at the same rate. So nothing has really changed.

When they talk about prevention, they are talking about early detection. If you find a lump in a mammogram, you already have cancer. You haven't prevented a damn thing. So you have to understand, they haven't come up with anything to prevent cancer, only things that detect it earlier, and then they pass it off as prevention.

---

* This was April 1991. As of November 1992, it was one in eight.

** Winnow was referring to the fact that the number of women dying has increased dramatically; the percentage of women dying compared to the number of women being diagnosed has remained the same.

We can do things to change, individually. We can
stop smoking. We can change our diets. We can
exercise. We can do some of those things to take care
of ourselves. But we can't think of ourselves as living
in a vacuum, in that we are responsible for our
health, because we cannot be ultimately responsible
for our health. We don't control everything in our
environment. We know that as lesbians we don't
control the society.

Prevention would be the proliferation of these
kinds of centers in the system that change the system,
that change the structure of the system. There should
be national health care in this society. We don't have
national health care. People are not getting health
care. Black women are being diagnosed with cancer
at a much greater rate than white women, and die
from it, are much more likely to die from it.

The Women's Health Trial was being developed for
eight years. It had to do with breast cancer and diet
and the fact that a low-fat diet might affect cancer.
Feminists tried to put the Women's Health Trial
through three different times, and on three different
occasions they were told it was too difficult for the
government researchers to carry it through, that
women would not change their diets, and that it was
too difficult to do a diet where women had to change
their diet, because you couldn't trust them. It wasn't
like giving them a pill. Of course, they've done a *lot*
of studies on heart disease and diet, and I guess men
can change their diets and they don't have to give
them a pill and they can trust them. But they would
not put the money into this, to see what would
happen with women. At the same time, women's
groups began lobbying the NCI (the National Cancer
Institute) and the National Institute of Health, and
they promised to give us more money and they
promised to fund a study, and the third time they

denied the study. And one of the reasons they said
they denied the study was because they wouldn't be
able to reach all socioeconomic groups because you
couldn't trust Black women to eat a low-fat diet.
That was one of the reasons that they gave.

But under some stress from people like us, because
we are organizing, because we have people like Pat
Schroeder in office, and we have Olympia Snow and
we have Barbara Milkulski, they have formed a
women's congressional committee and have proposed
the Women's Health Equity Act, which is twelve
separate bills dealing with women's health issues. It
was discovered that hardly any, *any* medical trials
were being done on women at all. Although we're
52 percent of the population, the National Cancer
Institute was spending 13 percent of its budget on
women. We're 52 percent of the population. They've
now doubled it to 26 percent, but it's still only 26
percent.

It's really important for us to look at that and keep
on pushing this feminist agenda in the Congress,
because it has gotten somewhere and we need to keep
on doing it. What I'm very concerned about right
now it that there's a new women's cancer national
organization being put together, but it's being put
together to deal with breast cancer and breast cancer
issues. I think at this point in our organizing, because
we are starting these organizations, we need to build
a national agenda to deal with women and cancer.
Not just breast cancer, because we don't only get
breast cancer and women are not just defined by their
tits, or their lack thereof. It's very important for us to
see and not exclude women who have all different
kinds of cancer and to make sure that everybody
knows that we do get other kinds of cancer besides
breast cancer, including lung cancer at increasing

rates, as the cigarette companies are targeting women in their ads to smoke.

We talk about prevention and we have a government that keeps on throwing out that we shouldn't be smoking, but they support the tobacco industry. So where are our tax dollars going?

We have to look very closely when we're talking about prevention and when we're organizing. At the petrochemical companies, we have to see what happened in 1950 that is so different from now. What happened in 1950 is that we had the beginning of the petrochemical companies. We had radiated Nagasaki and Hiroshima, and we had underground and overground and testing everywhere of radiation in this country, in the deserts. We had chemical companies starting to make chemicals; we had chemical dumping. We had toxic waste dumps, and they've found that toxic waste dumps are more likely to happen in neighborhoods where poor people and people of color live. We have no ozone layer—I mean we have an ozone layer, but we're having holes there.

We have a food chain that has become mass-produced. Before 1950, we didn't have a mass-produced food chain, and we have that now. The animals are fed massive antibiotics and toxins, and they live in incredibly terrible conditions. And they're bred simply for mass-production rather than for any nutritional value. And then you've got your vegetables that are sprayed with pesticides everywhere; you've got your farmworkers who are dying in the fields because they're being sprayed by the pesticides; and somehow, even though the farmworkers are dying of the pesticide spraying, we're not supposed to question that they are in fact picking the food that has those pesticides and we're eating it. And then we have all this stuff that's gone into the water.

So what we're talking about is changing the system that works for profits rather than people. That is the point. This society doesn't care whether we die. We are the throwaways, because we don't own chemical companies, and even if we did there are other major stockholders, and people are making profit. It's the profit-making system of this country that brings us into wars and that makes us kill our own people here at home. We need national health care. We need an end to the sexist, demeaning attitude toward women and health care, and we need it throughout this whole society. Otherwise, it's not going to work when we try to change health care. We need to clean up the environment. We need to make connections to other movements for social change rather than to think that it's an individual solution. And we have to start our own self-help programs because we have to take back our own health care.

We have to support our own local service centers. We have to build some more. One of the things that is really telling to me is when I have done speeches and women have called me up who are disabled to say that there are no longer any attendants. There used to be a lot of lesbian attendants for them, and there no longer are as many lesbian attendants because they're working with men who have AIDS. And I'm not pitting us against men who have AIDS, because I think men who have AIDS need help and women with AIDS need help. What I am saying is that we also have to put our energies into women's health care. We don't have to take it out. We need to put it back in. We need to be there for them.

When we are dealing with fundraising, when we are working for lesbians, we have to make sure that we understand the cancer politics and cancer realities. That goes for all of us. We need to be changing billboards, so that the presence is brought home.

Somebody changed a billboard in San Francisco for the movie *Marked for Death* to read "Marked for death. 1000 women a day marked for death by the NCI." It was very effective immediately.

How can you question the National Cancer Institute? I heard a figure given from the stage last night that six percent less funding is given to cancer research now than it was ten years ago. And we have to have research that's valuable research rather than research that just goes for a bullet type of cure. We have to have research that deals with the realities of people's lives. We have to elect women to office, and we have to move for legislation, and we really have to be marching in the streets. I think we really have to understand how urgent this is, because women are getting cancer, women are dying from cancer at ever-increasing rates, and our lives depend on what we do in this room today.

The Boob Trap:
Debunking Myths
About Breast Cancer

Virginia M. Soffa

I heard I had breast cancer when I was 38 years
old. Because I was young and the cancer was small,
only one centimeter, I classified this as early. When
the doctors told me I had an 85 percent chance of
living five years if I had a mastectomy, radiation, and
maybe even chemotherapy, I took another look at
how women are being sold a bill of goods about the
prognosis of breast cancer. What's with this early
detection stuff? Being cured, and having less invasive
treatment? Exactly who was getting these treatments
that were less deforming? Why was five years being
called "cured"? And why did my pea-sized tumor
require the treatment "works"?

Getting our facts clear about breast cancer, and
particularly about "early detection" isn't easy when
women are feeling both anxious and scared,
wondering if they will be next. Some women are
running to the doctor demanding a mammogram,
even when they are only in their 20s and 30s; others
are so afraid of what they might find that they won't
even do regular breast self-exams.

Early detection programs, often referred to as
prevention programs, have lulled society into being
both complacent and panicked about breast cancer.
This disease has the potential of being passed on to
still another generation, unless women begin to speak
up about how they feel about the betrayal. We are
being told we are being helped, when in reality we
are being victimized by the people we trust.

165

Why are one fourth of all women diagnosed still dying of this disease? Why has this been the situation for 60 years? Why are well-meaning public education programs suggesting that early detection saves lives?

MYTH 1: *Knowing the risk factors associated with breast cancer will help you avoid getting it.*

The idea is that understanding risk factors leads to prevention. For example, if you don't smoke or live in a smoky environment, you can decrease your change of getting lung cancer. But the major risk factors that have been identified for breast cancer relate to circumstances no woman has any control over. Knowing the risks does not help anyone avoid getting the disease, primarily because scientists have not determined what causes breast cancer.

Family history, menarche before age 12, and menopause after 55 are some risks associated with breast cancer. Knowing that your mother or sister had breast cancer may increase your anxiety, but it is not something you can change.

Although there are two risk factors that have been identified and that *can* be influenced, no one is currently rallying around these opportunities: having a child before 30, or 20, depending on what research you believe, and decreasing dietary fat.

Researchers have determined that breast cancer risk increases with the number of ovulation cycles, and women are most vulnerable from puberty to first pregnancy. It is still not clear why women who have a child before 30 can reduce their risk; however, this pattern has been observed. Additionally, women who have low body fat, have reduced their fat with exercise during their teenage years, or maintain a low fat intake as adults also have a lower incidence.

A study conducted by Rose E. Frisch, Ph.D. of the Harvard School of Public Health, noted a "disparity related to differences in the amount and type of estrogen produced in the body, resulting in less proliferation of cells in the breast and reproductive tissues."*

These risk factors are not aggressively publicized in breast cancer prevention efforts. Not enough substantive research exists to warrant public health officials encouraging women to either have children earlier or begin regular exercise programs in high school.

MYTH 2: *"Early detection is your best protection against breast cancer."***

This myth is not as innocent as it might appear: it uses women's fear of breast cancer to promote mammography screening. Initially, the message appeals to women who want to know what to do to protect themselves from getting this disease.

Mammography is promoted as a means of prevention; however, mammography does not prevent anyone from getting cancer. At best, it is a way of detecting cancer. At worst, a means of promoting it.

What is the best protection? Because no one seems to have this answer, the answer being promoted is to encourage women to "catch it early," because this will presumably improve their chances of survival. Improved survival is based primarily on three studies: the Health Insurance Plan of New York study (HIP), the Breast Cancer Detection Demonstration Project (BCDDP), and The Swedish Trial.

------

* Rose E. Frisch et al., "Lower Lifetime Occurrence of Breast Cancer and Cancers of the Reproductive System Among Former College Athletes," in *American Journal of Clinical Nutrition*, vol 45 (1987), p 328–35.

** Board of Sponsors of the October 1989 National Breast Cancer Awareness Month.

- The Health Insurance Plan of New York followed 62,000 women over 18 years, providing mammography screening for the test group and not for the control group. In this study, 163 women in the control group died of breast cancer, compared to 126 in the screened group—a difference of 23 percent. Many articles on mammography refer to this study as showing a "significant survival" resulting from screening. The study did not address whether the test women used other techniques to improve their survival; therefore, it does not appear conclusive that screening is what improved their chances of survival.

   Another peculiar finding, not commented upon by the HIP authors, is noted by Peter Skrabanek: "The subgroup of women in the mammography group who refused screening (35 percent) had a lower incidence and mortality due to breast cancer than either the mammography group or the control group."[*]

- The Breast Cancer Detection Demonstration Project (BCDDP) was a non-randomized, uncontroled study conducted by the National Cancer Institute, in conjunction with the American Cancer Society, in the 1970s. The BCDDP evaluated 280,000 women. More than 4,000 cancers occurred, of which approximately 3,500 were detected with mammography screening and 800 were present but undetected.

   The irony of early detection is that by the time a tumor is detectable with mammography it is approximately six years old and contains one

---

[*] Peter Skrabanek, "False Premises and False Promises of Breast Cancer Screening," in *Lancet*, August 10, 1985.

billion malignant cells.

Mammography—although extremely beneficial—has its limitations, yet health promoters dream that someday every woman over age 35 will be using mammography regularly.

- According to Dr. Kopans' book *Breast Imaging*, The Swedish Trial addressed concerns about the HIP study, particularly what "the relative contribution of mammography and physical examination [were] in mortality reduction."[*] The Swedish Trial demonstrated a 30-percent reduction in mortality for the screened population after seven years. "Since breast cancer is a slow growing disease" according to Dr. Susan Love,[**] studies that draw conclusions in less than 20 years offer incomplete data.

According to the American Cancer Society, 30 percent of the women diagnosed with breast cancer will survive less than five years. Of the remaining 70 percent, an additional 15 percent will perish before their 10-year anniversary, and still another 15 percent before the 20-year celebration. Therefore, only 40 percent of the women originally diagnosed will survive 20 years. Given these figures, which have remained stable for more than 50 years, it is difficult to place a great deal of credence in a seven-year trial.

---

[*] Daniel B. Kopans, *Breast Imaging* (Philadelphia: J.B. Lippincott Co, 1989).

[**] Susan M. Love, *Dr. Susan Love's Breast Book* (New York: Addison-Wesley Publishing Company, 1990).

At this time it is unclear whether early detection actually promotes survival or merely extends the amount of time a woman lives knowing about her breast cancer.

MYTH 3: *With early detection, the cancer can be caught while it is still local; therefore, the treatment will be less traumatic and deforming.*

Early detection is one of the primary reasons for encouraging breast self-examinatiom and mammography. Yet this concept has misled many to think that if their cancer is detected early they will be able to have a less invasive treatment.

According to a survey conducted by the American College of Surgeons in 1982, of the operations performed for carcinoma of the breast in 1977 and 1981, radical mastectomies decreased 24 percent, while modified radical mastectomies increased from 22.6 percent to 78.2 percent of the mastectomies performed. Partial mastectomies increased from 2.8 percent to 7.2 percent of the mastectomies performed.

Mastectomy, although not the radical Halsted method of removing the chest-wall muscles as well as the breast, is still the most common method of treatment. This fact inspired a study that revealed that "the majority of women (55 percent) who had breasts removed after an early diagnosis of breast cancer would not make the same decision if they had a chance to choose again."*

In addition, the National Institutes of Health (NIH) recommended in the spring of 1989 that all women with breast cancer, even women with negative lymph nodes, should be treated with chemotherapy or hormonal therapy. This order caused an outcry from

---

* *Psychomatics*, Spring 1989.

the medical community and cancer activists because of concerns that drugs with significant immune-system-weakening and cancer-causing side effects are being prescribed as "preventive treatment." What is more revealing about this recommendation is the fact that there is ongoing debate among medical professionals as to whether breast cancer is a local or systemic disease.

As a local disease, early detection should mean that the cancer can be treated by simply removing the tumor. Dr. Susan Love's Breast Book states that "with lumpectomy alone a woman has a 37 percent greater chance of recurrence."* Therefore, radiation is commonly recommended when lumpectomies are performed. These two methods of treatment address breast cancer on a purely local level.

By the time the tumor is detected, even if there is no node involvement, it is very likely the cancer cells have already entered the bloodstream, making breast cancer systemic. Systemic cancer will recur in another location at some later date. Vincent De Vitta** states that "a combined total of 33 percent of the patients with or without node involvement will have a local recurrence."

Another reason recurrence is difficult to predict is that many women have a condition known as extensive intraductal component (EIC). Three stages of cancer can exist simultaneously: the tumor, ductal carcinoma in situ in the area surrounding the tumor, and EIC in the ducts. The latter two are precancerous conditions.

---

* Susan M. Love, Dr. Susan Love's Breast Book (New York: Addison-Wesley Publishing Company, 1990).

** Vincent De Vitta, former director of the National Cancer Institute.

Other studies have suggested that by the time a woman has a breast tumor, all of her breast tissue is affected, in both breasts, and it is only a matter of time before this becomes detectable. Those studies conclude the only way to prevent recurrence is to remove both breasts at the earliest possible time.

Whether or not early detection affords a woman more protection, less invasive treatment, or even peace of mind remains under investigation. When it comes to breast cancer, the concept of "early" does not have the same definition for everyone. Presently, early is not early enough.

MYTH 4: *The medical profession is making progress concerning breast cancer.*

The cause of breast cancer remains unknown, and prevention is not possible because no one knows why breast cancer occurs. Research and education dollars are being spent on developing better detection equipment, attracting potential patients to use this expensive equipment, and developing new chemicals to kill the cancer before the chemicals kill the patient.

An estimated 46,000 women will have died of breast cancer in the USA in 1992. Each year the number increases. Yet many people are under the impression that breast cancer is curable and that great strides have been made in the treatment of this disease. These myths have lulled women into complacency about how they approach breast cancer physically, verbally, and psychologically. Often the treatment victimizes the patient more than the disease.

MYTH 5: *The doctor should decide what treatments are given to women with breast cancer.*

One corollary to Myth 5 is that women are emotionally helpless and can't make decisions themselves. Additional unspoken rules accompany this myth:

- Women will be "saved and taken care of" if in return they are dutiful and compliant.
- Women must not express anger.
- The male "rational" model is the model to emulate.

These rules, internalized from childhood, permit the following common scenario to unfold.

A woman is contacted by her doctor and told she has breast cancer. While still in shock, she is told she will need to have treatment. The bottom line is, take this treatment or you will die. A similar ultimatum is delivered to rape victims: do what I say or I [it] will kill you. In both cases, the women does the unthinkable to defend her life; she relinquishes control of her body to someone else.

Even a woman who has achieved professional and financial independence can fall into the "rescue me" trap. The doctor with authoritarian status represents her hope for survival. Above all else this relationship must be preserved. The fear of abandonment or isolation from her doctor, family, and friends is as great as her fear of the disease. Her dutiful obedience might reduce her to the status of a servant, because her defiance would cause her to be cast into the wilderness—alone.

Rarely will someone stop and ask the breast cancer patient what she wants or needs in order to make an intelligent and personal decision about what happens to her body. When conversation does take place between patient and doctor, the doctor is often patronizing. If the conversation lasts too long, the doctor (or a nurse) tells the patient she is taking up

too much of the doctor's time, and she is dismissed as
though she were a naughty girl.

A 40-year-old woman is reduced to a 10-year-old.
She typically addressses her physicians as Dr.
such-and-such, while they call her by her first name.
She may be expected to have conversations with her
doctor in the examination room, lying on her back,
partially clothed. The doctor remains fully clothed
and standing. Her breasts—formerly a private body
part associated with pleasure—and her femininity are
suddenly treated like a contaminated
accessory—unimportant and undesirable.

The doctor doesn't want the patient to spend too
much time thinking about what is about to happen,
whether it is breast-preserving or deforming. The
doctor wants things to move quickly. This, is
however, unnecessary; research has shown that breast
cancer is typically a very slow-growing disease.*
There is no need for the patient to make hasty
decisions. In fact, a second opinion is highly
desirable, and actually required by some insurance
companies.

Many women give away their right to choice of
treatment by allowing the doctor to schedule their
appointments for a second opinion. Other women are
so frightened by the diagnosis that they do not
explore their options. Some may feel they just want
the offending breast off—it has betrayed her,
therefore she strikes back swiftly, mentally detaching
from her body.

Both of these reactions are deeply influenced by the
cultural socialization that women need to be "fixed."
Women are not okay the way they are. Too often

---

* Susan M. Love, *Dr. Susan Love's Breast Book* (New York:
Addison-Wesley Publishing Company, 1990).

women's health concerns are dismissed as stress or as emotional problems. Now that she has breast cancer, there is really something wrong, something that can be repaired. In some respects, this diagnosis gives her the sense of being redeemed. She had known all along something was wrong, but nobody believed her.

Because of the insidious nature of this problem, it can be difficult for a woman to retain her self-respect and foster a mature relationship with her doctors. It might appear as though she has only two choices: Give in or give up. The current health-care setting is not conducive to a woman fighting for her life, for the preservation of her body, and for her right to choose what treatment she will undertake. The health-care system encourages patient helplessness.

Several psychological studies have examined the way "helplessness" and despair contribute to the progression of cancer.

Dr. Joan Borysenko states, "Feeling constantly helpless can upset our endocrine balance, elevating the immunosuppressant hormone cortisol and destroying its natural diurnal rhythm. Chronic helplessness also depletes the brain of the vital neurotransmitter norepinephrine, the chemical in our brains that is necessary for feelings of happiness and contentment."

If helplessness is so harmful to the cancer patient, shouldn't the health-care system, if not society in general, be encouraging women to become independent and self-actualizing thinkers?

MYTH 6: *Women with breast cancer don't need to incorporate psychotherapy as part of their treatment program.*

Theories that women with breast cancer have unique personality traits are as old as the disease itself. "Hippocrates, the ancient physician, notes that

unhappy women were more likely than happy women
to develop breast cancer," states author and physician
Arnold Fox.[*]

Dr. Peggy Boyd writes, in *The Silent Wound*, that
"researchers concluded in part that in life, as in the
situation of stress caused by biopsy and mastectomy,
these patients would admit to only a small amount
of anxiety, even when anxiety is quite understand-
able."[**] Breast cancer patients "were reluctant to
appear in any way socially unacceptable."

More and more research supports the theory that
there is an identifiable psychological link to cancer
growth or decline. The work of Bernie Siegel,
Norman Cousins, Lawrence LeShan, and Carl
Simonton demonstrates the effects of happiness on
the immune system and specifically refers to women
with breast cancer.

Dr. Winston Lewis, from the University of Vermont
Health Center, indicates in her doctoral thesis that
there is a relationship between psychological factors
and immune dysfunction in breast cancer patients.
Lewis refers to an unpublished study by Dr. Sandra
Levy, of the University of Pittsburgh School of
Medicine, who followed 36 breast cancer patients for
seven years. "The 'joy' factor [overall sense of
well-being] proved to be a more significant predictor
of survival than some physiological factors, such as
the number of metastatic sites."

Drs. Colette Ray and Michael Baum reported in
Psychological Aspects of Early Breast Cancer, that

---

[*]   Arnold Fox, "Cancer: It Doesn't Have to Be Deadly." Hippocrates
used the label *melancholy*; Fox affirms that this same concept is
presented in medical schools today.

[**] Dr. Peggy Boyd, *The Silent Wound: A Startling Report on Breast
Cancer and Sexuality* (New York: Addison Wesley Publishing Co.,
1984).

"conflicts about gender role and sexuality are cited in the breast-cancer literature, but are not commonly attributed to cancer patients in general."

In *The Silent Wound*, Boyd observed that women with breast cancer remained serene, compliant, and smiling, when that behavior was not expected. She explained this behavior as "a familiar defense, repression, [and] a way of denying painful experiences." After comparing 180 women with breast cancer to a control group, the study concluded that "women who had breast cancer have a significantly different life experience and psychosocial profile from their sisters." Interviews and examinations showed that "women who habitually suppressed their anger" were more prone to metastasis due to the "higher levels of immunoglobulin A in their blood."

We know that our emotions can affect our bodies directly, yet this information has not been incorporated into comprehensive breast cancer survival protocols. To add more evidence to this claim, Dr. David Spiegel of the Stanford University of Medicine, writes that "women with metastatic breast cancer, assigned to a psychotherapy support group lived twice as long as those in the control group."[*] Could it be that mortality would improve if these psycho-social concerns were integrated into treatment protocols?

MYTH 7: *Your doctor knows best.*

Medical professionals manipulate language to stretch the truth. Denial is an important element in this technique. As women began to be more educated

---

[*] Dr. David Spiegel, "Breast Cancer Study Shows Psychotherapy Improved Survival," in *Psychiatric Times*, January 1990.

and started to ask questions, wanting to participate in the decision-making, health professionals began to distort the accepted definitions of words like lumpectomy, mortality rates, and cure rates.

Lumpectomy became popular in the press in the 1970s with the two-step decision treatment process. Because of this awareness, more women started to request lumpectomies. Eventually research demonstrated that survival did not change for women undergoing less radical surgical procedures. However, "did not change" meant that if it wasn't worse, it also wasn't better.

According to the *Taber's Cyclopedic Medical Dictionary*, lumpectomy is "to remove only the tumor and no other tissue or lymph nodes." Nonetheless, many surgeons will refer to a procedure that removes the tumor and surrounding tissue, with or without lymph nodes, as a lumpectomy. That procedure is more accurately classified as a partial mastectomy—a description that did not go over well with breast cancer patients, so to be obscured by more acceptable—albeit misleading and inaccurate—terms.

Mortality rates for breast cancer in the United States have not improved in 50 years, according to the American Cancer Society (ACS). In this context, the ACS is talking about death rates. Most people understand mortality to mean death rates. However, in all of the early detection program literature, women are told that early detection has demonstrated a 30-percent improvement in mortality rates. In that context, mortality rates means that in trials that compared screened women with unscreened women, 30 percent more of the screened women survived for five to ten years after detection. Here improved mortality is substituted for improved survival.

Many women hear that if they are screened and their breast cancer is caught early, they have a 95 percent cure rate. Many people understand cure rate to mean they have a 95 percent chance of remaining free of disease. In reality, this 95-percent statistic is taken from an uncontrolled study that compared screened women in the Breast Cancer Detection Demonstration Project (BCDDP) with women who were part of another method of data collection—Surveillance, Epidemiology and End Results (SEER).

Several notions have been interchanged to create this misconception. First, people assume that the 95-percent survival statistic can be credited to a controlled study, as are all other statistics of this nature. This is not the case. *Survival* generally applies to throughout normal life expectancy; in this context, it means five years. Next, *cure* usually means disease-free; in this context, it means, "personal cure"—the patient will be free of disease symptoms and die of another cause before the breast cancer recurs. Hence, the widely publicized 95-percent cure rate for breast cancer is virtually meaningless.

▲ ▲ ▲

Myths such as these ring of betrayal and often raise the question of blame. No one involved wants to accept the guilt or shame associated with betrayal—no one wants to be a victim. It is easier to deny any findings that don't fit the fabricated reality.

To stop this cycle, everyone concerned needs to acknowledge that no one is to blame here—both women and their doctors are victims. Their actions are based on their collective limited knowledge. Henceforth neither needs to assume guilt, and there is no need to point a finger. Once this is understood, change can occur. Breast cancer is more than a disease of women's breasts, it is a disease of society—our collective attitudes of suppression, denial, and displaced reality.

"If I Live to Be 90 Still Wanting to Say Something": My Search for Rachel Carson

Sandra Steingraber

"The year 1960 ended on a somber note—Rachel learned that she had not been told the truth about a breast operation she had undergone the previous spring, 'even though I asked directly.' The tumor had been malignant and there was evidence that it had metastasized."
> —Paul Brooks, 1972, from
> *The House of Life: Rachel Carson at Work*

"For the first time in the history of the world, every human being is now subject to contact with dangerous chemicals, from the moment of conception until death. In the less than two decades of their use, the synthetic pesticides have been so thoroughly distributed throughout the animate and inanimate world that they occur virtually everywhere."
> —Rachel Carson, 1962, from *Silent Spring*

"I thought she was a spinster. What's she so worried about genetics for?"
> —member of the Federal Pest Control
> Review Board, 1962, on Rachel Carson

Until a few months ago, what I knew about Rachel Carson could be narrated in a paragraph or less. She was, of course, the author of *Silent Spring*, a book about the dangers of pesticides published when I was a child, a book that I had never entirely read but understood was significant in inaugurating the environmental movement, establishing the Environmental Protection Agency, and ruining the reputation of DDT. Everyone knows this. I vaguely remember reading her biography in junior high school. My image of her was as shy, bird-like woman. She had never married. Didn't she die shortly after her book came out?

It's strange to me now—how remote a figure Rachel Carson has been for me. Like me, she was both a biologist and a writer. I work within the environmental community she helped create. I even wrote about the ecological problems of a chlorinated pesticide similar to DDT in my dissertation. And yet, no teacher or colleague had ever suggested her work to me. I did not know that she had written five other books. Like Rosa Parks, Rachel Carson was a muse, a spark, an inspiration, a symbol, a myth, a single dramatic gesture, a vanishing presence. Rachel Carson was a name to be invoked at the beginnings of lectures, not an authority be reckoned with, not a woman to be known.

In October 1992, I received a phone call asking if I would speak at a literary reading commemorating the 30th anniversary of the publication of *Silent Spring*. A sweet idea, I thought, and so I agreed, although with an inward pang of shame that I did not know the text or the author more intimately. I did know the work of the environmental organization sponsoring the reading. A small group of activists, Terra has worked to expose the activities of Velsicol, a company in Chicago that sells pesticides banned for use in this country to the Third World.

Did I know that the Velsicol Chemical Company had tried to prevent *Silent Spring* from being published in 1962 because it raised the first questions about the safety of heptachlor and chlordane? I was stunned. No, I didn't. Did I know that Rachel Carson had died of breast cancer? No. I hung up the phone and stood by my office window for long time. So, we have more than just our careers in common. Rachel Carson, who are you?

The reading to commemorate *Silent Spring* never happened. But this phone call became the beginning of a personal search for a woman whose life I suddenly needed to know more about. Rachel Carson, the scientist, the writer, the cancer non-survivor. This is the story of that search. And of my own anger at what I found.

▲ ▲ ▲

In the video terminals and card catalogues of America's libraries, I am looking for Rachel Carson.

1. Carson, Rachel Louise 1907–1964
2. Ecologists—United States
3. Seashore biology
4. Nature study
5. Fisheries—U.S.
6. Fish as food

1. Carson, Rachel Louise 1907–1964
2. Pesticides—toxicology
3. Wildlife—conservation of
4. Insects—injurious and beneficial
5. Environmental pollutants

1. Carson, Rachel Louise 1907–1964
2. Ocean
3. Ocean—juvenile literature. Text first appeared in women's home companion under title: help your child to wonder

There is impressively little to find. No cross-references to cancer, although she had died from it and a good deal of *Silent Spring* is devoted to exposing the environmental root causes of the disease.

Moreover, there is no definitive biography of her life. In fact, the juvenile biography I read as a teenager remains the sole account. The handful of scholarly books and articles that do exist are attempts to locate her writing in a literary or historical tradition, and most were written twenty years ago in the wake of the first Earth Day. Carson's most recent commentator, Patricia Hynes, examines the chemical industry's backlash against *Silent Spring* in the early 1960s and documents how spurious notions of risk assessment involving pesticide use, first documented by Carson, have evolved and recurred under the pseudo-regulation of the EPA. Because much of the opposition to *Silent Spring* took the form of personal attacks on its author, we are privy to some of the details of Rachel's life, albeit through a hostile lens.

Interestingly, all the books I found emphasize in their introductions that Rachel Carson was "a private person." These statements seem to function as a way of excusing the one-dimensional portraits of her life that emerge from these pages: an unmarried bluestocking, predictably reclusive, childless, prim. Indeed, many of Carson's personal papers and letters were destroyed after her death or remain unavailable. However, only Hynes seems to find this alarming and questions the consensus among Carson's other commentators "that there is not much to know or tell about her person; that her life was her work, so people should read her work rather than probe her life."* After all, there was no science writer more reclusive than Charles Darwin—who, like Carson, wrote a book that lit the world on fire—and whose biographies and published diaries fill many library shelves. As Hynes observes, the insinuation seems to

---

* Hynes, p 2. In this article only, footnotes refer to the References listed at the end of the article.

be that an unmarried, childless woman has no life apart from her work—so what is there to write about?

▲ ▲ ▲

And if the life of such a woman is perceived as having no inherent value, then is the death of such a woman at the age of 56 to be viewed as equally unremarkable?

▲ ▲ ▲

My first real sense that there is something wrong with this picture came with the discovery that the "childless" Rachel Carson had in fact raised three children. As a young woman, she took over the care of her two nieces when her older sister died. Years later, when one of her nieces died, Rachel adopted her five-year-old son and became a single mother at the age of 50. Yet, "Rachel as mother" is not a listing in any of the indices of these books. There are, on the other hand, entries under the listing, "passion for cats."*

Now twenty years out of junior high school, I re-read Philip Sterling's biography, *Sea and Earth: the Life of Rachel Carson*. No wonder I had not rushed to embrace her as a role model. Sterling manages to project the full set of sexist stereotypes about

---

* Patricia Hynes has correctly observed a double standard inherent in biographical portrayals of the "solitary nature writer." For Henry Thoreau and John Muir, solitude was considered by their biographers to be conducive to their genius, or at the very least, as a tragic, existential condition of great proportion. But for Rachel Carson, loneliness was seen as psychological, spinisterly, eccentric. To male biographers, "Thoreau could enjoy 'the broad margins of life' without marrying; Carson could not. His homosocial world was sufficient; her female-centered world was not." (Hynes, pp 64-65)

unmarried, professional women onto a screen named
Rachel Carson.

Here is the young Rachel as an isolated egghead . . .

> Why worry about a girl who was so *different*? If
> she wanted to spend her weekends in the library
> studying and in her room. . . . Oh well, that was her
> business.[*]

. . . in training to be an asexual martyr to
science . . .

> She would have preferred to go through life calling
> freely on Minerva's courage and wisdom without turn-
> ing away from Venus' power. She knew, however, that
> she was better made to follow the stern goddess in ar-
> mor than the tender one draped in swirls of gauze.[**]

. . . stoically unphased by overt acts of gender
discrimination . . .

> There was a decided feeling against women in the
> sciences, which were largely male-dominated. . . .
> Rachel found nothing discouraging in these facts.[***]

. . . who succeeds through pluckiness, good
grooming, and good manners:

> "Do you have a position for which I might apply?"
> ". . . . Can you write?"
> "I also majored in English in college."
> "Were you any good?"
> "I got all As in all my English classes."
> Higgens kept a straight face but he smiled in-
> wardly. Quite a girl, he thought: lady-like appearance,
> modest manner, soft voice. She must be very sure of

---

[*] Sterling, p 43.

[**] Sterling, p 49.

[***] Sterling, pp 76–77.

herself to offer such brief, unflustered answers to his
challenging questions.[*]

And here is the adult Rachel as childlike scientist,
so devoted to her work that she is now detached not
only from her sexual and emotional life but from her
own biological body . . .

> She needed somebody to look after her when she
> really got wrapped up in her field work. . . . Half a
> dozen times at Boothbay Harbor, Hines [her assistant]
> lifted the frail, small-boned writer out of barnacle-
> covered tide pools.[**]

. . . who remains forever the invisible little girl,
even when testifying before Congress:

> Sitting at the long, witness table, she looked small,
> middle-aged, harmless. Her appearance gave no hint
> that she might indeed be capable of starting some-
> thing big enough to interest the Senate of the United
> States.[***]

So that when she is diagnosed with metastatic
breast cancer (soon after adopting a child and while
in the middle of writing a book that argues against
the passive acceptance of scientific authority), she
dutifully submits to her fate and to medical
paternalism:

> This was not time for self-pitying, fright-ridden
> guessing games. She had work to do against a dead-
> line not marked on any calendar but hidden in the life
> processes of her own perishable body. . . . Her doc-
> tors would make the best guesses and take the wisest

---

[*] Sterling, pp 88–89.

[**] Sterling, p 134.

[***] Sterling, p 1.

steps they could. She would be *their* responsibility. Hers was to get on with her job.[*]

Fortunately, she did not have to engage in any depressing conversations with her friends about the fact that she was dying in the middle of her life:

> Tactful by nature, they did not burden Rachel with any needless show of concern about her health. They successfully avoided the undertow of anxiety that might have dragged all of them downward through the buoyant surface of the summer tranquility.[**]

▲ ▲ ▲

Clearly, Sterling's biography exists more as a morality tale for young women than as an illumination of Carson's struggle to expose the covert "war on nature" waged by the chemical industry with the complicity of government and science. There is no way of reconciling his portrait of female passivity, obedience, and go-along aplomb with the voice of resistance that speaks from *Silent Spring*, a voice that contemporary naturalist Terry Tempest Williams describes as one of "sacred rage . . . fierce and compassionate."[***]

---

[*]   Sterling, p 154–155.

[**] Sterling, p 192.

[***] Williams, p 107. Interestingly enough, Sterling's portrait of the unflappable scientist also contrasts sharply with the vision of Carson put forth by the chemical industry in its attempt to discredit *Silent Spring*. In press releases and book reviews, Carson was called hysterical, overly emotional, fanatical, unscientific and—my favorite—"a priestess mystically attached to the balance of nature." Additionally, the Velsicol Chemical Company implied that Carson was a member of a network of "sinister parties" that sought to reduce the free world's food supply. (For more on the industry backlash against *Silent Spring*, see Brooks, pp 293-307; Gartner, pp 23-25; Graham, p 49; Hynes, pp 39-43.)

There is no way of reconciling a presumption that Carson accepted her own cancer diagnosis as natural or inevitable with the contents of chapter 14, entitled "One in Every Four."* Carson places blame for the rising rates of human cancers squarely on the activities of industry:

> No longer are exposures to dangerous chemicals occupational alone; they have entered the environment of everyone—even of children as yet unborn. It is hardly surprising, therefore, that we are now aware of an alarming increase in the malignant disease. . . . The chemical agents of cancer have become entrenched in our world in two ways: first, and ironically, through man's search for a better and easier way of life; second, because the manufacture and sale of such chemicals has become an accepted part of our economy and our way of life. . . . A large proportion are by no means necessities of life. By their elimination the total load of carcinogens would be enormously lightened, and the threat that one in every four will develop cancer would at least be greatly mitigated. The most determined effort should be made to eliminate those carcinogens that now contaminate our food, our water supplies, and our atmosphere, because these provide the most dangerous type of contact—minute exposures, repeated over and over throughout the years.**

There is no way of reconciling a vision of Rachel Carson the cancer patient as a trusting, childlike, saintly, selfless soul with the contents of her Congressional testimony, given in the last year of her

---

* The cancer incidence rate has risen from one in every four persons in 1960 to one in every three today. Nevertheless, Carson's description of how environmental carcinogens alter genetic structures to promote and initiate the development of tumors is still remarkably accurate. "One in Every Four" remains one of the most lucid accounts of the biology of cancer in print.

** Carson, pp 197-216.

life, which calls for a human rights approach to environmental contamination. Extending her analysis in *Silent Spring*, Carson urged legislation that would recognize (1) the individual's right to know about poisons introduced into one's environment by others; (2) the right to protection against these poisons; and (3) the right to legal redress when these rights are violated. She went on to criticize the federal government for its silence, passivity, and failure to protect its citizenry from the human consequences of environmental contamination:

> The problem I dealt with in *Silent Spring* is not an isolated one. It is merely one part of a sorry whole— the reckless pollution of our living world with harmful and dangerous substances. Until very recently, the average citizen assumed that "someone" was looking after these matters and that some little understood but confidently relied upon safeguards stood like shields between his person and any harm. But now he has experienced a rather rude shattering of these beliefs.[*]

Scholar Carol Gartner tells a different tale of Rachel Carson's breast cancer diagnosis. Narrated almost as an aside, her version indicates that Carson had in fact been lied to by her original physician in Washington D.C. about the nature of her tumor. Nine months went by before she obtained an accurate diagnosis of malignant breast cancer from another doctor and began radiation treatments:

> Late in 1960, Carson found that *even though she had asked about it directly*, she had not been told the truth about a growth removed from her breast the previous spring. It had been malignant.[**]

---

[*] Carson, quoted in Brooks, p 310.

[**] Gartner, p 26, my emphasis.

Gartner's version is corroborated by writer Paul Brooks. He goes on to note that Carson's cancer was already metastasized at the time of diagnosis; eventually, tumors formed in her cervical vertebrae causing numbness in her hands. Brooks does not offer any commentary on the impact such a side effect might have had on a woman who earned her living solely through writing, whose life was, as repeatedly emphasized, her work.

▲ ▲ ▲

Even though she had asked about it directly.
Again, I am standing by my office window. I cannot believe what I am reading, the implications of what it means. At the very least: bitter irony (of devoting your life to exposing deception . . . of offering to the world an eloquent explication of how false reassurances have led us down perilous paths . . . of advocating resistance to scientific arrogance). And at the very most?
If the life of such a woman is perceived as having no inherent value, then is the death of such a woman to be viewed as equally unremarkable?

▲ ▲ ▲

Rachel Carson died 29 years ago. She would be 85 today. Former Supreme Court Justice Thurgood Marshall, who will be buried tomorrow, was 84. As I am reading her Congressional testimony, the radio broadcasts his funeral service. The word "endurance" catches in my ears.

▲ ▲ ▲

The "real" Rachel Carson does not exist some-where beyond the mythologies and constructions and projections of her biographers and commentators. She is gone. Rachel Carson's experience with breast cancer—whatever her private struggle might have been—is gone with her. There is no public testimony. There are, however, fragments of other stories embedded in the remaining record which can be dug out and examined and recontextualized.

For example, published accounts describe Carson's death in 1964 as a natural closure—as if there were no real reason to go on living after the publication of her masterpiece, *Silent Spring*. As quoted above, Philip Sterling posits a predetermined "deadline" inscribed in Carson's "perishable" body. Similarly, Paul Brooks' chapter on Carson's work after *Silent Spring* is entitled "The Closing Journey" and emphasizes her feelings of satisfaction and relief at having stayed alive long enough to complete her book.

And yet, other quotes from Carson contained within these very same pages indicate both a great desire to go on living and writing and a maddening frustration at not being physically able to seize the opportunities that *Silent Spring* afforded:

> So many ironic things. . . . Now all the "honors" have to be received for me by someone else. And the opportunities to travel to foreign lands—all expenses paid—have to be passed up.[*]

> If only I could have reached this point ten years ago! Now, when there is an opportunity to do so much, my body falters and I know there is little time left.[**]

---

[*] Carson, quoted in Brooks, p 314.

[**] Carson, quoted in Brooks, p 314.

> I want to do what must be done, but no more. . . .
> After all, I still have several books to write and can't
> spend the rest of my life in hospitals!![*]

Far from viewing *Silent Spring* as her final
crowning achievement, Carson had been looking
forward to writing at least three other books. One
was to be a book of nature study for children.
Another was make the case for the conservation of
unspoiled shorelines—a project which, she happily
noted, would give her enough space "for being a
Cassandra." A third would examine the impact of
new technologies on the relationship between life and
the physical environment. She died before completing
any of these books.

The third project, what she called "the big man
and nature book," was to be her most ambitious
work and would develop her ideas on the inter-
locking economic structures that bound the direction
of scientific research to the interests of industry. She
had already begun to air some of this analysis in
public:

> We see scientific societies acknowledging as "sus-
> taining associates" a dozen or more giants of a re-
> lated industry. When the scientific organization
> speaks, whose voice do we hear—that of science?
> Or of the sustaining industry? It might be a less seri-
> ous situation if this voice were always clearly identi-
> fied, but the public assumes it is hearing the voice of
> science.[**]

---

[*] Letter from Carson to her doctor, quoted in Gartner, p 26.

[**] Carson, 1962, address to the Women's National Press Club,
quoted in Graham, p 170.

Additionally, this book would address the larger philosophical and psychological implications of living in a world in which natural forces themselves could now be altered and potentially ruined by human activities:

> It was pleasant to believe . . . that much of Nature was forever beyond the tampering reach of man. . . . These beliefs have almost been a part of me for as long as I have thought about such things. To have them even vaguely threatened was so shocking that . . . I shut my mind—refused to acknowledge what I couldn't help seeing. But that does no good, and I have now opened my eyes and my mind. . . . *So it seems time someone wrote of Life in the light of the truth as it now appears to us.* [*]

Literary critic Vera Norwood notes that Carson's later writing underwent an important shift from a position of simple reverence for and identification with nature to a focus on the consequences of our limited knowledge about nature. At the time of her death, Carson was discovering how to wed organic, celebratory metaphors of her earlier nature writings to the normative language of economics, thus constructing elegant tensions within her essays. [**]

Perhaps it is morbid to speculate about Rachel Carson's unfinished work, about what might have been. But I want us to see her life in a different light: not as a crusader who went gently into that good night, but as a brilliant woman who died an untimely death—perhaps a preventable one—at the peak of her scientific and literary career. As an ordinary woman who died shortly after radioactive implants were placed inside her body, who left behind her young

---

[*] Carson, quoted in Brooks, p 10, my emphasis.

[**] Norwood, pp 742–43.

son, several unfinished books, plans for summer field work. Not as a human sacrifice, but as a woman who died wanting more.

> But now that it seems that I shall somehow make this goal [of publishing *Silent Spring*], of course I'm not satisfied—now I want time for the Help Your Child to Wonder book, and for the big Man and Nature book. Then I suppose I'll have others—if I live to be 90 still wanting to say something.[*]

> She never really recovered from her last operation. . . . Her friend Shirley Briggs comments that no one expected her to die so quickly.[**]

▲ ▲ ▲

Dear Rachel,[***]

I recently attended a public hearing in Michigan that called for an industry phase-out of chlorinated hydrocarbons. If you had lived to be ninety, perhaps we could have sat together. Or perhaps you would have been the keynote speaker. I think you would have been impressed with the proceedings. Scientists, activists, physicians, writers, teachers, lawyers, clergy, union leaders, cancer survivors all speaking out "in the light of the truth as it now appears to us."

The apparent truth can be a slow light to dawn. Ten years after *Silent Spring*, the federal government finally restricted DDT, along with a handful of other chlorinated pesticides that you wrote about. Dieldrin.

---

[*] Carson, 1962, letter to a friend, quoted in Brooks, p 271.

[**] Gartner, p 26.

[***] This letter derives information from the following articles, for which bibliographic information appears at the end of this article: Falck, Feldman, Kolatta, Thornton. See also "Killing Us Quietly: Cancer, the Environment, and Women" by Rita Arditti and Tatiana Schreiber, pp 231-260 of this volume.

Chlordane. Lindane. Heptachlor. Unfortunately, the
law allows chemical companies to export these
pesticides to Third World countries that have no such
restrictions. The chemicals return to us in the fruit,
coffee, and meat that we import. A circle of poison.
The Velsicol Chemical Company, your old nemesis,
thus remains the world's sole manufacturer of
heptachlor and chlordane. In fact, two thirds of the
23 pesticides you profiled continue to be produced
and used around the world. I have learned that levels
of pesticides in some mothers' milk in the United
States now violates the federal standards for cows'
milk.

Other chlorinated compounds, chlorofluorcarbons,
have destroyed part of the earth's ozone layer. The
United Nations Environmental Program says the
resulting increase in UV light exposure may cause an
additional 300,000 people to contract skin cancer. If
you had lived to be ninety, we could talk about this.

Had you lived to be ninety, we could talk about
breast cancer, which is now striking one in every nine
women. Industry and government continue to
downplay the connection to environmental
contamination and portray the disease as a problem
of individual lifestyle, as a problem of cosmetics. But
this image is beginning to change as women demand
explanations. I feel a new awareness, a new sense of
urgency. You would be interested in one recent study
that shows that U.S. women with breast cancer have
higher levels of chlorinated pesticides in their breast
tissue than women without breast cancer. In Israel,
PCB levels in the breasts of women with cancer were
three times higher than in those of women without
breast cancer. And in Sweden, women with high levels
of lindane in their tissues were ten times more likely
to develop breast cancer than women with lower
levels.

The books all say you kept silent about your own diagnosis in order to retain the public perception of objectivity. Even your supporters feel the need to emphasize that you had drafted the chapter "One in Every Four" before learning that you yourself had cancer. (Still, after your death, critics claimed that your analysis of the carcinogenic effects of pesticides was distorted by your personal experience.) I would like to be able to tell you that those days are over—that today, people with cancer are considered no less objective on the topic than people without. That today, the opinions of women are no longer automatically labeled as emotional and overreactive. That today, feeling concern and passion and fear and desire is no longer considered the opposite of being factual and well-informed. That being motivated by self-preservation and respect for the inherent value of one's own living body is not considered a corrupting influence on science, but that being motivated by industry profits and patronage is. But this is wishful thinking.

It was interesting for me to learn that you began your investigation of pesticides by covering a DDT trial in Long Island for *The New Yorker*. Citizen groups eventually lost their lawsuit to stop blanket aerial sprayings by the federal government in Nassau and Suffolk counties, but the testimonies you heard on the potential dangers for people and wildlife compelled you to write a book. In a letter to a friend, you said you felt you had no choice, knowing what you did, but to set it down in writing for the public to read.

Today, Nassau County, Long Island has one of the highest incidence rates of breast cancer in the United States. But this is what I would want to tell you: some of the women who live there have organized and are demanding specific studies to investigate the root causes of breast cancer. The federal government has said the Long Island mortalities can be explained by demographics, but the women with breast cancer have replied that such conclusions will not put the issue to rest and are planning to form a committee of environmental experts to help them conduct their own research. This is what I can tell you: that groups like this are forming in many American cities, that women with cancer are reframing the debate on environmental protection, that our knowledge compels us.

These are the sea-changes that I feel. Sincerely yours.

▲ ▲ ▲

The fragments that remain urge us toward speech:

Incidentally, I'm convinced there is a psychological angle in all this: that people, especially professional men, are uncomfortable about coming out against something, especially if they haven't absolute proof that "something" is wrong, but only a good suspicion. So they will go along with a program about which they have acute misgivings.[*]

It is a great problem to know how to penetrate the barrier of public indifference and unwillingness to look at unpleasant facts that have to be dealt with if one recognized their existence. I have no idea whether I shall be able to do so or not, but knowing what I do, I have no choice but to set it down to be read by those who will.[**]

There would be no peace for me if I kept silent.[***]

---

[*] Carson, quoted in Brooks, p 241.

[**] Carson, quoted in Brooks, p 258.

[***] Carson, quoted in Brooks, p 228.

Rachel Carson died in April 1964 of breast cancer. A silent spring.

REFERENCES

Brooks, Paul. *The House of Life: Rachel Carson At Work.* Boston: Houghton Mifflin, 1972.

Carson, Rachel. *Silent Spring.* Greenwich, Connecticut: Fawcett Publications, 1962.

Falck, F. A. Ricci and M. Wolff, et al. "Pesticides and Polychlorinated Biphenyl Residues in Human Breast Lipids and Their Relation to Breast Cancer." *Archives of Environmental Health* 47: 143-146. 1992.

Feldman, Jay. "Thirty Years After *Silent Spring*, the Choice is Clear." *Global Pesticide Campaigner* 2: 11-12. November 1992.

Gartner, Carol. *Rachel Carson.* New York: Frederick Ungar Publishing Co., 1983.

Graham, Frank. *Since Silent Spring.* Boston: Houghton Mifflin, 1970.

Hynes, H. Patricia. *The Recurring Silent Spring.* New York: Pergamon Press, 1989.

Kolata, Gina. "Long Island Breast Cancer Called Explainable by U.S." *New York Times*, A-9, col. 5, Dec. 19, 1992.

Norwood, Vera. "The Nature of Knowing: Rachel Carson and the American Environment." *Signs* 12: 740-60. 1987.

Sterling, Phillip. *Sea and Earth: The Life of Rachel Carson.* New York: Dell, 1970.

Thorton, Joe. *Breast Cancer and the Environment: The Chlorine Connection.* Washington D.C.: Greenpeace U.S.A., 1992.

Thorton, Joe. *The Product is the Poison: The Case for a Chlorine Phase-Out.* Washington D.C.: Greenpeace U.S.A., 1991.

Williams, Terry Tempest. "The Spirit of Rachel Carson." *Audubon* 94:104-107. 1992.

Grassroots Healing

Ellen Crowley

I have some very clear ideas about how I would like to see women build community within the feminist movement in this desperate decade of the 1990s. My ideas are largely the result of my extraordinary experiences over the past two years as a member of the Political Action Committee of the Women's Community Cancer Project (WCCP), in Boston, and my observation of group process during my 30 years of combat and reward in the field of social work.

Formation of the WCCP was inspired in 1989 by Susan Shapiro, a young mother, feminist, and freelance writer. After being diagnosed and treated for breast cancer, Susan described in an article in *Sojourner* her view that dramatic changes were needed in the current medical, social, and political approaches to cancer, particularly as they affect women. In that article, she issued an invitation to interested women to attend a meeting at the Cambridge YWCA. Twenty-five women attended the first meeting of what was to become the WCCP. After only two meetings, Susan became even more seriously ill; she eventually died of cancer. However, she left behind the legacy of an excited, energized, and enraged group of women. Many of them had experienced some form of cancer. Others had loved ones who had experienced or died of cancer. Some, like me, were second-generation breast-cancer patients who, after being diagnosed, were shocked to realize that no real improvements in treatment and mortality expectation had occurred since our mothers' time of diagnosis, in some cases as many as 30 years earlier. Others, who were first-generation cancer patients, had been taken by surprise in middle age. They were terrified for themselves and for their children. All of us passionately wanted change, and we wanted it quickly.

The first action of the WCCP was to establish free, feminist support groups where women with cancer could share emotions and the complexities of decision making that affect every woman with cancer. Next, WCCP began doing research on cancer incidence. Simple truths about women and cancer were not easy to find, and this was a time-consuming process. The next step was getting to others the astonishing data that we were finding. We did this by choosing the most compelling facts and publishing them in brief, dramatic Fact Sheets. The first of these was the carefully researched "Shocking Facts About Women and Cancer." Next came "Alarming Facts About Women and Cancer," which was followed by "Terrifying Facts About Women and Breast Cancer." As we continued to share our personal experiences and talk to other women, we developed further hypotheses, which wee again carefully researched. This research led to "Appallinging Facts About Mammography and Women Under 50" and "Terrifying Facts About Cancer and the Environment." At each step in our research, we were shocked by what we were learning about the dramatic increases in the incidences of cancer since the 1950s and the lack of effort to explain and treat them.

The next phase of development was connecting with other grassroots groups nationwide who were concerned with women's cancers, in particular breast cancer. This connection was made in an unexpected way. In June 1990, fifteen women from our project,

holding cardboard signs, stood outside the Sixth
International Conference on Breast Diseases at the
Hynes Auditorium in Boston, Massachusetts. We
were demanding increased funding for breast cancer
research. A young woman reporter from *Newsweek*
magazine included a photograph of the rally taken by
a member of our group with an article she wrote on
breast cancer. That photograph was later carried by
The New York Times in all of its national editions.
Suddenly, similar grassroots groups across the
country knew about us, and we knew of them.
Telephones began ringing, fax machines began
grinding, and facts, feelings, histories, future goals,
and good will were shared by small, grassroots
groups all over the country.

At the same time, those women who, through the
most recent wave of feminism had attained a firm, if
limited, foothold in the audio, visual, and print
media, began to actively focus on breast cancer. With
anxiety, limited personal experience, and
determination, women from WCCP and other
grassroots groups across the country tackled local,
national, and international radio and TV shows. We
talked endlessly to any writer or reporter who called
from *Newsweek* to *Allure* to *McCalls* to *The
Progressive*, repeating our shocking facts and telling
our personal stories. The interviewers were always
women. Men never called.

Also around this time, a group of grassroots breast
cancer activists requested and received a meeting with
the entire staff of the NCI. And, because we were in
Washington anyway, we made our anger and
concerns clearly known to our representatives and
senators. While some were taken aback, other
Congresswomen and men were immediately devoted
to our cause, and provided grassroots women with
crash courses in understanding the political process.

The next step in the movement's progression was the formation of a coalition between grassroots cancer groups and more established women's health organizations. This was accomplished through the late 1991 establishment of the National Breast Cancer Coalition, of which WCCP was a founding member. This group quickly became a coalition of 160 groups. Immediately, NBCC held its own hearings on research priorities. Women from member groups testified and listened at all NIH hearings dealing with breast cancer. The NBC then organized a monumental action. On one day, women from member groups all over the country whose lives had been affected by breast cancer boarded buses, trains, and airplanes for Washington, DC, determined to make the breast cancer epidemic a matter of pressing concern to every senator and representative. On that day, over half a million letters were personally delivered to every state senator and representative, on up to the White House. When women with t-shrits saying "Do the Write Thing" were darting about the streets of Washington, a press conference was held in the shadow of the dome of the Capitol. At that press conference, one woman from every state read out loud a letter from someone in her state describing how breast cancer had affected her life. Bells tolled—for the nearly half million U.S. women who have died of breast cancer in just the past ten years.

Sincere and intense political pressure from women has brought unheard of increases in funding for breat cancer. Money was even appropriated through the Department of Defense. Women have let the NIH, and the DOD, and their senators and representatives know that women will be watching carefully how these monies are spent. We've come from a tiny rally to this in just a few years.

The latest project of WCCP has been the development of "A Women's Cancer Agenda: Demands for the U.S. Government and the National Institutes of Health."* This document deals with all women's cancers. It also incorporates the WCCP's increasing concern about the frightening role of environmental toxins in the current cancer epidemic sweeping the industrial world, to the point where one in three U.S. citizens will eventually develop a potentially fatal cancer.

The highly successful experience of the WCCP of Cambridge/Boston, and the women's cancer movement as a whole, has taught me several things:

- Women who are passionate about an issue and who have a clear expectation of immediate change can make tremendous progress with lightning speed by beginning with focused, consciousness-raising/action groups.

- In such groups, passion fosters hard work and creativity. Truths can be quickly determined, and societal structures that are maintaining the problem can be quickly identified.

- Even small demonstrations about timely issues can have a surprisingly powerful effect.

- Women who have gained a foothold in the media are often interested in a woman's message and are able to spread it quickly.

- Through media coverage, small grassroots groups can learn of one another's existence and form coalitions. Such networking is essential.

---

* "A Women's Cancer Agenda" appears on pages 261-264 of this volume.

- Grassroots groups can then form coalitions with more established women's groups concerned with the same issue.
- Though women senators and representatives are few, they can wield tremendous power when backed on a compelling issue by a huge voting block of women who are demanding change in a passionate, enlightened, and relentless way.

Groups of women such as I describe, forming in their own communities to identify "cancer clusters," could expedite the process of finding the cause of cancer. By following clues from cancer clusters, lay epidemiologists and scientists could greatly accelerate the cleaning up of the planet.

If women join together on issues like this, the 1990s will be a far better decade than any of us now expect.

Bringing It Home:
Lesbian Cancer Projects

Lynn Kanter

Every year, American women die of cancer by the tens of thousands. The statistics are horrifying. So are the shattering experiences of suffering and loss they represent. But you don't need to know the numbers. You only need to look at the women around you—the ones who have cancer, the ones who are caring for women with cancer, the ones we have lost to cancer—to realize that something terrible is going on.

Instead of dying quietly, women have begun to fight back. In communities across the country, women are establishing feminist cancer projects to provide direct services, to educate, to organize, to demand attention, funding, and research. And a growing number of these projects are created by and for lesbians.

It's not surprising that these groups are organized by lesbians. After all, lesbians have contributed the central vision, leadership, and energy for any number of causes. And there is some evidence that, because lesbians tend to fit the profile of women who are at higher risk, the incidence of breast cancer in particular may be greater in the lesbian community than among women in general.

But cancer projects designed specifically to serve lesbians—isn't that a little exclusive? And once a woman has been diagnosed with cancer, what difference does it make if she's a lesbian?

Obviously lesbians don't experience cancer itself differently from other women. What is different for

us is the social and economic context in which the
illness and all of its attendant burdens take place.
When cancer enters a woman's life, with its legion of
fears, concerns, and decisions, it presents lesbians
with a few additional worries.

A primary question is the issue of whether and
when to inform our doctors that we are lesbians.
Medical professionals can be highly homophobic.
Many lesbians don't come out to their doctors
because they fear the quality of their health care may
be compromised. Evidence suggests this fear is
well-founded.

Many women who do come out are shocked by
their doctors' ignorance and misconceptions about
lesbians and our way of life. A woman who is
battling cancer is generally not a woman who has the
energy or patience to start educating her doctor. Yet
she cannot afford to ignore incorrect assumptions
that may affect her doctor's attitude or her plan of
treatment.

Because lesbian couples have no legal standing, we
lack standing also in the policies of hospitals and
medical centers. The saga of Sharon Kowalski and
Karen Thompson[*] is only one dramatic example of a
common phenomenon. Many hospitals won't let a

---

[*] In 1983, Sharon Kowalski was severely injured in an auto
accident. Sharon's father, as legal next-of-kin, refused to
acknowledge her five-year relationship with her lover, Karen
Thompson. He obtained court orders to prevent Karen from
seeing her partner, and moved Sharon to a treatment center
hundreds of miles away from the home the two women shared. A
lengthy legal battle ensued, during which Sharon's father and her
partner vied for legal guardianship, while Sharon's own stated
wishes to stay with her partner were largely ignored by the courts.
In 1991, Karen Thompson was finally appointed as Sharon's
guardian.

sick woman's partner into the intensive care unit because she is not considered immediate family. And for even the most "out" lesbian couples, it is a constant and exhausting process to keep informing all of the many medical practitioners they encounter that their partners are to be present during treatments, included in meetings, and granted the same respect that would automatically be conferred on a heterosexual spouse.

Although a number of hospitals, hospices, and organizations offer support groups for women (and men) with cancer, heterosexuality is assumed to be the norm in most of these gatherings. Sometimes lesbians don't feel free to talk about personal issues in this kind of setting; sometimes it's just too tiring to have to deal with the prejudice or even well-meaning ignorance of others; and sometimes the other group members don't feel comfortable having lesbians participate. The same is true of bereavement groups.

Many lesbians, particularly those who are not out to their employers, colleagues, or families, find themselves excluded from informal support systems. A lesbian who feels she must guard her pronouns when chatting with coworkers is not likely to have a network of close workplace friends she can turn to if she is diagnosed with cancer. And women who are estranged from their families because of their lesbianism, or who have distanced themselves by not coming out to their families, cannot call on relatives for support in times of crisis.

For the partner of a lesbian with cancer, the social landscape is even more bleak. She is entitled to no time off from work to care for her partner or to mourn her if she dies. She must fight to be included in her partner's medical treatment. Her family and colleagues may not acknowledge or even understand the degree to which she is involved in the process her partner is undergoing.

Any catastrophic illness incurs catastrophic costs. Like all women, lesbians tend to have jobs that provide lower salaries and less adequate insurance and other benefits. While many heterosexual women are covered by their husbands' health insurance policies, this option is not available to most lesbian couples even if one of them has a job that provides excellent health insurance. And in general, a two-earner household which relies on women's salaries is going to have fewer financial resources than a household which brings in a woman's income and a man's usually higher income.

All of this is not to say that the experience of dealing with cancer is harder for lesbians than it is for heterosexual women—only that it is different for us. We have to negotiate certain difficulties that straight women do not. And at a time when we are sick and scared and urgently requiring information and assistance that is specific to our needs and our way of life, it is crucial for lesbians to be able to rely on support systems in which we are not "other." This is why lesbian cancer projects are essential.

The premier model is the Mary-Helen Mautner Project for Lesbians with Cancer, based in Washington, DC. A volunteer organization that provides direct services to lesbians with cancer and their chosen families, the Mautner Project also informs the lesbian community about cancer, educates the medical community about the special concerns of lesbians with cancer, and advocates for lesbian health issues.

The Project was envisioned by Mary-Helen Mautner, an attorney and long-time feminist activist, as she lay on a hospital table, undergoing a bone scan to assess the progress of her breast cancer. She thought of the tremendous assistance she had gotten from her partner, friends, and family. And she imagined an organization that could provide the same kind of support to other lesbians with cancer.

Mary-Helen died in 1989, at age 44. A few months later her partner, Susan Hester, and a number of Washington-area women transformed Mary-Helen's vision into action by founding the Mautner Project.

Because of the Mautner Project, a woman who has just been diagnosed with cancer doesn't need to interview a series of doctors to find one who is sensitive to lesbian issues; she can obtain a list of local practitioners who have treated lesbian patients with respect and professionalism. She doesn't need to explain to a heterosexual support group that her immediate family consists of an assemblage of unrelated women; she can join a lesbian group where both she and the women who care for her will find assistance and support. Through the Mautner Project, women can obtain rides to treatment centers, get help with insurance problems, receive donated medical equipment, talk to lesbians who have the same type of cancer, find answers to questions they may not yet have thought to ask.

Washington is not the only city in which lesbians are providing for one another. Chicago has the Lesbian Community Cancer Project, which offers direct services, sponsors a support group, and engages in political advocacy. Women in Philadelphia have founded The Lesbian Cancer Network (TLC Network).

Through the National Coalition of Feminist and Lesbian Cancer Projects, the lesbian groups work closely with women's cancer projects in Boston, Oakland, Santa Cruz, and other cities. They're sharing their skills and experiences with women around the country who want to start their own local projects. And they're joining forces with other organizations to demand increased funding, as well as attention and accessibility for cancer care and research. The Mautner Project, for example, is a founder and leading member of the National Breast Cancer Coalition, the advocacy organization that was largely responsible for 1992's unprecedented increase in research funds for breast cancer.

It requires a tremendous amount of energy to live with cancer, to form the questions, to determine the options, to make the decisions, to go through the treatments, to abide the pain, to face the terror. Lesbian cancer projects spare women the additional energy it costs to explain, to confront, to fit in. After decades of leadership in other movements, lesbians are coming home to take care of our own, in the way that only we can accomplish, and that experience tells us only we will attempt.

Cancer and Poverty:
Double Jeopardy For Women

Jean Hardisty and Ellen Leopold

It would be unusual to meet a woman over thirty who has not been touched either directly or indirectly by an episode of cancer or a cancer scare that has been mishandled in some way by the medical profession. Tales are legion of misdiagnosis, misinformation, and carelessness that, at best, have inflicted unnecessary additional suffering and, at worst, have cost women their lives. Even women with comprehensive insurance coverage who are well-informed and assertive have often fared poorly in the hands of the cancer establishment. Their mistreatment, coupled with the relatively higher incidence of breast cancer among educated white women has tended to reinforce our image of cancer as the great leveler. But while it is true that socioeconomic status may not necessarily determine how well a woman faces her cancer, how well she survives it, or how well she understands it, poverty is a powerful predictor of late diagnosis, poor treatment, and high mortality.

Women in this country are disproportionately poor; women of color are the most disproportionately poor. The recent mobilization of women against decades of silence and indifference to women's cancers must, therefore, actively incorporate poverty and its interaction with racism and sexism as a primary focus, since poverty so clearly influences women's experience of disease and their expectations of survival.

POVERTY

It is widely acknowledged that health care in the
United States is unevenly delivered and inadequate by
the standards set by other industrialized countries.
Great Britain, Canada, and Australia all have
national health insurance; in contrast, the United
States has 36 million uninsured persons (without
private insurance, Medicare, or Medicaid coverage)
and another 50 million underinsured. The uninsured
in the U.S. include 13 percent of the white
population, 30 percent of African Americans, and a
combined statistic for Asian Americans and Native
Americans of 20 percent. Of all Hispanics, 35 percent
are uninsured: one third of Mexican Americans, one
fourth of Cuban Americans, and one fifth of the
Puerto Rican community.*

A disproportionate number of the uninsured are
women and many of these women are single heads of
households. According to the 1990 Census, almost
three of every five female-headed households live
below the poverty line. Of course, poverty is
associated with lack of health insurance, but even
employed women are more likely than men to hold
low-income jobs which provide no health insurance.
A 1992 study by the Older Women's League found
that, of working women between the ages of 40 and
64, only 55 percent have health insurance benefits at
their jobs, compared with 72 percent of working men
in the same age group. Those who are covered by
their husband's health insurance face losing that

---

* F. M. Trevino, M. E. Moyer, B. Valdez, C. A. Stroup- Benham,
"Health Insurance Coverage and Utilization of Health Services by
Mexican Americans, Mainland Puerto Ricans, and Cuban
Americans," *Journal of the American Medical Association*, vol
265, no 2 (January 9, 1991), pp 233-237.

coverage if they become widowed or divorced.* Poor
working women, whose jobs are insecure and often
without benefits, are more likely to risk losing their
jobs if they agitate or organize for health benefits, or
take too much time from work for their health needs.
Further, recent Federal court rulings allow employers
to use the increasingly popular option of "self-
insurance." Under these plans, employers provide
health insurance coverage themselves, by creating
their own in-house insurance operation rather than
relying on a third party insurance company.
Employers are then allowed to reduce coverage for
employees, and simply refuse to provide coverage for
cancer, AIDS, and other serious illnesses.**

Lack of insurance becomes a health threat in itself
when a woman receives a diagnosis of cancer.
Uninsured women are more likely to die of breast
cancer and less likely to receive hospital care, making
lack of insurance an important risk factor.***
Common cancer treatments are expensive and
time-consuming. Radiation treatments often require
daily visits over a six-week period. Chemotherapy can
leave the patient ill and unable to work, and
treatment can last for many months, even years. Poor

---

* "Critical Condition: Midlife and Older Women in America's
   Health Care System," Older Women's League, Washington, DC,
   May 1992.

** "Employers Winning Right to Cut Back Medical Insurance," *The
   New York Times*, March 29, 1992.

*** M.B. Wenneker, J.S. Weissman, Ph.D., A.M. Epstein, MD,
   "Association of Payer with Utilization of Cardiac Procedures in
   Massachusetts," *Journal of the American Medical Association*,
   September 19, 1990, pp 1255-60. Reported in "Study Finds
   Uninsured Receive Less Hospital Care," *The New York Times*,
   September 12, 1990. Also see study in progress by John Z.
   Ayanian of Brigham and Women's Hospital, Boston which finds
   that uninsured women are more likely to die of breast cancer.

women facing cancer without insurance are often penalized by another serious disadvantage, limited education, which restricts their access to information about cancer prevention and warning signs.* Lack of general awareness about risks and symptoms and delayed access to health care are associated with late diagnosis, which is directly linked to higher cancer mortality rates.** Five-year survival rates among women who did not finish high school are 64 percent for white women and 61 percent for African American women, compared with 81 percent among white women who graduated from college.***

Further barriers to health care access which are impossible to measure but are often associated with poverty, are lack of transportation and childcare, a wariness of all authorities, fatalism based on past experiences, language and cultural barriers, the threat of deportation, and lack of doctors willing to practice in poor urban neighborhoods. Further, women living in poverty are increasingly forced to rely on emergency rooms, overtaxed clinics, and underfunded and inadequately equipped public hospitals. This is one result of the withdrawal of Federal funds from

---

* In a pertinent 1992 study of the effect of socioeconomic status on cardiovascular risk factors, level of education is identified as the most important parameter predicting high risk factors. See M.A. Winkleby, D.E. Jatulis, Erica Frank, and S.P. Fortmann, "Socioeconomic Status and Health: How Education, Income and Occupation Contribute to Risk Factors for Cardiovascular Disease," in *American Journal of Public Health*, vol 82, no 6 (June 1992), pp 816-820.

** C.R. Baquet and K. Ringen, eds., "Cancer Among Blacks and Other Minorities: Statistical Profiles." National Institutes of Health Publication No. 86-2785. 1986.

*** D. Gaiter, "Although Cures Exist, Poverty Fells Many Afflicted with Cancer," *Wall Street Journal*, May 1, 1991, p 1, citing unpublished NCI SEER data.

urban clinics which once provided the basic health care that more affluent people get from their family doctors.*

In New York City, for instance, a 1990 report released by Elizabeth Holtzman, the New York City Comptroller, revealed that eight of the eleven municipal hospitals offered no programs for the detection of breast cancer, and that 65 percent of breast cancers diagnosed in city hospitals were not picked up until the cancers had reached an advanced stage. This contrasts with a national figure of advanced stage diagnosis of 20 to 25 percent. Further, of those who were diagnosed with possible breast cancer, 30 percent were "lost to follow up." As Elizabeth Holtzman put it, this "means that thousands of poor women will suffer and die from a very treatable disease."**

According to the National Cancer Institute, the five-year breast cancer survival rate for white women earning less than $15,000 is 63 percent compared with 78 percent for white women earning more than $30,000. The corresponding figures for African American women (64 vs. 68 percent) show less of a spread between low and higher income women, perhaps reflecting the overriding influence of racism across socioeconomic status.*** For all racial groups, the discrepancy between the survival rates of low and higher income women is confirmed by a recent study of 4,750 women with breast cancer which found that

---

* "Escape the Emergency Room Trap," *The New York Times*, May 4, 1992; "City Plans $3m Cut in Health-Center Aid," *Boston Globe*, May 23, 1992; and "Panel Seeks Cut in Funds for Care of Poor," *Boston Globe*, September 20, 1991.

** "Poverty and Breast Cancer in New York City," Office of the Comptroller, City of New York, October 1990.

*** D. Gaiter, *op. cit.*

uninsured women are 66 percent more likely to die of
the disease than women with private insurance.[*]

A review of the research on women, socioeconomic
status, and cancer confirms our worst suspicions
about a health care system in which the social "safety
net" has been decimated: low income correlates with
late diagnosis and a higher rate of death from cancer.
The risk posed by poverty may be even greater for
rural poor women, who suffer from the same severe
cutbacks in Federal funding of health care services as
those in urban areas. The great distances to be
traveled to obtain health care in rural areas, the
inability of rural hospitals to maintain an
infrastructure of expensive advanced equipment due
to the lack of economies of scale, and the drastic
shortage of either specialists or general practitioners
in rural areas often make the health care situation of
low-income rural women even more precarious than
that of poor urban women.[**]

RACISM

Although the links between poverty and illness are
well established, most of the historical and current
studies of these links exclude specific reference to
cancers, concentrating instead on conditions such as
infant mortality, tuberculosis and heart disease. The
disturbing contrast between death rates for rich and
poor in these areas are regularly highlighted in the
media. Cancer statistics, on the other hand, have
traditionally been handled differently. Here, the

------

[*] "Breast Cancer Takes a Bigger Toll Among Poor," Ron Winslow,
Wall Street Journal, June 19, 1992, p B1; cites presentation of a
study in progress by Dr. John Z. Ayanian, Brigham and Women's
Hospital, Boston.

[**] "Rural New Englanders Find Medical Care in Short Supply,"
Boston Globe, March 22, 1993.

attempts to break down the global figures have commonly been based on *race* rather than income, and in particular, on the contrast in rates between Blacks and whites. This trend has, unfortunately, often produced misleading results, making it appear that African Americans are genetically predisposed to cancer.

According to Dr. Harold Freeman, a past president of the American Cancer Society, this view is untenable; there is "no known genetic basis to explain the major racial differences in cancer incidence and outcome. . . . Within one race, economic status is the major determinant of cancer outcome. Therefore the target for correction is poverty, regardless of race."* In fact, it turns out that cancer statistics for middle-class Blacks show a pattern similar to those for middle-class whites. And once the raw statistics are adjusted for age and income differences between the two populations, whites show higher incidence rates for some cancers, particularly lung cancer.**

Because Blacks are disproportionately poor, and suffer from housing discrimination, job and wage discrimination, and other effects of racism, Black culture is often used as a proxy for poverty. All those aspects of life that contribute to reduced survival— lack of education, lack of access to health care, unemployment, substandard living conditions, poor nutrition, an inadequate social support network, etc. are accurately described as symptoms of poverty

---

* H.P. Freeman, "Cancer in the Socioeconomically Disadvantaged," *Cancer*, vol 64 (supplement; 1989), p 324-334.

** C.R. Baguet, J.W. Horm, T. Gibbs, P. Greenwald, "Socioeconomic Factors and Cancer Incidence Among Blacks and Whites," *Journal of the National Cancer Institute*, vol 83, no 8 (April 17, 1991), p 551-557.

rather than as aspects of Black culture. To confuse poverty with Black culture encourages the public to lose sight of the role of racism in creating poverty. Race itself is not a known cause of cancer.

The exclusive comparison between Blacks and whites obscures the threat that cancer poses to other minorities who are also disproportionately poor. Native American women, for example, have a higher rate of cervical cancer and a lower survival rate from breast cancer than African Americans or white Americans. Hawaiian- and Japanese-Americans both have higher rates of stomach cancer than whites or African Americans.* Hispanic women have higher than average rates of stomach and gallbladder cancer and twice the rate of cancer of the cervix as white, non-Hispanic women.**

Most statistics presented to the general public fail to make any adjustments to accommodate demographic or socioeconomic differences. The results— which show Blacks and other people of color dying more often of all cancers—inevitably carry with them an unstated but nonetheless powerful imputation of blame. This could create the impression that people of color are genetically or behaviorally more prone to cancer. Patterns of behavior that are known to be harmful—such as smoking, diet, and occupational exposure to toxins—are identified as the cause of higher rates of cancer. These practices are viewed as forms of willful self-destruction that characterize the lifestyles of low income people, instead of being

---

*   H.P. Freeman, *op. cit.*

**   National Cancer Institute, "Cancer in Hispanics" (Bethesda, MD: National Institutes of Health, 1988). Cited in Eli Ginzberg, Ph.D., "Access to Health Care for Hispanics," *Journal of the American Medical Association*, vol 265, no 2 (January 9, 1991).

viewed as a response to lack of employment options, stress, chronic economic recession, or, in the case of smoking, as the result of relentless campaigns by tobacco advertisers targeting poor communities. Explanations for the restricted educational and job opportunities that are both cause and effect of poverty are rarely sought. Instead, the focus is placed on the individual.

The idea of individual responsibility for health through the pursuit of a healthful lifestyle and lowered stress is without doubt a boon to the health of the nation as a whole. However, the positive effects of changes in individual behavior (with the exception of cigarette smoking) on overall health and longevity are often overstated, and the ability to comply with current wisdom on a healthy lifestyle depends on a wide range of external factors, both environmental and social. Responsibility for health can tend, if we are not careful, to be privatized without regard for the unequal ability of people to "follow the rules." Living near toxic dumps, working in chemical plants, coping with job insecurity, low income, poor diet, and inadequate medical insurance—all these factors can easily overwhelm the most valiant efforts of the individual to take charge of her health.

It has been known for some time that toxic waste, radioactive materials, and the production of pollutants are related to cancer. Since the 1970s, people of color have become more politically aware that their communities are disproportionately the targets of toxic dumping and the location of the most hazardous industrial operations and that this is affecting their health. This realization has crystallized into the concept of "environmental racism," which has begun to generate its own research. The first study (1979) to link environmental hazards to the race of those exposed to them revealed that all the city-owned landfills built in Houston since the 1920s were located in Black neighborhoods, even though Houston was once an overwhelmingly white city.* A 1987 study found that the pattern was a national one; three out of the five largest commercial hazardous waste landfills in the United States are located in mostly Black or Hispanic communities, accounting for 40 percent of the nation's estimated commercial landfills.**

This sort of injustice has inspired grassroots organizing within communities of color, notably a national conference in October 1991, the First National People of Color Environmental Leadership Summit. The raised awareness of environmental racism has also led to a dramatic increase in the number of lawsuits and protests against local, state, and federal agencies, which often argue that Blacks and Hispanics are more likely to be found in areas with high concentrations of cancer (cancer clusters) caused by toxic pollutants.

The crucial contribution of this new movement is that it integrates an analysis of environmental racism with broader issues of social and racial justice. Thus, environmental degradation is not seen as one "issue area," but is redefined as part of the larger pattern of exploitation and victimization of poor urban and rural communities, especially communities of color and indigenous communities.

---

* "Pollution-Weary Minorities Try Civil Rights Tack," *The New York Times*, January 11, 1993, p A1.

** Charles Lee, *Toxic Waste and Race in the United States* (New York: United Church of Christ Commission for Racial Justice, 1987). Also see Dana Alston, ed., "We Speak for Ourselves: Social Justice, Race and Environment," The Panos Institute, December 1990, p 9.

The concerns of the environmental racism movement overlap with those of the burgeoning women's cancer movement. Pressure from both movements may be required to spur long-overdue research on the relationship among environmental toxins, race, and cancer. We need to know much more, for instance, about the effect of chemical pesticides on men and women farmworkers, the causes of cancer clustering, and the relationship among workplace hazards, race and gender of employees, and cancer incidence.[*]

SEXISM

One of the first issues explored by the contemporary women's movement was sexism within the medical establishment. The patronizing attitude of doctors, the overuse of hysterectomy and mastectomy, the medication of women deemed "nervous" were all practices exposed through feminist activism. Feminists resurrected the practice of midwifery and changed the norms of childbirth.

More recently, feminists, many of them lesbians, have taken up the issue of increasing rates of cancer among women, particularly focussing on the staggering increase in the rate of breast cancer.[**]

---

[*] See Judith Brady, ed., *One in Three: Women With Cancer Confront an Epidemic* (Pittsburg and San Francisco: Cleis Press, 1991) and Rita Arditti and Tatiana Schreiber, "Killing Us Quietly: Cancer, the Environment, and Women," pp 231-260 of this book.

[**] According to The American Cancer Society, one in twenty women developed breast cancer in 1940. This rate increased to one in fourteen in 1960, and as of early 1993 it is one in nine. Addressing the overall cancer rate for the years 1950 to 1988, P. J. Landrigan states in "Commentary: Environmental Disease: A Preventable Epidemic" that among U.S. whites, age-adjusted incidence for all forms of cancer rose by 43 percent. *American Journal of Public Health*, vol 82, no 7 (July 1992), p 942.

In the late 1980s, grassroots groups began to
emerge across the country arguing that indifference to
these alarming changes is part of the broader sexist
neglect of women within the medical establishment.*
Writing in *Sojourner* in 1989, Susan Shapiro, a
Boston area writer and feminist activist, analyzed her
own and other women's experience of cancer as a
feminist issue.** This was the catalyst for the
founding of the Boston/Cambridge-based Women's
Community Cancer Project. Earlier that same year in
Out/Look magazine, Jackie Winnow described the
founding of the Women's Cancer Resource Center in
Berkeley: "I took some of what I learned doing AIDS
work and a lot of what I learned from feminist
organizing and women's liberation, and with other
women, created the Women's Cancer Resource
Center."*** Both Susan Shapiro and Jackie Winnow
have died of breast cancer. There are now at least a
dozen grassroots groups across the country that
organize, protest, and research the neglect of women's

---

* For descriptions of the growth of the feminist cancer movement
see Mary Jo Foley, "Cancer Organizers Push Feminist Agenda,"
New Directions for Women, vol 19, no 3 (May/June 1990); Jane
Gross, "Turning Disease Into Political Cause: First AIDS, and
Now Breast Cancer," *The New York Times*, January 7, 1991, p
A12; Ellen Crowley, "Grassroots Healing," in this book, p
201-206; and Lynn Kanter, "Bringing It Home: Lesbian Cancer
Projects," in this book, p 207-212.

** Susan Shapiro, "Cancer as a Women's Issue," *Sojourner: The
Women's Forum*, September 1989, pp 181-19.

*** Jackie Winnow, "Lesbians Working on AIDS: Assessing the
Impact on Health Care for Women," *Out/Look*, no 5 (summer
1989); reprinted as "Lesbians Evolving Health Care: Our Lives
Depend on It," in *Cancer As a Women's Issue: Scratching the
Surface*, Women/Cancer/Fear/Power series, vol 1, Midge Stocker,
ed. (Chicago: Third Side Press, 1991), pp 23-36.

cancers and angrily demand that more research money be allocated, especially for breast cancer.

In 1990, just as this women's cancer movement was emerging, a Government Accounting Office (GAO) report documented continued sexist neglect within medical research at the National Institutes of Health, despite the existence of a 1986 policy intended to correct it. Women, the GAO reported, have been systematically excluded from controlled experiments, long-term studies, and clinical studies of new drugs.[*]

Also in 1990, the Physicians Insurers Association of America chided doctors for not taking women seriously when they report self-discovered breast lumps. The cost of dismissive and/or patronizing medical attention has been high in terms of claims paid in malpractice suits; the Physicians Insurers Association reports that in 69 percent of cases where claims were paid in response to charges of unnecessarily delayed diagnosis, the female patient discovered the breast lump herself, but had not been taken seriously by her physician.[**]

In large part due to the activism of feminist health groups, Congress, in 1991, allocated $50 million to establish the Women's Health Initiative at the National Institutes of Health. This is an impressive beginning for the young and vigorous women's cancer movement, but it does not address an important set

---

[*] "Our Bodies, Their Selves," *Newsweek*, December 17, 1990, p 60, and "Health Research Largely Excludes Women, GAO Says," *Boston Globe*, June 19, 1990.

[**] "Physicians Chided in a Cancer Study," *The New York Times*, July 9, 1990, and "Doctors Faulted on Reply to Patient Breast Checks," *Boston Globe*, July 9, 1990. Physicians Insurers Association of America, *Breast Cancer Study*, Lawrenceville, NJ, March 1990.

of issues that are peculiar to women when they must
deal with cancer.

For women who are the caretakers of children,
the ill, and the elderly, as well as the principle
homemakers, a diagnosis of cancer imposes enormous
practical as well as emotional burdens. There is often
no one available to step in to help with caretaking,
and, for poor women, no money to hire caretakers.
This can create family crisis, and added stress for the
ill woman. In addition, women usually find
themselves in a medical world of male values, where
the side effects of cancer treatment assaulting their
bodies are not considered significant, crying is
discouraged, and women, especially poor women, are
often treated with condescension or paternalism.

ADDRESSING THE INEQUITY

Frequent stories in print, TV, and radio media tell
of families bankrupted by the crushing burden of
medical debt. Families in which the parent or parents
are unemployed are particularly vulnerable, but 80
percent of children who have no health insurance
have at least one parent who is working.* After years
of neglect and footdragging by Republican administrations, popular support for major reform of the
health care system has forced the issue onto the
legislative agenda. It would be comforting to think
that, should a system of universal health care be
instituted, the problem of unequal access to quality
health care according to socioeconomic status would
be solved. However, what is needed is an affirmative
action health care program for low income people
and people of color, especially women. This is

---

* "At Risk: Middle-Class Families Often Lack Insurance For
   Children's Health," *Wall Street Journal*, June 5, 1992, p 1.

necessary because, even when universal health care is provided, obstacles remain to taking full advantage of its services.

In Great Britain, which has operated a universal health care service since 1948, cancer incidence rates of those in the lowest socioeconomic group remain consistently and significantly higher than those in the highest income group.* Four different cancers among women—invasive and *in-situ* cervical cancers, stomach and lung cancer—showed the greatest difference in rates between rich and poor, with cervical cancer showing the greatest difference. Mortality rates follow the same pattern.**

The long-term persistence of these disparities suggests that, even when there is less economic discrimination in treatment after a diagnosis of cancer, late diagnosis of otherwise curable cancers may remain the overriding determinant of long-term survival rates. This in turn is a reminder that the repercussions of poverty (through restricted education and employment opportunities) affect the way women approach health care. Even if free and in principle universally available, health care may be hard to reach without access to a car or a babysitter or in the context of an insecure job. Universally available health care may be delivered in a way that stereotypes and alienates patients. Further, fatalism can

---

* D.A. Leon, Office of Population Censuses and Surveys, *Longitudinal Study, Social Definition of Cancer* (London: HMSO, 1988).

** L. Doyal and S. Epstein, *Cancer in Britain: The Politics of Prevention* (London: Pluto Press, 1983), p 13.

sometimes play a role in the relationship between the patient and the medical establishment.

Hampered by limited knowledge of the system, discouraged by past encounters with that system, or faithful to religious tenets to follow God's will, a woman may see cancer itself as a death sentence, leading to overwhelming fear of the diagnosis and of any possible treatment.[*] These disadvantages must be overcome by culturally-specific and targeted outreach, support, and education, as well as by efforts to reduce the extreme inequities in the distribution of income in the United States.

This is, of course, not to minimize the absolute necessity of universal health insurance. However, universal health insurance will not on its own eliminate the consequences of poverty, racism and sexism on either incidence or mortality rates of cancer for women. Cancer education and outreach efforts to those who do not now have access to high quality health care must be systematic, well-funded, culturally informed, and relevant to low-income people to be effective.

Many of those who study and advocate for reform of the United States medical system understand this need.[**] Even mainstream organizations such as the

---

[*] This point was made in the Findings of Regional Hearings conducted by the American Cancer Society in May and June 1989 in seven states. See the report from these Hearings, "Cancer and the Poor: A Report to the Nation," American Cancer Society.

[**] See Eli Ginzberg and Miriam Ostow, "Beyond Universal Health Insurance to Effective Health Care," *Journal of the American Medical Association*, vol 265, no 19 (May 15, 1991), pp 2559-2562; Matthew Menken "Caring for the Underserved," *Archives of Neurology*, vol 48 (1991), pp 472-475; and James E. Dalen and Jose Santiago, "Insuring the Uninsured Is Not Enough," *Archives of Internal Medicine*, vol 151 (1991), pp 860-862.

American Cancer Society see a need for culturally-specific outreach and education in poor communities about the risk factors and warning signs of cancer. More farsighted advocates see additional needs—for people to organize to oppose criminal profiteering by pharmaceutical corporations, governmental indifference to the health needs of all its people, and the poisoning of the environment which leads to increased cancer rates. Universal health insurance without accompanying legislation to end environmental degradation and environmental racism will not bring an end to the rapidly increasing rates of cancer we are now experiencing. Similarly, universal health insurance will not end corruption within the medical system unless accountability to the public in the areas of profit-making and public health care policy are established. Finally, greater access to expensive drugs and medical procedures must be accompanied by a reassertion of the role of primary care and preventive care.

The devastation to women's health caused by poverty does not mean that women with money, education, access, and private insurance are never misdiagnosed, treated carelessly and stupidly, or even that they do not occasionally have cancer at higher rates. It does not mean we should not care about men, who sometimes have cancer at higher rates than women. It does not mean that we advocate decreasing the federal budget allocation to AIDS research and treatment. This must be stressed because the conservative media often stir up discord between groups of activist women and sometimes play off AIDS advocates against cancer advocates. It is *not* a matter of pitting one against the other, but of recognizing and supporting multiple layers of demands that must be promoted simultaneously.

CONCLUSION

Statistical research speaks a painful truth about health care for women with cancer in the United States. To a shocking extent, a woman's health reflects her ability to pay for it. This is a morally unacceptable condition. Adequate health care is a fundamental right. As a movement for women's health, we must refuse to accept inadequate health care for poor women. We must demand not only health care reform that equalizes access to medical care, but also insist on affirmative outreach to those women who have been paying with their health— even their lives—for their race, their socioeconomic status, and their gender.

Thanks to the members of the Women's Community Cancer Project for their assistance.

Killing Us Quietly: Cancer, the Environment, and Women[*]

Rita Arditti and Tatiana Schreiber

Today in the United States we live in the midst of a cancer epidemic. One out of every three people will get some form of cancer, and one out of four will die from it. Cancer is currently the second leading cause of death; by the year 2000 it will likely have become the primary cause of death. More than two decades have passed since the National Cancer Act was signed, yet the treatments offered to cancer patients are the same as those offered fifty years ago: surgery, radiation, and chemotherapy (or "slash, burn and poison," as they are called bitterly by both patients and increasingly disappointed professionals). And in spite of sporadic, optimistic pronouncements from the cancer establishment, survival rates for the three main cancer killers—lung, breast, and colo-rectal cancer—have remained virtually unchanged.

In the 1960s and 1970s, environmental activists and a few scientists emphasized that cancer was linked to environmental contamination, and their concerns began to make an impact on public

---

[*] The original version of this article, titled "Breast Cancer: The Environmental Connection," appeared in the May/June 1992 newsletter of Resist, a national foundation funding grassroots social change projects. RESIST, One Summer St., Somerville, MA 02143.

231

understanding of the disease.* In the 1980s and 1990s, however, with an increasingly conservative political climate and concerted efforts on the part of industry to play down the importance of chemicals as a cause of cancer, we are presented with a new image of cancer. Now it is portrayed as an individual problem that can only be overcome with the help of experts, and then only if one has the money and know-how to recruit them for one's personal survival efforts. This emphasis on personal responsibility and lifestyle factors has reached absurd proportions. People with cancer are asked why they brought this disease on themselves and why they don't work harder at getting well.

While people with cancer should be encouraged to do everything possible to strengthen their immune systems (the primary line of defense against cancer) and not to fall into victim roles, the socio-political and economic dimensions of cancer have been pushed completely out of the picture.** Blaming the victim is a convenient way to avoid looking at the larger environmental and social issues that frame individual experiences. This article probes environmental links to cancer in general and to breast cancer in particular, the kinds of research that should be going on, why it's not happening, and the political strategies needed to turn things around.

Extensive evidence exists to indicate that cancer *is* an environmental disease. Even the most conservative scientists agree that approximately 80 percent of all

---

* See, for instance, *The Politics of Cancer* by Samuel S. Epstein (San Francisco: Sierra Club Books, 1978; rev. ed. Garden City, NJ: Anchor Press/Doubleday, 1979) and *The Cancer Connection* by Larry Agran (New York: St. Martin's Press, 1977).

** See *Understanding the Immune System*, National Cancer Institute. NIH Publication No. 90-529, revised March 1990.

cancers are in some way related to environmental factors.* Support for this view relies on four lines of evidence:

1. Dramatic differences in the incidence of cancer between communities (Incidence of cancer among people of a given age in different parts of the world can vary by a factor of 10 to 100.)

2. Changes in the incidence of cancer (either lower or higher rates) in groups that migrate to a new country

3. Changes in the incidence of particular types of cancer with the passage of time

4. The actual identification of the specific causes of certain cancers (like the case of beta-naphthylamine, responsible for an epidemic of bladder cancer among dye workers employed at duPont factories)

Other well-known, environmentally-linked cancers are lung cancer (linked to asbestos, arsenic, chromium, bischloromethyl ether, mustard gas, ionizing radiation, nickel, polycyclic hydrocarbons—in soot, tar, and oil—and, of course, smoking); endometrial cancer (linked to estrogen use); thyroid cancer (often the result of childhood exposure to irradiation); and liver cancer (linked to exposure to vinyl chloride).

---

* Richard Doll and Richard Peto, *The Causes of Cancer. Quantitative Estimates of Avoidable Risks of Cancer in the United States Today* (Oxford and New York: Oxford University Press, 1981).

The inescapable conclusion is that, if cancer is largely environmental in origin, it is largely preventable.

OUR ENVIRONMENT: A HEALTH HAZARD

Environment as we use it here refers not only to air, water, and soil, but also to our diets, medical procedures, and living and working conditions. That means the food we eat, the water we drink, the air we breath, the radiation to which we are exposed, where we live, what kind of work we do and the stress that we suffer: these are responsible for at least 80 percent of all cancers.

The 1958 Delaney Clause of the Food, Drug, and Cosmetics Act banned the deliberate addition to foods of *any* level of carcinogens but has been ignored by the EPA. Until challenged by a recent court decision, EPA regulations allowed dozens of cancer-causing pesticides to be used in the most commonly eaten foods, claiming that the Delaney Clause did not apply to processed foods. Some of these foods are allowed to contain 20 or more carcinogens, making it impossible to measure how much of the substances a person actually consumes.[*] As Rachel Carson wrote in *Silent Spring* in 1962, "This piling up of chemicals from many different sources creates a total exposure that cannot be measured. It is meaningless, therefore, to talk about

---

[*] "Presumed Innocent: A Report on 69 Cancer-causing Pesticides Allowed in Our Food" by Rick Hind, Environmental Program Director, and Jim Baek, Staff Intern. U.S. Public Interest Research Group, September 1990. Available for $10 from US PIRG, 215 Pennsylvania Avenue, SE, Washington DC, 20003.

On July 8, 1992, a federal court of appeals in San Francisco affirmed the Delaney Clause, striking down the EPA's policy. The EPA was expected to appeal.

the 'safety' of any specific amount of residues." In other words, our everyday food is an environmental hazard to our health.

Recently, a study on the trends in cancer mortality in industrialized countries has revealed that while stomach cancer has been steadily declining, brain and other central-nervous-system cancers, breast cancer, multiple myeloma, kidney cancer, non-Hodgkin lymphoma, and melanoma have increased in persons aged 55 and older.[*]

Given this context, it is not extreme to suspect that breast cancer, which has reached epidemic proportions in the U.S., may be linked to environmental ills. In 1992, estimates were that 180,000 women would develop breast cancer, and 46,000 would die from it.[**] In other words, in that year nearly as many women died from breast cancer as Americans died in the entire Vietnam War.

Cancer is the leading cause of death among women ages 35–54, about a third of which are due to breast cancer. Breast cancer incidence data meet three of the four lines of reasoning linking it to the environment:

1. The incidence of breast cancer can vary between communities by a factor of seven.

2. The risk for breast cancer among populations that have migrated becomes that of their new residence within a generation, as is the case for Japanese women who have migrated to the United States.

---

[*] Devra Lee Davis, David Hoel, John Fox, and Alan Lopez, "International Trends in Cancer Mortality in France, West Germany, Italy, Japan, England, and Wales, and the USA" in *The Lancet*, vol 336 (August 25, 1990), pp 474-481.

[**] Actual figures for 1992 are not yet available.

3. The incidence of breast cancer in the United States
   has swelled from one in twenty in 1940 to one in
   eight in the early 1990s.

A number of factors have been linked to breast
cancer: a first blood relative with the disease, early
onset of menstruation, late age at first full-term
pregnancy, higher socio-economic status, late
menopause, and Jewish lineage, for example.
However, for the overwhelming majority of breast
cancer patients (70–80 percent), their illness is not
clearly linked to any of these factors. Research
suggests that the development of breast cancer
probably depends on a complex interplay among
environmental exposures, genetic predisposition to
the disease, and hormonal activity.

Research on the actual identification of causal
factors, however, is given low priority and proceeds
at a snail's pace. We still don't know, for example,
the effects of birth control pills and the hormone
replacement therapy routinely offered to menopausal
women. Hormonal treatments are fast becoming the
method of choice for the treatment of infertility, while
we know nothing about their long-range effects. And
the standard addition of hormones into animal feed
means that women (and men) are exposed to
hormone residues in meat. Because a general
consensus exists about the importance of estrogen
metabolism for the induction of breast cancer,
hormonal interventions (through food or drugs) are
particularly worrisome.

A startling example of the lack of interest in breast
cancer prevention is the saga of the proposed study
on the supposed link between high fat diets and
breast cancer. The Women's Health Trial, a 15-year
study designed to provide conclusive data about the
high fat–cancer link was denied funding by the

National Cancer Advisory Board, despite having been revised to answer previous criticisms and despite feasibility studies indicating that a full-scale trial was worth launching. Fortunately, it now appears that the study will be part of the Women's Health Initiative, a $500-million effort that will look at women's health issues. That success story is a direct result of women's activism and pressure from women's health groups across the country.

The evidence of a relationship between breast cancer and fat intake is so far inconclusive. A study in 65 Chinese counties with low levels of industrialization found that fat intake varied widely (from 5 to 47 percent of total calories) but had no relation to breast cancer rates, which were at most one-tenth of the U.S. rates.[*]

Even if new studies establish a correlation between high-fat diets and breast cancer risk in the U.S., that link is unlikely to fully explain how breast cancer develops. The breast is rich in adipose cells, and carcinogens that accumulate in these fat tissues may be responsible for inducing cancer rather than the fat itself, or the fat alone. Environmental contamination of human breast milk with PCBs, PBBs, and DDE[**] is a widely acknowledged phenomenon. These fat-soluble substances are poorly metabolized and have a long half-life in human tissue. They may also interact with one another, creating an additive toxic effect, and they may carry what are called "incidental contaminants": compounds like dibenzofurans and dioxins, each with its own toxic properties. (The most infamous of the dioxins [2, 3, 7, 8-tetra-

---

[*] W. Willett, "The Search for the Causes of Breast and Colon Cancer" in *Nature*, vol 338 (1989), p 389-393.

[**] DDE is a metabolite of the pesticide DDT.

cholorodibenzo-p-dioxin or TCDD] is considered
the most toxic synthetic chemical known to science).[*]
   Among the established effects of these substances
are liver dysfunction, skin abnormalities, neurological
and behavioral abnormalities, immunological
aberrations, thyroid dysfunction, gastrointestinal
disturbances, reproductive dysfunction, tumor
growth, and enzyme induction. Serious concerns have
been raised about the risks that this contamination
entails for infants who are breast-fed.
   What is outrageous in the discussion about human
breast milk poisoning is that little or no mention is
made of the possible effects on the women themselves, particularly since it is known that most of
these substances have estrogenic properties.[**] It is
as if the women, whose breasts contain these
carcinogens, do not exist. We witness the paradox of
women being made invisible, even while their toxic
breasts are put under the microscope.

THE PESTICIDE STUDIES

   Very recently some scientists have begun to look at
the chemical–breast cancer connection. In 1990, two
scientists from Hebrew University's Hadassah School
of Medicine, Elihu Richter and Jerry Westin, reported
a surprising statistic. They found that Israel was the
only country among 28 countries surveyed that
registered a real drop in breast cancer mortality in the

---

[*] Mason Barr, Jr., "Environmental contamination of Human Breast
    Milk," *AJPH*, vol 71, no 2 (February 1981). Joe Thornton, "The
    Dioxin Deception," *Greenpeace*, May/June 1991. For recent
    attempts from the paper and chlorine industries to loosen
    regulations on dioxin, see Jeff Bailey, "Dueling Studies: How Two
    Industries Created a Fresh Spin on the Dioxin Debate" in *The
    Wall Street Journal*, February 20, 1992.

[**] They behave like estrogen in the body.

decade 1976–1986.[*] This was happening in the face
of a worsening of all known risk factors, such as fat
intake and age at first pregnancy. As Westin noted,
"All and all, we expected a rise in breast cancer
mortality of approximately 20% overall, and what
we found, was that there was an 8% drop, and in the
youngest age group, the drop was 34%, as opposed
to an expected 20% rise, so, if we put those two
together, we are talking about a difference of about
50% which is enormous."

Westin and Richter could not account for the drop
solely in terms of demographic changes or improved
medical intervention. Instead, they suspect it may
have been related to a 1978 ban on three
carcinogenic pesticides (benzene hexachloride,
lindane, and DDT) that heavily contaminated milk
and milk products in Israel. Prior to 1978, Westin
said that "at least one of them [pesticides] was found
in the milk here at a rate 100 times greater than it
was in the U.S. in the same period, and in the worst
case, nearly a thousand times greater." This
observation led them to hypothesize that there might
be a connection between the decrease in exposure
following the ban and the decrease in breast cancer
mortality.

The pesticides that were contaminating Israeli milk
are known as inducers of a superfamily of enzymes
called the cytochrome P450 system. These enzymes
can promote cancer growth, weaken the immune
system, and destroy anti-cancer drugs. Westin and
Richter believe that these induced enzymes could have
increased the virulence of breast cancer in women and

[*]   Jerome B. Westin and Elihu Richter, "The Israeli Breast-Cancer
      Anomaly," in *Trends in Cancer Mortality in Industrial Countries*,
      edited by Devra Davis and David Hoel (Annals of the New York
      Academy of Science, 1990, pp 269-279).

therefore increased the mortality rates. When the pesticides were removed from the diet, they speculated, much less virulent cancers occurred and the mortality from breast cancer fell.

Westin and Richter are convinced that there is a critical need to increase awareness about environmental conditions and cancer. Health care clinicians, for example, could play an important role in the detection of potential exposures to toxic chemicals that might be missed in large studies. "It's a question of a mindset and of programming and training and activating the medical profession and the health professions to keep their eyes and ears open for such possible associations," said Richter. "This is not necessarily expensive. It's a question of awareness and professional commitment."

This is a refreshing view. It encourages individual physicians to ask questions about work environments, living quarters, dietary habits, and other factors, that could provide important clues about the cancer–environment connection. Epidemiological studies, as currently conducted, are not that sensitive in identifying low levels of risk, and the long latency periods of some cancers may not adequately be taken into consideration. Needless to say, the relevant questions are not usually asked of cancer patients.

In the United States, only one study we know of has directly measured chemical residues in women who have breast cancer compared to those who don't. Dr. Mary Wolff, a chemist at New York's Mount Sinai School of Medicine recently completed a pilot study with Dr. Frank Falck (then at Hartford Hospital in Hartford, Connecticut) that was

published in *The Archives of Environmental Health.*[*]
In this case-controlled study, Falck and Wolff found
that several chemical residues from pesticides and
PCBs were elevated in cases of malignant disease as
compared to nonmalignant cases.

The study involved 25 women with breast cancer
and the same number of women who had biopsies
but did not have breast cancer. The results showed
differences significant enough to interest the National
Institute for Environmental Health Sciences which
will fund a larger study, a collaboration between
Wolff and Dr. Paolo Toniolo, an epidemiologist at
New York University School of Medicine and one of
the authors of a study conducted in Italy on the role
of diet in breast cancer.[**] Wolff and Toniolo's new
study will look at the level of DDT and its
metabolites in the blood samples of 15,000 women
attending a breast cancer screening clinic in New
York, and it will take into consideration reproductive
factors, dietary habits, family history, and hormone
levels in the body. This study could provide valuable
data clarifying any link to chemical exposures and
stimulating further research.

A Finnish study published in 1990 lends support to
Falck and Wolff's findings. In that study, a group of
44 women with breast cancer had significantly higher

---

[*] Frank Falk, Andrew Ricci, Mary S. Wolff, James Gobold and
Peter Deckers, "Pesticides and Polychlorinated Biphenyl Residues
in Human Breast Lipids and Their Relation to Breast Cancer," in
Archives of Environmental Health, vol 47, no 2 (March/April
1992), pp 143-146.

[**] Toniolo Paolo, Elio Riboli, Fulvia Protta, Martine Charrel, and
Alberto P.M. Cappa, "Calorie Providing Nutrients and Risk of
Breast Cancer" in *Journal of the National Cancer Institute* vol 81
(1989), pp 278-286. This study linked animal fat to the incidence
of breast cancer. This finding could support the pesticide link if in
fact the pesticides have concentrated in the animal fat.

concentrations of the pesticide beta-hexachlorocyclohexane (b-HCH) in their breast fat than a set of
33 women without cancer. The authors found that
women whose breast tissue contained more than 100
parts per billion of b-HCH were 10.5 times more
likely to have breast cancer than women with lower
levels of the pesticide in their tissues.[*]

In the U.S., levels of pesticides residues in adipose
tissue have been decreasing since the 1970s (following
the banning of DDT and decreased use of other
carcinogenic pesticides), while the breast cancer rate
continues to rise. This observation would seem to
contradict the pesticide hypothesis. However, Paolo
Toniolo points out that the chemicals could act
differently at different exposure levels; they are
unlikely to act alone; and time of exposure may be
important. For example, if a child is exposed during
early adolescence, when breast tissue is growing
rapidly, the result may be different than exposure
later in life.

In late 1992, Greenpeace gathered together much
of the recent research in a report entitled "Breast
Cancer and the Environment: The Chlorine
Connection," that argues for the complete phase-out
of all organochlorine based substances, a principle
called Zero Discharge. The report outlines the history
of industrial production of chlorine and
organochorines in this country, which now produces
about 40 million tons of chlorine per year. Most of
that is combined with petrochemicals to make
products such as plastics, solvents, pesticides, and
refrigerants. Organochlorines have the insidious

---

[*] Mussalo-Rauhamaa, H.E. Hasanem, et al. (1990), "Occurrence of
beta-hexachlorocyclohexane in breast cancer patients" in *Cancer*,
vol 66, pp 2124-2128.

property of great stability, resisting breakdown in the environment for decades or centuries. At least 177 organochlorines have been identified in human tissue. Greenpeace notes that banning organochlorines means "phasing out the substance that is their root—chlorine—since wherever chlorine is used organochlorines result."*

RADIATION AND MAMMOGRAPHY

Another area that demands urgent investigation is the role of radiation in breast cancer development. It is widely accepted that ionizing radiation causes breast cancer at high doses, while low doses are generally regarded as safe. Questions remain, however, regarding the shape of the dose-response curve, the length of the latency period, and the importance of age at time of exposure. These questions are of great importance to women because of the emphasis on mammography for early detection. Evidence exists that mammography screening reduces breast cancer death in women age 50 or older. However, Dr. Rosalie Bertell, director of the International Institute of Concern for Public Health and well-known critic of the nuclear establishment, raises serious questions about mammography screening.**

In a paper entitled "Comments on Ontario Mammography Program," Bertell criticized a breast cancer screening program planned by the Ontario Health Minister in 1989. Bertell argued that the

---

* Thornton, Joe, "Breast Cancer and the Environment: The Chlorine Connection," a Greenpeace Report, available from Greenpeace, 1017 W. Jackson, Chicago, Illinois 60607.

** Dr. Rosalie Bertell, *No Immediate Danger: Prognosis for a Radioactive World* (TN: Book Publishing Co, 1985).

program, which would potentially screen 300,000
women, was a plan to "reduce breast cancer death by
increasing breast cancer incidence."* She presented an
independent risk-benefit assessment of the program
and concluded that even if breast cancer deaths were
reduced, only a very small number of the lives saved
would be exclusively due to the screening. The
overwhelming majority of the cancers could have
been detected by other means, including monthly
self-examination. She added that a significant number
of women (163) would have unnecessary breast
surgery due to the program and a very high number
(10,000) would have retests because of false positive
mammograph readings. Despite these criticisms, the
program was put into place and is now ongoing.

Bertell's critique of mammography is supported by
a recent multi-million dollar Canadian study that
examined cancer rates in 90,000 women between
1980 and 1988.** The study found that for women
aged 40 to 49, mammograms have no benefits and, in
fact, the number of deaths was higher in the group
that received mammograms than in the control
group. Although the authors of the study say the
difference wasn't "statistically significant," the
numbers are still troubling. The study also suggests
that for women aged 50 to 69, many of the benefits
attributed to mammography in earlier studies "may
have been provided by the manual breast exams that
accompanied the procedure and not by the

_____

*   The paper can be obtained by writing to Dr. Rosalie Bertell,
    President, International Institute of Concern for Public Health,
    830 Bathurst Street, Toronto, Ontario, Canada, M5R 3G1.

** A.B. Miller, C.J. Baines, T. To, C. Wall, "Canadian National
    Breast Screening Study: Breast Cancer Detection and Death Rates
    Among Women Aged 40-49 Years," in *Canadian Medical
    Association Journal*, vol 147 (1992), pp 1459-76.

mammography," as Bertell noted in her paper. Not surprisingly, the study has been mired in controversy. As study director Dr Anthony Miller remarked, "I've come up with an answer that people are not prepared to accept." *

According to Bertell, the breast cancer epidemic is a direct result of "above ground weapons testing" done in Nevada between 1951 and 1963, when 200 nuclear bombs were set off and their fallout dispersed across the U.S. Because the latency period for breast cancer peaks at about 40 years, this is an entirely reasonable hypothesis.

Other studies have looked at the effect of "low-level" radiation on cancer development. A study investigating the incidence of leukemia in south-eastern Massachusetts found a positive association with radiation released from the Pilgrim nuclear power plant.** In adult cases diagnosed before 1984, the risk of leukemia was almost four times higher for individuals with the greatest potential for exposure to the emissions of the plant.*** Other types of cancer take a greater number of years to develop, and there is no reason to assume that excessive radiation emission was limited to the 1978–1986 time frame. In other words, it is entirely possible that as follow-up

---

* For a critique of the Canadian study and the statistical significance of the data for women 40-49, see "Mammography: Uncertainty Clarified," *The Lancet*, vol 340 (November 21, 1992), pp 1261-1262.

** The study was limited to cases first diagnosed between 1978 and 1986.

*** Southeastern Massachusetts Health Study Final Report. Investigation of Leukemia Incidence in 22 Massachusetts Communities 1978-1986. Massachusetts Department of Public Health. Division of Environmental Health Assessment. October 1990.

studies continue, other cancers, (including breast
cancer) will also show higher rates.*

BIOLOGICAL EFFECTS OF
ELECTROMAGNETIC FIELDS

In the past few years, questions have also arisen
about the possible biological effects of electromagnetic fields. Studies looking at EMF and
childhood leukemia are inconclusive, but two
studies of telephone company and electrical workers
have raised the possibility of a connection between
EMF exposure and breast cancer in males. Genevieve
Matanoski of Johns Hopkins University studied
breast cancer rates in male New York Telephone
employees between 1976 and 1980, observing a
dose-response relationship to cancer. There were two
cases of breast cancer, a very high number for such a
small group. Breast cancer in men is rare; in the U.S.,
the annual incidence is 1 in 100,000.

Another study, by Paul Demers and others at the
Hutchinson Cancer Research Institute in Seattle,
Washington, found a strong correlation between male
breast cancer and jobs that involved exposure to
EMFs. They reported that "men whose jobs involved
some exposure to EMFs were nearly twice as likely to

---

* The NCI grouped the following cancers according to how closely
their incidence was associated with exposure to radiation: Group I
(most closely): leukemia, multiple myeloma, Hodgkin's disease;
Group II: breast and lung cancer and Group III (less closely):
bone, brain, and liver cancer, lymphomas. With respect to latency,
the NCI presented the following data as to where cancer was
likely to occur: possible leukemia, after two years; possible
leukemia and other cancers, after ten years. Commentary by the
Duxbury Nuclear Affairs Committee presented to the Duxbury
Board of Selectmen relative to the Department of Public Health
Recommendations regarding the Southeastern Massachusetts
Health Study.

have breast cancer as those men with no exposure, and men likely to have the highest exposures—electricians, utility linemen, and power plant workers—had six times the risk of developing breast cancer as men who worked in occupations with no EMF exposure."[*] Individuals exposed at least 30 years prior to diagnosis and earlier than age 30 were at higher risk than other EMF-exposed workers. According to Dr. Robert Pool, EMFs can produce changes in the cellular metabolism, including changes in hormone production, protein synthesis and ion flow across cell membranes.

Ironically, most of the studies on EMF exposure have been done on men, while EMFs are generated by household appliances and video display terminals largely used by women.

THE SURVEILLANCE THEORY

Current theory supports the concept that cancerous mutations are a common phenomenon in the body of normal individuals and that ordinarily the immune system intervenes before mutated cells can multiply. Known as the "surveillance" theory of cancer, the basic premise is that cancer can develop when the immune system fails to eliminate mutant cells. Carcinogenic mutations can be induced by radiation or chemicals, for instance, and if immunological competence is reduced at a critical time, the mutated cells can thrive and grow.[**]

---

[*]   Quoted by Dr. Robert Pool, "Is There an EMF-Cancer Connection?" in *Science*, vol 249 (September 7, 1990).

[**] Victor Richards, MD, *The Wayward Cell—Cancer—Its Origins, Nature and Treatment* (Berkeley and Los Angeles: University of California Press, 1978).

Given the apparent importance of the immune system in protecting us from cancer, we ought to be concerned not only with eliminating carcinogens in our environment, but also with making certain that our immune systems are not under attack. Recent evidence that ultraviolet radiation depresses the immune system is therefore particularly ominous. At a hearing on "Global Change Research: Ozone Depletion and Its Impacts" held in November 1992 by the Senate Committee on Commerce, Science, and Transportation, a panel of scientists reported that ozone depletion is even more serious than previously thought. According to the data, the ozone layer over the U.S. is thinning at a rate of 3–5 percent per decade, resulting in increased ultraviolet radiation, which "will reduce the quantity and quality of crops, increase skin cancer, *suppress the immune system,* and disrupt marine ecosystems" (our emphasis).[*] As the writers make chillingly clear, this is happening literally over our heads, and there is no place we can hide.

In other words, our basic mechanisms of defense against cancer are being weakened by the chemical soup in which we are immersed. Dioxin, an extremely toxic substance that has been steadily building up in the environment since the growth of the chlorinated chemical industry following World War II, can produce alterations that disrupt the immune system.[**]

---

[*] The report also states that a 10-percent decrease in ozone will lead to approximately 1.7 million additional cases of cataracts per year, worldwide, and at least 250,000 additional cases of skin cancer.

[**] A.M. Jennings, G. Wild, et al. "Immunological Abnormalities Seventeen Years After Accidental Exposure to 2,3,7,8-tetrachlorodobenzo-p-dioxin," in *British Journal of Industrial Medicine*, vol 45 (1988), pp 701-704, and R.W. Clapp,

"Free radicals" created by exposure to low-level
radiation can cause immune system abnormalities.[*]

CANCER PREVENTION STRATEGY

It follows that an intelligent and long-range cancer
prevention strategy would make a clean environment
its number one priority. Prevention, however, has a
low priority in the U.S. national cancer agenda. In
1992, out of an almost $2 billion National Cancer
Institute (NCI) budget, $132.7 million was spent on
breast cancer research, but only about 15 percent of
that was for research on cancer prevention.
Moreover, research on the cellular mechanism of
cancer development, where much of the "prevention"
effort goes, does not easily get translated into actual
prevention strategies.[**]

In *The Cancer Industry*, his 1989 expose of the
cancer establishment, Ralph Moss writes that until
the late 1960s the cancer establishment presented the
view that cancer is "widely believed to consist of a
hereditable, and therefore genetic" problem.[***] That
line of thinking is still with us, but with added
emphasis on the personal responsibility we each have

B. Commoner, et al., "Human Health Effects Associated with
Exposure to Herbicides and/or their Associated Contaminants," in
Agent Orange and the Vietnam Veteran, April 1990. Both articles
are available from National Veterans Legal Services Project, 2001
S. Street NW, Washington, DC 20009-1125.

[*] A. Petkau, "Radiation Carcinogenesis From a Membrane
Perspective," in *Acta Physiologica Scandinavia, Supplement,* vol
492 (1980), pp 81-90.

[**] Figures were obtained from the budget office of the National
Cancer Institute.

[***] W. Ralph Moss, *The Cancer Industry: Unraveling the Politics*
(New York: Paragon House, 1989), p 348 (quoting a 1969 Sloan
Kettering Report).

for our cancers (smoking and diet), and little or no
acknowledgment of the larger environmental context.
In a chapter appropriately named "Preventing
Prevention," Moss provides an inkling of why this
is so.

The close ties between industry and the National
Cancer Advisory Board* and the President's Cancer
Panel, two of the most influential groups determining
the U.S. national cancer agenda, are revealing. For
example, the chair of the President's Cancer Panel
throughout most of the 1980s was Armand Hammer,
head of Occidental International Corporation. Among
Occidental's subsidiaries is Hooker Chemical
Company, implicated in the environmental disaster in
Love Canal.

Moss, formerly assistant director of public affairs
at Memorial Sloan-Kettering Cancer Center
(MSKCC), the world's largest private cancer center,
outlines the structure and affiliations of MSKCC's
leadership, and the picture that emerges borders on
the surreal. In 1988, 32.7 percent of its board of
overseers were tied to the oil, chemical, and
automobile industries; 34.6 percent were professional
investors (bankers, stockbrokers, venture capitalists).
Board members included top officials of drug
companies—Squibb, Bristol-Myers, Merck—and
influential members of the media—CBS, *The New
York Times*, Warner's communications, and *The
Reader's Digest*—as well as leaders of the $55-billion
cigarette industry.

Moss's research leaves little doubt about the
allegiances of the cancer establishment. Actual cancer

---

* The National Cancer Advisory Board is an 18-member board
   appointed by the U.S. President that reports every three months to
   the director of the NCI.

prevention would require a massive reorganization of industry, hardly in the interest of the industrial and financial elites. Instead of preventing the generation of chemical and toxic waste, the strategy adopted by industry and government has been one of "management." But, as Barry Commoner rather succinctly put it, "The best way to stop toxic chemicals from entering the environment is to not produce them."[*]

Instead, the latest "prevention" strategy for breast cancer moves in a completely different direction. A trial has been approved that will test the effect of a breast cancer drug (an anti-estrogen, tamoxifen) in a healthy population, with the hope that it will have a preventive effect. The trial will involve 16,000 women considered at high risk for breast cancer; the women will be divided into a control group and a tamoxifen group. The National Women's Health Network is unequivocal in its criticism of the trial. Adrienne Fugh-Berman, a member of the Network Board, wrote in their September/October 1991 newsletter, "In our view the trial is premature in its assumptions, weak in its hypothesis, questionable in its ethics, and misguided in its public health ramifications."[**] The criticisms center around the fact that tamoxifen causes liver cancer in rats, liver changes in all species tested, and that a number of endometrial cancers have been reported among tamoxifen users. Berman

---

[*]   Barry Commoner, director of the Center for the Biology of Natural Systems at Queens College, in Brooklyn, New York, quoted in *Greenpeace Toxics*, non-dated two-page article entitled "U.S. Industry's Toxic Chemical Dependency: Causes, Effects and the Cure." For more information, write to Greenpeace, 1436 U Street, NW, Washington DC 2000, (202) 462-1177.

[**]   National Women's Health Network is a national public-interest organization dedicated solely to women and health. NWHN, 1325 G Street NW, Washington, DC 20005.

points out that approving a potent, hormonal drug in healthy women and calling that "prevention" sets a dangerous precedent.

This drug-oriented trial symbolizes, in a nutshell, the paradoxes of short-sighted cancer prevention strategies: more drugs are used to counteract the effect of previous exposures to drugs, chemicals, or other carcinogenic agents. It is a vicious circle and one that will not be easily broken.

GRASSROOTS PRESSURE

In the mid-1980s, women living on Long Island learned that Nassau and Suffolk county had a cancer rate 13–14 percent higher than the state average.[*] When journalist Joan Swirsky learned that a major study would be undertaken to look for associations, she was pleased at first, but in no time found herself in the role of activist, as she discovered flaws in the study design.

From her column in The Women's Record, Swirsky noted that the original study (a joint effort of the state Health Department and SUNY-Stoneybrook) "omitted at least two important environmental variables—the source of drinking water and proximity to toxic dumpsites."[**] Because of the questions she and other women raised, the study was redesigned twice. When finally released in 1991, the study's results were inconclusive but indicated that environmental factors do not account for Long Island's high breast cancer incidence. Instead, residents were told, their cancers were probably

---

[*] Since that time, statistics indicate an even more dramatic "hot spot" for breast cancer in Nassau County.

[**] Joan Swirsky, "Breast Cancer Update" in The Women's Record, October 1988.

attributable to affluence or diet, and that no further research was warranted.

Partly in response to the study, a group of Long Island breast cancer survivors and their supporters formed a group called "One in Nine."* Women were enraged at being told that this was "the end" of the issue and met several times with the NY Department of Health, pointing out that their counties are actually areas of mixed income, and at the same time, neighboring affluent counties have not been found to have particularly elevated breast cancer rates. Marie Quinn, founder of the group commented, "Is water studied enough? . . . Electromagnetic fields, dishes that take in TV and radio waves? . . . How about homes that have been built on top of waste dumps that have been closed, . . . areas where there were factories years ago, [and] dumped toxic materials . . . I don't think that these things have been examined closely enough."

A new report on breast cancer on Long Island was released in late 1992 by a panel of the Centers for Disease Control. It rejected the women's requests for a new study and reiterated the idea that the high incidence of cancer was due to affluence and other "established" risk factors. Swirsky and members of One in Nine were outraged and have announced plans to convene their own panel to investigate unexplored variables (such as electromagnetic fields, actual chemical levels in drinking water, hormones in meat, observed "clusters," and others) that have yet to be studied. The New York City Commission on the Status of Women also organized a public hearing on the issue. Swirsky's criticisms were instrumental in

---

* The name was based on Nassau County's breast cancer rate, which at the time was higher than the national average.

helping other women to speak out and to try to make
public officials accountable for their actions.

CANCER, POVERTY, POLITICS

It is ironic that women in Long Island are being
told that their high breast cancer rates are due to
their affluent lifestyle, when breast cancer is on the
rise (both in incidence and in mortality) among
African-American women, hardly an "affluent"
population, as a whole. The African American Breast
Cancer Alliance of Minnesota, organized in October
1990, has noted this steady increase and the limited
efforts that have been made to reach
African-Americans with information and prevention
strategies. Many people of color live in the most
polluted areas of this country, where factories,
incinerators, garbage, and toxic waste are part of the
landscape.*

Native American nations are particularly targeted
by waste management companies that try to take
advantage of the fact that "because of the sovereign
relationship many reservations have with the federal
government, they are not bound by the same
environmental laws as the states around them."**

Poverty and pollution go hand in hand. The 1988
Greenpeace report *Mortality and Toxics along the
Mississippi River* showed that the "total mortality
rates and cancer mortality rates in the counties along

---

* For more information, see *Toxic Wastes and Race in the United
States* by Charles Lee, which is available from United Church of
Christ Commission for Racial Justice, 475 Riverside Drive, New
York, NY 10115. 212-870-2077.

** Conger Beasley, Jr., "Dances with Garbage," in *E*,
November/December 1991. See also, *We Speak for
Ourselves-Social Justice, Race and Environment*, The Panos
Institute, December 1990.

the Mississippi River were significantly higher than in the rest of the nation's counties" and that "the areas of the river in which public health statistics are most troubling have populations which are disproportionately poor and black."* These are also the areas that have the greatest number of toxic discharges. Louisiana has the dubious distinction of being the state with most reported toxic releases—741.2 million pounds a year. Cancer rates in the Louisiana section of the "Chemical Corridor" (the highly industrialized stretch of river between Baton Rouge and New Orleans) are among the highest in the nation. Use of the Mississippi River as a drinking water source has been linked to excess rates of cancer in Louisiana. The rates of cancer of the colon, bladder, kidney, rectum, and lung all exceed national averages. Louisiana Attorney General William J. Guste, Jr., has criticized state officials who claimed that people of color and the poor *naturally* have higher cancer rates. You can't "point out race and poverty as cancer factors" said Guste, "without asking if poor people or blacks . . . reside in less desirable areas more heavily impacted by industrial emissions."**

It follows that for African-American women, living in the most contaminated areas of this country, there would be a disproportionate increase in breast cancer

---

* Pat Costner and Joe Thornton, *We All Live Downstream: The Mississippi River and the National Toxic Crisis*, Greenpeace report (December 1989).

** "Baton Rouge, Louisiana" in *Greenpeace*, Oct/Nov/Dec 1991, p 12.

incidence.[*] However, widespread epidemiological
studies to chart such a correlation have not been
undertaken. For instance, given the evidence
implicating pesticides in the development of breast
cancer, it would seem imperative to study migrant
(and other) farm workers who have been exposed to
such chemicals.

ORGANIZING

Women's groups around the country have started
organizing to fight the breast cancer epidemic. In
1991, a National Breast Cancer Coalition was
founded, with a threefold agenda: increase the
funding for research, organize, and educate. All the
recently formed groups consider prevention a priority,
and one of their tasks will undoubtedly entail
defining what effective prevention really means. In
Massachusetts, the Women's Community Cancer
Project (WCCP), which defines itself as a "grassroots
organization created to facilitate changes in the
current medical, social, and political approaches to
cancer, particularly as they affect women," has
developed a Women's Cancer Agenda to be presented
to the federal government and the NCI.[**] Several of
its demands address prevention and identification of
the causes of cancer. WCCP hass received endorse-
ments of the Women's Cancer Agenda from many

-----

[*] According to *Cancer Statistics Review, 1937-1987*, L.A. Ries, B.F.
     Hankey, and B.K. Edwards, editors, U.S. Dept. of Health and
     Human Services. NIH Pub. 90-2789, for Black women under age
     50, a 22.7 percent increase occurred in the period 1973-1987,
     compared with a 10.4 percent increase for white women. For
     women over age 50, the increases were roughly similar, 30.2
     percent for white women and 29.1 percent for Black women.

[**] "A Women's Cancer Agenda" appears on pages 261–263 in this
     book.

organizations and individuals working in the areas of environmental health, women's rights, and health care reform. This effort will provide a networking and organizing tool, bringing together different constituencies in an all-out effort to stop the cancer epidemic.

Cancer *is* a political issue and needs to be seen as such. The women's health movement of the 1970s made that strikingly clear and gave us a roadmap to the politics of women's health. In the 1980s, AIDS activists showed the power of direct action to influence research priorities and treatment deliveries. In the 1990s, an effective cancer prevention strategy demands that we challenge the present industrial practices of the corporate world, which are based solely on economic gains for the already powerful, and that we insist on an end to the toxic discharges that the government sanctions under the guise of "protecting our security." According to Lenny Siegel, research director of the Military Toxic Network, the Pentagon has produced more toxic waste in recent years than the five largest multinational chemical companies combined, between 400,000 tons and 500,000 tons annually.

If we want to stop not just breast cancer, but all cancers, we need to think in global terms and build a movement that will link together groups that previously worked at a respectful distance. At a world-wide level, the Women's World Congress for a Healthy Planet, meeting in Miami in November 1991 (attended by over 1500 women from 92 countries from many different backgrounds and perspectives), drafted a position paper, Agenda 21, and presented it at the 1992 United Nations Earth

Summit conference in Brazil.* It articulates a women's
position on the environment and sustainable
development that stresses pollution prevention,
economic justice, and an end to conflict resolution
through war and weapons production.**

In an inspiring example of collaboration between
environmentalists and women's health activists,
Greenpeace and a coalition of other groups sponsored
a national conference on breast cancer and the
environment in November 1992. Invited speakers
included researcher Mary Wolff, poet and biologist
Sandra Steingraber, other researchers, activists,
legislators, and cancer survivors. The conference was
an important first step in developing a prevention-
oriented approach to fighting cancer.

On February 4, 1992, a group of 65 scientists
released a statement at a press conference in
Washington, DC, entitled, "Losing the 'War Against
Cancer': Need for Public Policy Reforms" that calls
for an amendment to the National Cancer Act that
would "re-orient the mission and priorities of the
NCI to cancer causes and prevention."*** The seeds
of the anti-cancer movement have been sown. It is
now our challenge to nourish this movement with
grassroots research, with demonstrations, and with
demands that our society as a whole take

---

*   Copies of this document are available from Women's Environment
and Development Organization, 845 Third Avenue, 15th floor,
New York, NY, 10022. (212) 759-7982. Ask for the Official
Report of the Congress. $5 per copy, bulk rates available.

** War and weapons production are probably the greatest force in
destroying the environment.

*** For a copy of this statement, write to Samuel S. Epstein, MD,
Professor of Occupational and Environmental Medicine, School of
Public Health, University of Illinois, Chicago, Illinois, 60680

responsibility for the environmental contamination that is killing us.

Many thanks to the women of the Women's Community Cancer Project in Cambridge for their help and support.

A Women's Cancer Agenda

Demands to the NCI and the U.S. Government

The Women's Community Cancer Project of Boston/Cambridge, MA has compiled the following list of demands, to be presented to the National Cancer Institute and the U.S. government. Demands 1–4 refer to research; 5–10 refer to public policy.

1. Increase funding, **through new allocations**, for research on cancers of the female reproductive organs: breast, cervical, uterine, vaginal and ovarian, to whatever level is necessary to allow for <u>meaningful</u> research resulting in <u>decreased incidence and decreased mortality among women of all races, ethnic groups and social classes</u>. Increase funding, **through new allocations**, for research focused on identifying the causes of the recent 12–13% increase in childhood cancer incidence, which could be due to toxic exposures to either or both parents.

2. Fund research, **through new allocations**, on all other types of cancer with an emphasis on similarities and differences between men and women, and between women of different races, ethnic groups and social classes, in the causes and course of the disease and the effectiveness of treatment.

3. Develop an integrated and interdisciplinary approach to research that takes into account the whole individual and her social and political context, not just the cancer cells in her body. Study the interrelationship between the immune system, the neuroendocrine system, and cancer,

and the importance of support networks in enhancing the length and quality of life.

4. We demand decision-making power for women, minorities, and the poor, including those with cancer and at high risk for cancer, in all NCI decision-making bodies, especially the councils which decide research funding allocations.

5. Pass the Women's Health Equity Act (H.R. 1161, S. 513, 1991), a set of legislative initiatives drafted by the Congressional Caucus for Women's Issues concerned with research, services and prevention related to women's health.

6. Enact a comprehensive and universal national health plan that will allow access to conventional health care and alternatives for people of all socioeconomic groups. In the meantime, enact legislation to allow for health insurance coverage of experimental cancer treatments and end insurance discrimination against people with cancer.

7. Enforce the Americans With Disabilities Act which was signed into law on July 13, 1990, as it pertains to employment discrimination against people with cancer.

8. Direct research to focus on prevention, the environmental causes of cancer, and new, nontoxic therapies. Make the identification and removal of all carcinogens from our environment an all-time high priority. Ban the production and dumping of toxic wastes.

9. Ban cigarette advertising (as has been done in Canada, France and other countries). Ban the export of U.S. tobacco.

10. Implement the recommendations of a recent report
    from the Office of Technology Assessment,
    Congress of the United States, 1990
    (*Unconventional Cancer Treatments*, G.P.O.
    #052-003-01207-3), describing unconventional
    cancer treatments, such as herbal substances,
    vitamins, and dietary changes, and offering
    suggestions to the cancer establishment, such as
    providing funds and expertise for the evaluation
    of these treatments. The present highly polarized
    situation between mainstream and alternative
    treatments is not in the best interests of people
    with cancer.

Resources

Alternative Women's Cancer Resource Groups

National Coalition of Feminist and Lesbian
  Cancer Projects
  P.O. Box 90437
  Washington, DC 20090-0437
  202-332-5536
Mautner Project for Lesbians with Cancer
  P.O. Box 90437
  Washington, DC 20090-0437
  202-332-5536
Lesbian Community Cancer Project
  Pat Parker Place
  1902 West Montrose
  Chicago, IL 60613
  312-561-4662
Los Angeles Shanti Foundation
  Emotional Support Services Department
  6855 Santa Monica Blvd. Suite 408
  Los Angeles, CA 90038
  213-962-8197
  Contact: Deborah Openden
National Women's Health Network
  1325 G Street NW
  Washington, DC 20005
TLC Network
  P.O. Box 18914
  Philadelphia, PA 19119
Women's Community Cancer Project
  c/o The Women's Center
  46 Pleasant Street
  Cambridge, MA 02139
  617-354-9888

Women's Cancer Resource Center
    3023 Shattuck Avenue
    Berkeley, CA 94705
    510-548-9272

National Breast Cancer Organizations

African-American Breast Cancer Alliance
    1 West Lake St. # 423
    Minneapolis, MN 55408
National Breast Cancer Coalition
    P.O. Box 66373
    Washington, DC 20035
    202-296-7477
National Alliance of Breast Cancer Organizations
    1180 Avenue of the Americas, 2nd floor
    New York, NY 22036
Reach To Recovery
    American Cancer Society
    1-800-ACS-2345
Y-Me National Organization for Breast Cancer
    Information and Support
    18220 Harwood Avenue
    Homewood, IL 60430
    1-800-221-2141

National Ovarian Cancer Organization

Ovarian Cancer Prevention & Early Detection
    Foundation
    P.O. Box 447
    Paauilo, HI 96776-0447
    808-776-1696 (voice), 808-776-1266 (fax)

National Women's Cancer Newsletter

What We Know About Cancer
Louder Than Words
P.O. Box 90934
Washington, DC 20090

Selected Recommended Publications

Bits of Ourselves: Women's Experiences With Cancer. Fairbanks, AK: Vanessapress Publishers, 1986.

Brady, Judy, editor. *1 in 3: Women with Cancer Confront an Epidemic.* San Francisco: Cleis Press, 1991.

Butler, Sandra, and Rosenblum, Barbara. *Cancer in Two Voices.* San Francisco: Spinster Books, 1991.

East West Foundation, with Ann Fawcett and Cynthia Smith. *Cancer-Free: 30 Who Triumphed Over Cancer Naturally.* Tokyo and New York: Japan Publications, Inc., 1991.

Givens, Carol and Fortier, L. Diane. *Practicing Eternity.* San Diego: Paradigm Publishing Company, 1992.

Kauffman, Danette G. *Surviving Cancer: A Practical Guide for Those Fighting TO WIN!* Second edition. Washington, DC: Acropolis Books, Ltd., 1989.

Lifshitz, Leatrice H., editor. *Her Soul Beneath the Bone: Women's Poetry on Breast Cancer.* Urbana: University of Illinois Press, 1988.

Lorde, Audre. *The Cancer Journals,* Second edition. San Francisco: Spinsters/Aunt Lute, 1980.

Lorde, Audre. *A Burst of Light.* Ithaca, NY: Firebrand Books, 1988.

Morra, Marion and Potts, Eve. *Choices: Realistic Alternatives in Cancer Treatment.* Revised edition. New York: Avon Books, 1987.

Morra, Marion and Potts, Eve. *Triumph: Getting Back to Normal When You Have Cancer.* New York: Avon Books, 1990.

Mullan, Fitzhugh, M.D.; Hoffman, Barbara, J.D.; and the Editors of Consumer Reports Books. *Charting the Journey: An Almanac of Practical Resources for Cancer Survivors / The National Coalition for Cancer Survivorship.* Mount Vernon, NY: Consumers Union, 1990.

Pitzele, Sefra Kobrin. *We Are Not Alone: Learning to Live with Chronic Illness.* New York: Workman Publishing, 1986.

Sontag, Susan. *AIDS and Its Metaphors.* New York: Farrar, Straus and Giroux, 1988.

Sontag, Susan. *Illness as Metaphor.* New York: Farrar, Straus and Giroux, 1978.

Stocker, Midge, ed. *Cancer As a Women's Issue: Scratching the Surface.* Women/Cancer/Fear/Power series, vol. 1. Chicago: Third Side Press, 1991.

Other books are referred to in articles throughout this book.

Contributors

Contributors to this volume are listed here in alphabetical order by first name.

ANDRÉE O'CONNOR is a published poet/writer (included in *Amateur People* Geo. Braziller/fiction collective First Novel Prize 1977), sculptor (including ornate dada van she lived & travelled in, collected by Mendocino County Museum 1988), ecofeminist timber activist, talkradio host, breast cancer activist, child of Pan.

ANN MARI BUITRAGO, an FOIA document specialist and former director of the Fund For Open Information and Accountability, is the coauthor of *Are You Now Or Have You Ever Been In the FBI Files?* (Grove Press, 1980). She now lives in Maine and continues to help people secure files under the Freedom of Information Act as director of the Institute for Public Access to Government Information.

BETH KUPPER-HERR works with the Ovarian Cancer Prevention and Early Detection Foundation, a national group based in Hawaii, to raise consciousness about and funding for ovarian cancer. She taught English in Indonesia, Malaysia, and Japan for seven years, and now teaches writing at a community college in Hawaii.

CANDICE HEPLER is a 47-year-old lesbian from a blue-collar family in Long Beach, California. She was diagnosed with ovarian cancer in February 1991.

ELLEN CROWLEY is a member of The Women's Community Cancer Project. This volunteer grassroots organization is working toward radically changing the current medical, social, and political approaches to cancer, particularly as they affect women.

ELLEN LEOPOLD served as an economic policy advisor to the Greater London Council until its abolition by the

Thatcher government in 1986. She currently lives in Boston where she is a member of the Women's Community Cancer Project.

ELISSA RAFFA was born in the Bronx in 1959 but has lived half her life in Minneapolis. She writes prose and plays, teaches at an alternative high school, and is an activist for disability rights and the rights of young lesbians.

JACKIE WINNOW, was born 1947 in New York City; she lived in Oakland, California from 1975 until her death in 1991. She was coordinator of the Lesbian/Gay and AIDS Unit of the San Francisco Human Rights Commission and founder of the Women's Cancer Resource Center in Berkeley, California.

JEAN HARDISTY, director of Political Research Associates and a founding member of the Women's Community Cancer Project in Cambridge/Boston, Massachusetts, is on the board of directors of Grassroots International, the Civil Liberties Union of Massachusetts, and the Center for Democratic Renewal. She formerly served on the board of directors of the Illinois Justice Foundation and the Ms. Foundation for Women. She was also a founding member of the Institute for Affirmation Action, the Chicago Abused Women Coalition, and the Crossroads Fund.

LOUISE LANDER writes, processes words part-time on the night shift to stay afloat, and travels south of the border as frequently as possible. Her most recent published work is *Images of Bleeding: Menstruation as Ideology* (Orlando Press, 1988). Her most recent unpublished work is *Intensity and Irony: A Memoir of Guatemala and Breast Cancer* (1991).

LYNN KANTER's novel, *On Lill Street*, was published in 1992 by Third Side Press. She also wrote the award-winning ERA documentary *Fighting for the Obvious*. She lives in Washington, DC, where she volunteers for the Mary-Helen Mautner Project for Lesbians with Cancer.

PAMELA FERGUSON is a New York- and Dallas-based journalist and author of six published books, a shiatsu teacher in Europe and North America, and a breast cancer activist worldwide.

PORTIA CORNELL lives and writes in Canton, CT. Her story "Air Born" was published in *Cancer As a Women's Issue: Scratching the Surface*, volume 1 of the Women/Cancer/Fear/Power series. Another short story, "The Eleanor Roosevelt Erotic Letter Writing Club," appears in *The Time of Our Lives: Women Write on Sex After 40* (Crossing Press, 1993). She is working on a novel about what happens to two lesbians when they decide to get married.

RITA ARDITTI is a biologist, a woman with breast cancer, and a founding member of the Women's Community Cancer Project in Cambridge, MA. She is a member of the graduate faculty of the Union Institute.

SANDRA BUTLER, a 20-year veteran of grassroots activism, is author of *Conspiracy of Silence: The Trauma of Incest* (Volcano Press, 1978) and coauthor with Barbara Rosenblum of *Cancer in Two Voices* (Spinsters Ink, 1992). She is currently affiliated with the International Institute for Advanced Feminist Training, which specializes in training, supervision, and program consultation with individuals working in all forms of feminist psychological theory and practice, political organizing, and cross-cultural work. She is writing essays for a book that will be both memoir and analysis of her activism in the movement to end violence against women and children.

SANDRA STEINGRABER is a professor of biology at Columbia College in Chicago. She writes and lectures frequently on environmental issues and is the author of

"Post-diagnosis," a manuscript of poems currently seeking a publisher.

SUZANNE JOI is a Jewish Lesbian Feminist/Womanist who is striving to be a writer while being healthy, woman-loving, a mother of an adult daughter, and a visionary-activist for diverse women's land-rule "where we have the freedom, respect, and responsibility to shape all aspects of our lives, our health, our love, our values."

TATIANA SCHREIBER is the editor of the *Resist* newsletter and a freelance public radio journalist. Her work focuses on health, education, and language issues, particularly as they affect women and communities of color.

VICTORIA A. BROWNWORTH is a Philadelphia writer and editor. She is a nationally syndicated columnist for the Philadelphia *Daily News*, where she writes the only lesbian column for a daily newspaper in the country. She is also a columnist for the *Advocate Magazine*. Her work on health, AIDS, and women's issues has appeared in numerous national newspapers and magazine in both the mainstream and queer press, including *The Advocate*, the *Village Voice, Utne Reader, The Nation, SPIN, OUT*, the *Philadelphia Inquirer*, and others. She lives with her partner of five years, filmmaker Judith Redding.

VIRGINIA M. SOFFA, was diagnosed with breast cancer in 1989. She is president and founder of the Breast Cancer Action Group. Living in South Burlington, VT, she divides her time among writing, speaking, and acting as a political activist for the eradication of breast cancer. She is author of *The Journey Beyond Breast Cancer: From the Personal to the Political* (Healing Arts Press, 1993).

Index

Circle symbolism, 31-44
  and spider web, 42
Clinton Administration, 124-125
Colbin, Annemarie, 81, 87
Colon cancer, 137
Colostomy, 144
"Comments on Ontario
    Mammography Program" (Bertell),
    244
Commoner, Barry, 251
Conference on Breast Diseases, Sixth
    International, 203
Congress, influencing, 160, 203-204
Constipation, 120
Cornell, Portia, 45, 271
Cousins, Norman, 34, 176
Cramping, 120
Creative imagery. *See* Visualization
Creative visualization, 38
Crossroads Farm, 87
Crowley, Ellen, 201, 270
Cuban Americans and poverty, 214
Cytoxin, 129

D

Dagmar, Sister, 108
Dalton, Carla, 155
D&C, 84
DDE, 18, 237
DDT, 18, 181, 195, 197, 239
Death
  as an alternative, 51-73
  equated with cancer, 140
  facing, 51-73
  getting used to idea of, 102-103
Death bed vigils, 70-72
Demers, Paul, 246
Denial, 177-178, 180
DES, 1
Detoxification, 92, 93-96
De Vitta, Vincent, 171
Dieldrin, 195
Diet, 2, 43, 80, 87-89, 110, 159, 220
  chocolate, 3
  dairy, 110
  and fat, 166, 236-237
  low-fat, 160
  macrobiotics, 17, 42-43, 81, 87-89,
    115
  recommended by American Cancer
    Society, 87
  search for nutritionist, 89-93
Dioxin, 238, 248
Doctor
  attitude toward women, 225
  examination, 135

and homophobia, 137
  questions to ask, 76
Doctor-patient relationship, 172-175,
    177-180
Drevecki, Dave, 15
Drinking water, 255. *See also*
    Environment
duPont factories, 233
Dye workers, 233

E

East/West, 100
EIC. *See* Extensive intraductal
    component
Electrical workers, 246-247
Electromagnetic fields, 246-247
EMFs. *See* Electromagnetic fields
Empowerment, 155
Encounter groups, 46
Endometrial cancer, 233
Environment, 161-162
  and cancer, 181-200 *et passim*,
    231-259
  definition, 234
  toxins, exposure to, 220-223
Environmental Protection Agency, 181
Erotica, 16-17
Esko, Wendy, 81
Estrogen, 18-19, 43, 167, 236
  replacement, 118
Eurythmy, 96, 108, 115
Exercise, 22, 37, 159
  breathing, 35
  circle movements, 38-44 *et passim*
Extensive intraductal component, 171

F

Faith Daniels Show, 11, 12-20
Falck, Frank, 241
Family history, 166. *See also* Heredity
Fatalism, 227
Feminism, 46, 159
  agenda in Congress, 160
  cancer projects, 207-212
  grassroots healing, 201-205
Feminist health centers, 154
Feminist rationalization, 25
Ferguson, Pamela, 31, 271
Fibroids, 1
  and menopause, 4
Fink, John, 80, 100
First National People of Color
    Environmental Leadership Summit,
    222
Food. *See* Diet
Food, Drug, and Cosmetics Act, 234